JONAH & NAHUM

GRACE IN THE MIDST OF JUDGMENT

Jonah & Nahum

The Master's Seminary Press is an imprint of the John MacArthur Publishing Group and is committed to producing trusted resources that anchor believers in sound doctrine and biblical truth.

Designed by WeKREATIVE Co.

ISBN-13: 978-1-883973-05-6

Printed in China

THE MASTER'S
SEMINARY
PRESS

Los Angeles, California
www.tms.edu

THE MACARTHUR OLD TESTAMENT
COMMENTARY ON THE BOOKS OF

JONAH & NAHUM

EDITED BY
JOHN MACARTHUR

LOS ANGELES, CALIFORNIA
THE MASTER'S SEMINARY PRESS

CONTENTS

Preface

PSALM 1:1–3
HOW BLESSED IS THE MAN WHO DOES NOT WALK IN THE COUNSEL OF THE WICKED, NOR STAND IN THE WAY OF SINNERS, NOR SIT IN THE SEAT OF SCOFFERS! BUT HIS DELIGHT IS IN THE LAW OF YAHWEH, AND IN HIS LAW HE MEDITATES DAY AND NIGHT. AND HE WILL BE LIKE A TREE *FIRMLY* PLANTED BY STREAMS OF WATER, WHICH YIELDS ITS FRUIT IN ITS SEASON AND ITS LEAF DOES NOT WITHER; AND IN WHATEVER HE DOES, HE PROSPERS.

JEREMIAH 15:16
YOUR WORDS WERE FOUND, AND I ATE THEM, AND YOUR WORDS BECAME FOR ME JOY AND GLADNESS IN MY HEART, FOR I HAVE BEEN CALLED BY YOUR NAME, O YAHWEH GOD OF HOSTS.

Both preaching through every verse of the New Testament and writing the *MacArthur New Testament Commentary* series over the past half-century have been an incomparable gift of divine grace that has allowed me to live in the blessedness of Psalm 1:1–3 and the joy of Jeremiah 15:16. I have now been blessed with the opportunity to continue the commentary series into the Old Testament.

In studying Scripture, my desire has always been to behold and to proclaim the beauty of our Lord to His people (Neh 8:8; Ps 27:4). Understanding that the knowledge of God affects the life of the believer, I pray that the exaltation of God in these commentaries will transform lives. The Apostle Paul wrote: "All Scripture is God-breathed and profitable for teaching, for reproof, for correction, for training in righteousness, so that the man of God may be equipped, having been thoroughly equipped for every good work" (2 Tim 3:16–17). This is the purpose of these commentaries: to explain the Word of God so that the people of God would continue to grow in their knowledge and love of the Lord Jesus Christ (2 Pet 3:18).

In producing the *MacArthur Old Testament Commentary* series, I have been delighted to partner with Abner Chou, Iosif Zhakevich, and Nathan Busenitz to examine the biblical text word by word. Faithful to the approach of expository preaching, the commentary is based on thorough exegesis of the text in the original Hebrew. The aim is to bring out the meaning and theology of Scripture with accuracy, precision, and clarity. While each section is arranged to aid the preacher, the commentary is also intended to be read and applied by every believer for personal edification, blessing, and joy.

JONAH

Introduction to Jonah

The dominant theme of the book of Jonah is God's compassion for the lost, both Jew and Gentile. As Jonah himself exclaimed, "I knew that You are a gracious and compassionate God, slow to anger and abundant in lovingkindness, and one who relents concerning evil" (Jonah 4:2). That the Lord saved not only a Gentile people but specifically the Ninevites, the archenemies of Israel (cf. 2 Kgs 15:19–29; 16:7–18; 17:3–6, 23–27; 18–19; Jonah 1:1–2), demonstrated the height and depth of divine grace. About fifty years before the northern kingdom would be exiled by the Assyrians, the Lord showed the Israelites that even their adversaries were not beyond the reach of His mercy. Through Jonah's example, God prepared His people to be sown among the nations, like Jonah briefly was, so that they might point the Gentiles to Him (cf. Zech 10:9).

From the outset of the story, God manifested His heart for the lost. Instead of executing immediate judgment on the Ninevites for their wickedness, the Lord graciously sent them a warning of their pending destruction if they did not repent (Jonah 1:2; 3:5–9). Yet, God showed compassion not only to Nineveh but also to His wayward prophet Jonah, sending a storm to discipline him (1:4) and a fish to deliver him from the sea (1:17; 2:10). Additionally, Yahweh spared the pagan sailors whom Jonah had hired to take him to Tarshish. Though they deserved death, being steeped in idolatry and self-dependence (1:5),

God preserved their lives and drew them to Himself (1:16). The Lord continued to demonstrate His mercy by giving Jonah a second opportunity to obey (3:1–2). When the prophet finally arrived in Nineveh, as he had originally been commissioned, the Lord put His saving grace on full display. The result was the largest revival in recorded history, as the entire city of Nineveh repented of their evil ways, turned to God, and received His mercy and forgiveness.

While God delighted in being gracious to the Gentiles, His prophet disdained such magnanimity, calling it evil (4:1) and claiming that death would be better than watching God extend His goodness to Israel's enemies (4:3). But the Lord gave Jonah still more grace, teaching him through a leafy plant that divine grace is inherently good and that life without it would be unbearable. If Jonah was right to care about a withering weed in the wilderness, how much more should God care about an entire city of souls whom He had created! Because Yahweh is Lord over the whole earth and every nation on it, He is therefore the God of both Jew and Gentile.

The story of Jonah is so powerful that it reverberates throughout history. While in Jonah's generation Nineveh experienced God's goodness, the city would later face His wrath. In a sequel to the story, more than a hundred years later, Nahum prophesied that this city would be destroyed. Nahum reminded Nineveh that though God is gracious, He is also righteous and just. Because that generation of Ninevites returned to their evil ways and became a "city of bloodshed, completely full of deception *and* pillage" (Nah 3:1), they became the objects of God's judgment. (For more on the theme of Nahum's prophecy, see the Introduction to Nahum in this volume.)

As God granted repentance to the Ninevites in Jonah's day, so He ordained that salvation would come to the Gentiles centuries later through prophets parallel to Jonah. Peter Bar-Jonah found himself at Joppa, akin to Jonah, commissioned by God to go to the Gentiles (cf. Acts 10:1–23). But unlike Jonah who fled from God's calling, Peter obeyed his commission. He went to the Gentiles, preaching the gospel to Cornelius and those of his household, demonstrating the triumph of God's intention to reach the nations (cf. 11:18). Paul too was like Jonah, finding himself aboard a ship caught in a terrible storm (cf. 27:1–38). But unlike Jonah, Paul journeyed specifically to the Gentiles rather than fleeing away from them. Similar to Jonah, both Peter (Acts 10:13–16) and Paul (Phil 3:1–6) had at one point been reluctant to minister to the Gentiles. But being commissioned by the Lord Jesus, they did not follow in Jonah's footsteps. Instead, they emulated the example of Christ, who Himself represents the ultimate antithesis of Jonah. Unlike the wayward prophet, Jesus boarded a storm-bound boat precisely to minister in a Gentile region (Luke 8:22–25). The Lord Jesus miraculously calmed that storm, thereby demonstrating that He is God, the very One who subdued the sea for Jonah centuries earlier (8:24–25). He also declared that He would fulfill the sign of Jonah, which He did by overcoming death in His resurrection on the third day (Matt 16:39–40). Before ascending to heaven, He commissioned His disciples to go into all the world and to be His witnesses to the ends of the earth (Matt 28:18–20; Acts 1:7–8). Thus, what was prefigured in Jonah came to pass in Jesus. While Jonah attempted to impede God's saving purposes, he actually served to illustrate their ultimate fulfillment through the Messiah. The book of Jonah, therefore, points to the work of Christ and unveils the heart of God to seek and save the lost.

Title and Author

The book is titled after the name of the prophet Jonah, whose name means "dove." In Scripture, the dove represents either a messenger of peace (Gen 8:11) or a symbol of foolishness (Hos 7:11). Both descriptions apply to Jonah's ministry. On the one hand, Jonah was a messenger of warning and repentance, calling the Ninevites to make peace with God. On the other hand, through his disobedience and disdain, he often proved to be a foolish prophet.

According to both Jewish and Christian tradition, the author of the book is Jonah, the son of Amittai and the servant of God (Jonah 1:1; cf. 2 Kgs 14:25). Second Kings 14:25 records that Jonah was from Gath-hepher, a town from the tribe of Zebulun (Josh 19:10–16) in the region of Galilee near Nazareth. This indicates that Jonah was a prophet to the northern tribes of Israel. However, the Pharisees overlooked or ignored the fact that Jonah came from Galilee, for in rejecting the messiahship of Jesus they claimed, "Search and see that no prophet arises out of Galilee" (John 7:52; cf. 7:41). Within Jewish tradition, although without Scriptural evidence, Jonah is believed to be the son of the widow from Zarephath, that is, the boy who died and whom Elijah raised from the dead (1 Kgs 17:8–24).[1]

Even though the text refers to Jonah mostly in the third person (but cf. Jonah 2:2–9), Jonah's authorship of this book should be affirmed. Writing or speaking in reference to oneself in the third person was not unknown, and at times in Scripture, the biblical author shifts between first and third person for effect (e.g., Exod 11:3; Ezra 5:3–5; Neh 1:1; Amos 1:1; 7:1–2, 10–17; 8:1–2; and see Exod 34:6–7; 1 Sam 25:18–31, 39–41; 2 Cor 12:1–6). The details revealed about Jonah in the book—both in the third person (chs. 1, 3, and 4) and in the first person (ch. 2)—suggest that Jonah himself wrote this as an autobiographical account. Moreover, the introduction to the book of Jonah ("Now the word of Yahweh came to Jonah") follows the general formula that appears in other prophetic books, in which the prophet himself records a message from Yahweh (cf. Hos 1:1; Joel 1:1; Mic 1:1; Zeph 1:1; Hag 1:1; Zech 1:1).

1 See Uriel Simon, *Jonah*, JPS Bible Commentary (Philadelphia: Jewish Publication Society, 1999), xxxiv, 38.

Date

According to 2 Kings 14:23–25, Jonah prophesied during the prosperous reign of Jeroboam II (ca. 793–758 BC), perhaps between 784–774 BC. In Assyria, the king would likely have been either Adad-nirari III (ca. 810–783 BC) or Ashur-dan III (ca. 772–755 BC). Jonah was preceded by Obadiah (ca. 850–840 BC) and Joel (between ca. 835–796 BC), overlapped with Amos (ca. 763–755 BC), and was succeeded by Hosea (ca. 755–710 BC).

Historical Context

Jonah ministered during the reign of Jeroboam II (ca. 793–758 BC), a time when Israel enjoyed peace and prosperity. While Assyria had previously subjugated Israel and required tribute during the reign of Jehu (841–814 BC), Jeroboam II succeeded in establishing autonomy and security. Under the prophetic direction of Jonah, the king restored Israel's territory up to Lebo-hamath in the north and the Sea of the Arabah in the south (2 Kgs 14:25). With such expansion, the northern and southern kingdoms of Israel regained all the territory that Israel had possessed in the days of Solomon (1 Kgs 8:65; cf. Num 34:7–9; Josh 13:5). The nearly forty-year reign of Jeroboam II represented a second golden age for the nation.

This time of success, however, would be short-lived because Israel did not repent but continued to live in rebellion against the Lord. Along with Jeroboam II, Israel did what was evil in the sight of Yahweh (2 Kgs 14:24). God nonetheless restrained judgment because He had promised that Jehu would have four sons to sit on the throne (15:12), providing continuity and stability for the northern kingdom. But once that period was over, Amos, along with other prophets, declared that Israel would be exiled by Assyria (Amos 5:27; cf. Isa 7:17–18, 20; Hos 9:3; 11:5, 11). Since Jeroboam II was the third of Jehu's four sons, the time of stability was approaching its end. Jehu's fourth son, Zechariah, ruled for only six months (2 Kgs 15:8), and over the subsequent three decades the stability of the northern kingdom waned until it fell to Assyria in 722 BC.

Since oppression by Gentile nations was a historical reality and exile was a prevailing threat (cf. Deut 4:25–31; 28:64–67), Israel was characterized by an anti-Gentile sentiment. While many of the prophets rightly condemned the nations for their wickedness (cf. Isa 13–27; Joel 3; Mic 7:16–17) and prophesied that God's judgment would fall on them (Obad 17), the Israelites became self-righteous and assumed they were innately superior to the people groups around them (Amos 1–2).

Of the nations Israel hated, perhaps the most detested was Assyria, given its military prominence and reputation for cruelty. The empire had a long history of brutal conquest and expansion. Early on, various kings, including Adad-nirari I (ca. 14th–13th c. BC), Shalmaneser I (ca. 13th c. BC), and Tukulti-Ninurta I (ca. 13th c. BC), aggressively conquered territory in Mesopotamia to establish the kingdom of Assyria. After a period of instability, Assyria returned to dominance under Ashur-dan II (ca. 10th c. BC), giving rise to the Neo-Assyrian Empire under the auspices of Adad-nirari II (ca. 911–859 BC) and Ashurnasirpal II (ca. 883–859 BC). Having consolidated power in Mesopotamia, Shalmaneser III (ca. 859–824 BC) ruled from Nineveh, turning his attention toward other nations, notably at the battle of Qarqar (853 BC), also fighting Israel during the reign of King Ahab (ca. 874–853 BC; 1 Kgs 16:28–33; 22:1). Shalmaneser III later subjugated the Israelite king Jehu. His victory is depicted on the Black Obelisk of Shalmaneser III, which records that Israel paid tribute to Assyria (ca. 841 BC; cf. 2 Kgs 9–10; Hos 1:4).

Assyria was barbaric to every nation at that time. An image from the reign of Shalmaneser III portrays the king with piles of dismembered heads, hands, and feet around him along with bodies impaled on stakes.[2] Such brutality would have been well-known to the Israelites when God called Jonah to minister to Nineveh. Roughly fifty years after Jonah's ministry, Israel's suspicions about

2 JoAnna M. Hoyt, *Amos, Jonah, & Micah*, Evangelical Exegetical Commentary (Bellingham, WA: Lexham, 2018), 354.

Assyria were confirmed when the Assyrian army conquered Israel and exiled the people in barbaric fashion (722 BC). Ancient reliefs from the conquests of Sennacherib (ca. 701 BC), depicting a pile of decapitated heads or even soldiers skinning their captives, reveal the kind of graphic violence for which Assyria was known.[3] The Assyrians also attempted to conquer the southern kingdom of Judah, only being halted by the Angel of Yahweh who killed 185,000 enemy soldiers (2 Kgs 19:35–37; Isa 37:36–38). Without question, Assyria was a bloodthirsty nation, eager to dominate by force.

Because Assyria was so violent, the fact that its aggression against Israel subsided during the reign of Jeroboam II is significant. This was due, in part, to internal unrest and the rise of a rival kingdom named Urartu, which put pressure on the Assyrian empire.[4] But a major reason that peace between Israel and Assyria continued during Jeroboam II's reign was that Jonah's preaching led to Nineveh's repentance. The continued lull in Assyria's aggression was evidence of the mercy of God and the genuineness of Nineveh's conversion.

At the time of Jonah, the major center of Assyria and the surrounding Gentile world was the city of Nineveh. The city had a long and storied history. It first appears in Scripture in Genesis 10:11–12, when Nimrod went to Assyria to build "Nineveh and Rehoboth-Ir and Calah, and Resen between Nineveh and Calah." Nineveh was briefly mentioned in a record in the context of ancient Akkadian kings, indicating that a temple was built there for Ishtar, the goddess of love and war (ca. 2300 BC).[5] Hammurabi (ca. 1792–1750 BC) also recognized Nineveh as a place of importance, and in the reign of Tiglath-pileser I (ca. 1115–1071 BC), Nineveh was developed into a

3 Ibid., 354–55.

4 Daniel DeWitt Lowery, "Assyria," *The Lexham Bible Dictionary* (Bellingham, WA: Lexham, 2016); and Brian Neil Peterson, "Urartu," *The Lexham Bible Dictionary* (Bellingham, WA: Lexham, 2016).

5 C. T. Fritsch, "Nineveh," *The International Standard Bible Encyclopedia*, revised edition (Grand Rapids: Eerdmans, 1979–1988), 3:539.

grandiose metropolis.[6] About 550 miles from the Israelite town of Joppa (cf. Jonah 1:3), the city was situated on the east bank of the Tigris River (in modern-day Iraq), making it well situated for prosperous trade and rich agriculture. There appears to have been religious significance to the city as well, as the name Nineveh has been linked to the Sumerian word for "fish" and associated with the river-goddess Nina.[7]

As the capital of Assyria, Nineveh was home to the royal palaces of Assyrian rulers, culminating with the magnificent palace of Sennacherib (cf. 2 Kgs 19:36; Isa 37:37). The city was also an academic center as Ashurbanipal (ca. 669–633 BC) assembled a great library there.[8] While the inner city was about three to four square miles, the rest of the city extended to fifty-five miles all around.[9] And with a population in Jonah's day of about six hundred thousand people (cf. Jonah 4:11), Jonah would have needed three days to travel through the metropolitan area as he preached (cf. 3:3).[10] All of this demonstrates why God called Nineveh "the great city" (1:2). As one ancient writer declared, "No one afterward built a city of such compass or with walls so magnificent."[11]

At a time when Israel's animosity against the Gentiles was growing, the Lord called Jonah to go and minister in the capital of the hated Assyrians. In God's providence, as noted above, Nineveh was suffering from internal strife and weakness at the time. Famine and plagues in 765 BC and 759 BC added to Nineveh's woes, and a full eclipse of the sun occurred in 763 BC, which the Assyrians interpreted as an omen of doom.[12] While none of these circumstances caused the conversion of the Ninevites, the Lord

6 Ibid.

7 Ibid., 3:538. See also Marvin A. Sweeney, *The Twelve Prophets: Hosea, Joel, Amos, Obadiah, Jonah*, Berit Olam (Collegeville, MN: Liturgical, 2000), 310; but Hoyt, *Amos, Jonah, & Micah*, 351–52.

8 A. Kirk Grayson, "Nineveh," *The Anchor Yale Bible Dictionary* (New York: Doubleday, 1992), 4:1118.

9 Billy K. Smith and Frank S. Page, *Amos, Obadiah, Jonah*, New American Commentary (Nashville: Broadman & Holman, 1995), 257.

10 Douglas Stuart, *Hosea–Jonah*, Word Biblical Commentary (Dallas: Word, 1987), 487–88; and Hoyt, *Amos, Jonah, & Micah*, 354; Grayson, "Nineveh," 4:1118.

11 Leslie C. Allen, *The Books of Joel, Obadiah, Jonah, and Micah*, New International Commentary on the Old Testament (Grand Rapids: Eerdmans, 1976), 221.

12 Hoyt, *Amos, Jonah, & Micah*, 354; Stuart, *Hosea–Jonah*, 487–88.

used them to pave the way for His prophet to be heard. As the book of Jonah emphasizes, the greatest sign God gave to Nineveh was to send a prophet who was delivered from a great fish (1:17). The Lord sovereignly orchestrated these circumstances surrounding the prophet's ministry to ensure that the message of His marvelous grace was clearly heard.

Themes

Several theological themes drive the story of Jonah and its main purpose. These include the Person of Yahweh and the divine perfections of God's sovereignty, omnipresence, grace, and judgment of sinners. The book also highlights the need for sinners to repent and the Lord's willingness to forgive the penitent, whether Jew or Gentile.

Yahweh

The covenant name of God, Yahweh, appears twenty-one times in this concise book. The account of Jonah's ministry amplifies the character of Yahweh, declaring that He is the only true God who created heaven and earth (Jonah 1:9), who is omnipresent (1:3, 10; 2:2, 7), who reigns over all creation (1:4, 15, 17; 2:3, 10; 4:6–7), who sits in judgment over mankind (1:2, 14; 2:3, 8; 3:2, 4, 5–10; 4:2, 11), and who alone is able to offer salvation (2:9; 3:9–10; 4:11). God's personal name Yahweh, moreover, emphasizes His loyalty and love, particularly with Israel whom He chose to be His people (Exod 3:14–16). In the past, God revealed Himself as "Yahweh, Yahweh God, compassionate and gracious, slow to anger, and abounding in lovingkindness and truth" (34:6). Jonah affirmed this in saying, "I knew that You are a gracious and compassionate God, slow to anger and abundant in lovingkindness, and one who relents concerning evil" (Jonah 4:2).

The book of Jonah emphasizes that Yahweh extends His covenant love not only to Israel but also to the Gentiles. Yahweh who showed mercy and salvation to Jonah the Israelite

(Jonah 2:9) is the same One who extended mercy and salvation to the pagan sailors (1:14) and the Ninevites (3:1, 3, 10). While the name Yahweh does not appear in the portion that describes Nineveh's repentance (cf. 3:5–10), underscoring the Lord's unique relationship with Israel, God still demonstrates that He is the Savior of both Jew and Gentile by granting repentance to the Ninevites. Their salvation serves as a preview of heaven, where the redeemed include those "from every nation and *all* tribes and peoples and tongues" joyfully proclaiming that "salvation *belongs* to our God who sits on the throne, and to the Lamb" (Rev 7:9–10; cf. Jonah 2:9).

SOVEREIGNTY OF GOD

Throughout the narrative, Yahweh is presented as the Creator and Ruler of the universe. He is in full control of every aspect of life. Jonah proclaimed this truth, saying, "I am a Hebrew, and I fear Yahweh, the God of heaven, who made the sea and the dry land" (Jonah 1:9). The Lord demonstrated His sovereignty when He sent the storm precisely against Jonah's ship (1:4), and then subsequently calmed the sea after Jonah was thrown overboard (1:15–16). When Jonah was in the water, he confessed that God's sovereign hand was behind this event, declaring, "For You had cast me into the deep" (2:3). He reiterated the Lord's supremacy while sinking beneath the waves, acknowledging that the sea belonged to God: "All Your breakers and waves passed over me" (2:3). God appointed a fish to swallow Jonah to deliver him from drowning (1:17) and He commanded the fish to vomit Jonah up on dry land so that he could complete his mission (2:10). In the same way, God appointed the plant to grow and provide shelter for Jonah (4:6), and God appointed the worm to devour the plant (4:7). It was also God who whipped up the scorching wind of the Sirocco specifically where Jonah was sitting outside of Nineveh (4:8). Even though Jonah initially resisted God's commission (1:3), he ultimately submitted because he could not withstand the Lord's sovereign hand (3:3). As with all history, God's sovereign will and power directed and drove the events of Jonah's ministry.

OMNIPRESENCE OF GOD

God's omnipresence is a key truth that manifests itself throughout the entire story. At the outset, Jonah's flight proved that God was not limited to any physical space, as the Lord was present at Joppa (Jonah 1:3), on the ship (1:4–7), in the sea (1:17), and in the fish (2:1–9). At Nineveh (3:10), God was present to prompt the repentance of the Ninevites (3:10), and outside of Nineveh, God was present to hear the prayer of His prophet (4:5). Despite his flagrant attempt to flee, Jonah himself recognized God's omnipresence, declaring that Yahweh is "the God of heaven, who made the sea and the dry land" (1:9), and then praising God because "from the belly of Sheol," He heard Jonah's voice (2:2). God's omnipresence is a reminder of man's inescapable accountability (1:3–17), the Lord's unrestricted availability to hear and answer prayer (2:2), and His ever-readiness to save (2:3–9; 3:10; 4:2, 11). Above all, the theme of divine omnipresence serves as a vivid reminder that God reigns not only over Israel but over all the earth. Because He is Lord over all mankind, He not only had the authority to send Jonah to the Ninevites, but He also had the ability to bring them to repentance and salvation.

GRACE OF GOD

From its beginning to its end, the story of Jonah abounds with the grace of God. Yahweh demonstrated His grace when He commissioned Jonah to bring a message of warning to Nineveh in order to save the Ninevites (Jonah 1:2). God expressed grace by persisting with His plan even though Jonah rebelled against Him (1:4; 3:2). The Lord also extended His grace to the sailors by bringing them to repentance (1:16). When Jonah was thrown into the sea, God showed grace to His wayward prophet by delivering him from death (1:17; 2:2, 6, 9, 10).

God also extended grace to Jonah by giving him a second opportunity to go and preach to Nineveh (3:2). When Jonah declared the message to the Ninevites, God caused a revival, saving more than half a million people (3:5–10). Despite Jonah's wicked and heartless response to Nineveh's repentance, God demonstrated further grace by patiently confronting His prophet and expounding the wonder of His grace (Jonah 4:9–11; cf. Eph 2:8). The breadth and variety of instances in which God exercised patience and extended grace throughout this book underscore the extent of His mercy and lovingkindness (cf. Exod 33:19; 34:6).

The book of Jonah displays not only the breadth but also the depth of God's grace. When the prophet was about to drown, the Lord rescued him from sure death (Jonah 1:17–2:9), which then served as a sign that God's grace can overcome even the grave (cf. Matt 12:39). As for the sailors and the Ninevites, God's grace transformed their hearts so that they would repent and be saved (Jonah 1:10, 14; 3:5–10). God's grace in those cases was magnified by the fact that Jonah was either minimally involved in or resistant to their conversion (1:9; 3:4). The story of Jonah illustrates the abundance and the power of divine grace, and reiterates the truth that salvation is rooted solely in the grace of God (cf. Jonah 2:9; Eph 2:8).

JUDGMENT OF SINNERS

This narrative also reveals that the Lord is the supreme Judge. At the beginning of the story, God declared judgment against Nineveh because their evil had reached Him (Jonah 1:2). He then illustrated that His judgment is destructive, ravaging the sea (1:4) and nearly destroying the sailors (1:6–16). God showed that the wages of sin is death, as He nearly killed His prophet who disobeyed Him (1:17; 2:1–5). The Lord also displayed the fearsomeness of His wrath, as evidenced in the terror-stricken reaction of the Ninevites at God's threat of their destruction (3:4). Accompanied with God's grace, the warning of judgment ultimately moved the Ninevites to repentance (3:5–9; cf. Matt 10:28), and God relented from His burning anger (Jonah 3:9). Thus, the book of Jonah demonstrates not only the severity of God's wrath against sin but also the reality that His wrath should cause all sinners to repent (Acts 2:37–38; 17:29–31).

REPENTANCE OF SINNERS

Powerful illustrations of repentance appear throughout this book. Jonah's prayer in chapter 2 exhibits numerous components of righteous repentance, including the fundamental element of calling on the Lord in desperate dependence (Jonah 2:1). Jonah repented of His perversion of God's nature, acknowledging that though he had fled from God's presence (1:3), he could not evade the Lord's omnipresence (2:1–4). Sincere repentance recognizes the wonder of God's salvation, as Jonah did when he exclaimed that he should have died in the storm but was spared because God rescued him (2:5–6). Repentance also acknowledges the mercy and grace of God which He shows because of His compassion (2:7). As Jonah's prayer demonstrates, those who repent turn away from sin and idolatry, and turn, instead, toward the Lord and His salvation (1:16; 2:9).

The Ninevites manifested such repentance. They understood the urgency of their situation and grounded their repentant faith in the one and only God (3:5a). They bore fruit in keeping with repentance by forfeiting food and drink to focus on their relationship with the Lord (Jonah 3:5b; cf. Matt 3:8). Thus, they demonstrated the humility that accompanies genuine repentance, recognizing that it is not merely in word but also in deed (Jonah 3:7–8). Ultimately, however, the fact that the entire city of Nineveh repented—which was clearly a divine miracle—affirms that God alone is the source of repentance (cf. 2 Tim 2:25).

Nevertheless, Jonah's life illustrated that while repentance must be earnest and vigorous, it can also be dangerously partial. Even though the prophet repented in the fish, his repentance proved to be incomplete, for he still detested the Ninevites (Jonah 4:1). God, therefore, continued refining His servant (4:6–11), chastening him and driving him to further repentance. Thus, the Lord affirmed that repentance is not merely a single act but a lifestyle that bears fruit (cf. Matt 3:8; 1 John 1:8).

SALVATION OF GENTILES

The main thrust of the book of Jonah deals with God's saving love for Gentiles. The very first words of God's commission to Jonah ("Arise, go") demonstrate the heart of Yahweh for those outside of Israel (Jonah 1:2). Instead of immediately judging the Ninevites for their wickedness, the Lord showed them grace by giving them a warning (1:2; 3:2); and instead of abandoning them when Jonah refused to go (1:4), God persisted until His reluctant servant submitted and went (3:3). Throughout Jonah's journeys, the Lord saved the Gentiles that the prophet encountered, from the sailors (1:16) to the Ninevites (3:10). The entire plot of Jonah is driven by the unrelenting compassion of God for those outside of Israel.

The book of Jonah, moreover, defends God's love for the Gentiles. This narrative exposes the hypocrisy of Jonah who loved divine grace when his life was spared (1:17), but who hated divine grace when his enemies were delivered (4:1–2). It reveals Jonah's pride in that he believed he was more deserving of God's grace than the Gentiles, when in fact it was the sailors who feared Yahweh more than Jonah did (1:8–10, 16). It discloses that Jonah's hatred so twisted his theology that he called God's mercy evil (4:1) and selfishly demanded to die (4:3). No one has the prerogative to object to God's grace (cf. Rom 9:20–23), for all are sinners in need of salvation. If one can rightly care about a plant that he neither toiled over nor caused to grow, then the Lord most certainly has the right to care for those He created in His own image (Jonah 4:10–11).

As noted above, this theme of God's salvation of the Gentiles is so pervasive that it echoes throughout redemptive history. Like Jonah, Peter too would one day journey from Joppa to bring the gospel to the Gentiles (Acts 10:1–23). Paul also would travel on a ship through a storm while preaching God's Word to the Gentiles (Acts 27:1–44). They did this because Jesus had commissioned them, and all His disciples, to go throughout the world and proclaim the gospel (Matt 28:18–20). Thus, what God accomplished in the time of Jonah did not end with Jonah. Rather, God has continued to work out His saving purposes through history to the present, pointing sinners to the Lord Jesus Christ, the One who fulfilled the sign of Jonah through His death and resurrection (Matt 12:39).

Purpose

The book of Jonah demonstrates that Yahweh is the Savior of both Jews and Gentiles. The Lord sent His servant not only to bring a message to Nineveh but also to serve as a message to His own people. Through Jonah, God declared that He has the sovereign prerogative to show compassion on whomever He wishes, and that He lavishes His grace freely upon those who acknowledge their unworthiness, repent of their sin, and believe in Him. The wondrous grace that God revealed through the ministry of Jonah ultimately culminates in the One who fulfilled the sign of Jonah and accomplished salvation for all who repent and believe in Him.

Outline

1. An Unwilling Missionary (1:1–6)
    a. The Lord's Directive (1:1–2)
    b. The Prophet's Defiance (1:3)
    c. The Lord's Discipline (1:4)
    d. The Sailors' Dread (1:5a)
    e. The Prophet's Disregard (1:5b)
    f. The Captain's Desperation (1:6)

2. A Great Fish and the Fishing of Men (1:7–17)
   a. The Sailors' Discovery (1:7–8)
   b. The Prophet's Declaration (1:9)
   c. The Crew's Dismay (1:10–13)
   d. The Gentiles' Deliverance (1:14–16)
   e. Jonah's Detainment (1:17)
3. The Marks of a Penitent Prayer, Part I (2:1–4)
   a. A Humble Condition (2:1)
   b. A Heartfelt Cry (2:2)
   c. An Honest Confession (2:3–4)
4. The Marks of a Penitent Prayer, Part II (2:5–10)
   a. A Hope-filled Confidence (2:5–7)
   b. A Heart of Consecration (2:8–9)
   c. God's Hand of Compassion (2:10)
5. The Grace of Repentance, Part I (3:1–5)
   a. A Restored Missionary (3:1–3a)
   b. A Rebuking Message (3:3b–4)
   c. A Repentant Multitude (3:5)
6. The Grace of Repentance, Part II (3:6–10)
   a. A Remorseful Monarch (3:6)
   b. A Royal Mandate (3:7–8)
   c. A Reliant Meekness (3:9)
   d. A Relenting Mercy (3:10)
7. God's Forgiveness and Jonah's Fury (4:1–4)
   a. A Fierce Anger (4:1)
   b. A Flagrant Accusation (4:2–3)
   c. A Forbearing Answer (4:4)
8. A Prophet, a Plant, and a People (4:5–11)
   a. A Flawed Anticipation (4:5)
   b. A Fitting Analogy (4:6–8)
   c. A Final Admonition (4:9–11)

An Unwilling Missionary

1

JONAH 1:1–6

Now the word of Yahweh came to Jonah the son of Amittai saying, "Arise, go to Nineveh, the great city, and call out against it, for their evil has come up before Me." Yet Jonah arose to flee to Tarshish from the presence of Yahweh. So he went down to Joppa, found a ship which was going to Tarshish, and paid its fare and went down into it to go with them to Tarshish from the presence of Yahweh. But Yahweh hurled a great wind on the sea, and there was a great storm on the sea so that the ship gave thought to breaking apart. Then the sailors became fearful, and every man cried to his god, and they hurled the cargo which was in the ship into the sea to lighten *it* for them. But Jonah had gone down *below* into the innermost part of the vessel, lain down, and fallen deep asleep. So the captain came near to him and said to him, "How is it that you are deeply sleeping? Arise, call on your god. Perhaps *your* god will be concerned about us so that we will not perish."

The Old Testament consistently presents Israel as God's chosen nation. The Lord set His love on the people that descended from Abraham (Deut 7:7), giving them special prominence (7:6), covenant promises (Gen 15:1–21; Jer 31:31–34), and a distinct future (Zech 14:1–21; Rev 7:4–8; 14:1–5). In light of that dominant focus, one might wonder if God's compassion and concern extended only to Israel. But that was not the case. Israel was to be a beacon of hope to the nations, so that people from every tribe and tongue might learn the saving truth about Yahweh (cf. Isa 60:3). In His plan to reach the world, God ascribed a unique role to Israel—so that through them and their Messiah every nation on earth would be blessed (Gen 12:1–3).

God positioned Israel to be a kingdom of priests to the nations, demonstrating His glory to the world (Exod 19:5–6). To that end, Moses wrote in Deuteronomy 4:5–6: "See, I have taught you statutes and judgments just as Yahweh my God commanded me, that you should do thus in the land where you are entering to possess it. You shall keep and do *them*, for that is your wisdom and your understanding in the sight of the peoples who will hear all these statutes and say, 'Surely this great nation is a wise and understanding people.'" The Old Testament is filled with bold proclamations of God's glory to the nations. The psalmist declared, "Recount His glory among the nations, His wondrous deeds among all the peoples" (Ps 96:3; cf. 117:1–2), and God Himself exclaimed, "The people whom I formed for Myself will recount My praise" to the world (Isa 43:21). Because of God's concern for all peoples, Yahweh said to the Messiah, "It is too small a thing that You should be My Servant to raise up the tribes of Jacob and to cause the preserved ones of Israel to return; I will also give You as a light of the nations so that My salvation may reach to the end of the earth" (49:6; cf. 42:6). From the beginning, God designed Israel to be a nation that would display His majesty to every corner of the earth.

While Israel was called to be a witness nation to a watching world, God also selected individuals to address Gentile nations directly. For example, the Lord directed Abraham to prophesy to his pagan neighbors (cf. Gen 20:7); Moses proclaimed divine truth to the Egyptians (cf. Exod 3:10; 4:16; 7:1); Elijah confronted the Phoenician princess Jezebel (1 Kgs 17–2 Kgs 2); Elisha issued divine instructions to the Syrian leper Naaman (2 Kgs 5); and Daniel operated as a missionary-statesman in Babylon and Medo-Persia (cf. Dan 2:1–45; 4:19–27). The Old Testament prophets also addressed the surrounding nations in their writings. Isaiah wrote concerning Babylon, Assyria, Philistia, Moab, Damascus, Ethiopia, Egypt, Dumah, Arabia, and Tyre (Isa 13–23). Jeremiah penned prophecies about Egypt, Philistia, Moab, Ammon, Edom, Damascus, Kedar, Hazor, Elam, and Babylon (Jer 46–51). Ezekiel preached about Ammon, Moab, Edom, Philistia, Tyre, Sidon, and Egypt (Ezek 25–32). Daniel, Obadiah, Nahum, and Zephaniah also declared the truth of God concerning Gentile nations. As repeatedly illustrated throughout the Old Testament, God chose Israel to be the messenger of His truth to all nations because He is the Lord over all people.

The New Testament writers also testified to God's care for both Jews and Gentiles (cf. Mark 7:26–30; John 4:7–26). Paul emphasized this point with a series of rhetorical questions: "Is God *the God* of Jews only? Is He not *the God* of Gentiles also?" (Rom 3:29; cf. Acts 18:6). Because the Lord has chosen to save both Jews and Gentiles, heaven will consist of saints "from every nation and *all* tribes and peoples and tongues" (Rev 7:9). A song of worship will resound in heaven, directed to the Lord Jesus Christ, "Worthy are You to take the scroll and to open its seals, because You were slain and purchased for God with Your blood *people* from every tribe and tongue and people and nation" (Rev 5:9). That heavenly anthem reflects the fulfillment of Christ's Great Commission (Matt 28:18–20), a call that demonstrates God's heart for sinners from Jerusalem and Judea to the very ends of the earth (cf. Acts 1:8).

The Great Commission in Matthew 28 was not the first time God issued a command to go and preach repentance to those beyond the borders of Israel. In the book of Jonah, the Lord directed His prophet to depart for another land (Jonah 1:2) and declare a message of impending judgment so that the people of Nineveh might repent and be saved. In that way, the book of Jonah previews the Great Commission, exhibiting Yahweh's great lovingkindness toward the nations.

Though God's heart on the matter was clear, Jonah callously refused to reflect that love to those outside Israel. When God commanded him to go and preach to Nineveh, he ran in the opposite direction. Jonah's disobedience has earned him a place of distinction among Old Testament prophets, as the only one who deliberately defied his divine commission. He knew that if he obeyed and preached to Nineveh, and if the people repented, the Lord would grant them mercy and stay His wrath. Jonah despised the notion that God might show compassion to a city as wicked as Nineveh. Preferring to see Israel's enemies perish, the prodigal prophet went absent without leave, evidencing a heart staunchly opposed to God's desire to save the nations.

In the opening section of this book, Yahweh graciously commissioned His prophet to warn the Gentiles in Nineveh of His impending judgment, so that they might repent. But Jonah had other ideas. Verses 1–2 present the Lord's compassionate directive regarding the Ninevites. Verse 3 reveals the prophet's calculated defiance, as he deliberately disobeyed. Verse 4 describes God's cataclysmic discipline on His wayward prophet, by means of a severe storm. In verse 5, the sailors reacted to the tempest with complete dread, while Jonah slept with calloused disregard. Finally, in verse 6, the captain of the ship responded with a cry of confounded desperation, confused as to why Jonah was sleeping, but also expressing the true need of every Gentile sinner: "Perhaps *your* god [the God of Israel] will be concerned about us so that we will not perish." An examination of these elements highlights the Lord's gracious compassion toward the nations, in contrast to the hard-hearted prejudice and pride of a petulant prophet who was supposed to represent Him.

The Lord's Directive

Now the word of Yahweh came to Jonah the son of Amittai saying, "Arise, go to Nineveh, the great city, and call out against it, for their evil has come up before Me." (1:1–2)

The opening verses introduce two drastically different characters: Yahweh and His prophet Jonah. As in other minor prophets (Hos 1:1; Joel 1:1; Mic 1:1; Zeph 1:1), **the word of Yahweh came** to the prophet, indicating that this book is divine truth (Deut 18:18–20; 2 Pet 1:20–21). Its contents are fundamentally God's own revelation,[1] being inspired by Him and therefore profitable for sanctification in the life of every believer (2 Tim 3:16–17). Scripture elsewhere uses this phrase (**the word of Yahweh**) to refer to more than a message, but in fact a Messenger (cf. Gen 15:1–6; Num 12:6–8; Jer 1:4–10; John 1:1–3; Col 1:16–17; Heb 1:1–2; Rev 19:13). When referencing a Person, the Word of Yahweh refers to the second Member of the Trinity, God the Son (cf. Isa 61:1; Zech 2:8–9; John 1:1; 5:24, 37; 7:29; 8:42; 10:36; 17:3; Rev 19:13). The Word of Yahweh created the world (Gen 1:1–3; Ps 33:6), upholds the natural order (1 Kgs 17:16), and governs history (Jer 47:1). In the case of Jonah, this connection between the message and the Messenger is vital. The gracious words of Yahweh through Jonah to Nineveh were only possible because of what the incarnate Word of Yahweh (John 1:14) would later accomplish on the cross (cf. 1 Tim 2:3–7). Thus, Yahweh's gracious commission reflected His saving character and pointed to the Person and work of the incarnate Word—the One who would come to redeem sinners from every tribe, tongue, and nation (Dan 7:13–14; Rev 7:9).

The recipient of this message, **Jonah the son of Amittai,** stood in stark contrast to the divine Messenger. Jonah was from Gath-hepher, located in Galilee. He ministered around 784–774 BC, during the reign of Jeroboam II (ca. 793–758 BC;

1 Stuart, *Hosea–Jonah*, 446.

cf. 2 Kgs 14:25; see Introduction for discussion). The name Jonah means "dove," a bird that represented either a messenger of peace (Gen 8:11) or a person acting foolishly (Hos 7:11). In this book, Jonah lived up to both contrasting meanings of his name. Though he brought a message of repentance to the Ninevites, indicating they could be pardoned by God if they turned from their wickedness, he also exhibited the folly of defiant disobedience. Perhaps it was Jonah's lack of faithfulness that centuries later caused the Pharisees of Jesus' day to discount his prophetic ministry. In attempting to discredit Jesus, the Jewish leaders issued this challenge: "Search and see that no prophet arises out of Galilee" (John 7:52; cf. 5:39). Whether intentional or not, they overlooked the ministry of Jonah, who was in fact a Galilean prophet. Despite Jonah's lack of faithfulness, God remained faithful, a reality reflected in Jonah's full name: the **son of Amittai,** meaning "truth." Throughout this book, the Lord repeatedly proved true to Jonah and to the people of Nineveh whom He sent Jonah to reach.

In commissioning His prophet, the Lord commanded Jonah to **arise,** calling him to **go** (cf. Gen 19:15; 27:43; 1 Kgs 17:9; Jer 13:6). In Israel's history, the Lord commissioned many prophets to proclaim His truth to the surrounding nations (see discussion above). Most did so without leaving the place where they lived. But God called Jonah to **go.** He was not to stay in his homeland, but to travel to a foreign city, bringing a warning of impending judgment.

God sent Jonah to Nineveh for several reasons. First, He desired to display His mercy and grace toward sinners, even those considered detestable by human standards (cf. Ezek 18:23). Second, God wished to expose Israel's calloused complacency and wicked hatred toward the Gentiles. Third, the Lord intended to use Nineveh's ready response to rebuke Israel for her stubborn refusal to repent. The wicked city of Nineveh repented at the proclamation of one prophet, but Israel stubbornly resisted

God's message though the Lord sent many prophets to His people (cf. Luke 10:13–15; Acts 7:52).

That Yahweh commanded Jonah to go to **Nineveh** certainly demonstrated His profound love for the lost. The city was the capital of Assyria, a major world power and one of Israel's greatest enemies. Israel's hatred for the Assyrians only intensified their animosity toward Gentiles in general, an attitude that continued into New Testament times (cf. John 4:9–10). In commissioning Jonah to go to Nineveh, God called His prophet to declare His message to Israel's foremost adversaries, the very people who would later conquer and destroy the northern kingdom (cf. 2 Kgs 17:1–6).

The Lord described Nineveh as **the great city,** in part because of its massive size. The city was founded by Nimrod (cf. Gen 10:8–9; Mic 5:6) on the east bank of the Tigris River, a location that provided the city with ample irrigation for crops and natural protection from potential invaders. Archaeological discoveries indicate that the population of Nineveh in Jonah's day was approximately 600,000 people. The fifty-five-mile-wide metropolitan area required a three-day journey to cross (Jonah 3:3).[2] Nineveh was not merely *a* great city, but **the** great city. Because of its size, infrastructure, wealth, and political power, it was one of the most formidable metropolitan centers of the ancient Near East. The city was also of importance to God who cared about its many inhabitants (cf. 3:5, 10; 4:11). By sending Jonah to this Gentile capital, the Lord demonstrated His compassionate commitment to the nations (cf. Gen 12:1–3; 22:18; Isa 49:6; Rom 3:29).

Though He intended to show mercy to the Ninevites, Yahweh summoned Jonah to **call out against** the city. God commissioned His spokesman to proclaim both judgment and mercy (cf. Jonah 4:2), but that full declaration was not given here. Nevertheless, judgment was an essential part of Jonah's message

2 Smith and Page, *Amos, Obadiah, Jonah*, 257; Grayson, "Nineveh," 4:1118.

especially since Nineveh's **wickedness** had **come up before** God. Like Sodom and Gomorrah, which were described with similar language (cf. Gen 18:20–21), Nineveh's depravity was rampant and repugnant. The prophet Nahum depicted Nineveh as a bloody city full of fraud, lies, theft, sensuality, violence, witchcraft, and idolatry (Nah 3:1, 4). Their soldiers were infamous for barbarism and brutality (3:1–3). God knew their wickedness, and His wrath was kindled against them. But the deep darkness of their iniquity would provide a vivid backdrop against which God's saving grace would shine (cf. Pss 51:1–19; 130:3–4; Isa 6:5–7; Acts 2:37–40; Rom 1–3; Eph 2:1–10). No presentation of the message of God's grace is complete without a clear explanation of God's judgment against sin (cf. Isa 53:5, 10–12; Rom 6:23; 1 Cor 15:3). For this reason, Jonah's message of divine mercy began with the truth of divine wrath being stored up against sinners for their wickedness.

The Prophet's Defiance

Yet Jonah arose to flee to Tarshish from the presence of Yahweh. So he went down to Joppa, found a ship which was going to Tarshish, and paid its fare and went down into it to go with them to Tarshish from the presence of Yahweh. (1:3)

In response to God's calling, Jonah **arose,** just as God had commanded him to do. But there his obedience ended. Jonah took urgent action not to heed God's directive but to head in the opposite direction. Instead of arising to "go" (cf. 1:2), Jonah arose **to flee,** running away to avoid his God-given mission. Rather than travel to Nineveh, he boarded a ship bound for **Tarshish** (cf. 1 Kgs 10:22; 22:48; Isa 23:1, 6, 10, 14), a city some 2,500 miles in the opposite direction, located likely off the coast of Spain.

In his disobedience, Jonah displayed both defiance and delusion by attempting to flee **from the presence of Yahweh.** The rebellious prophet was well aware of God's omnipresence. In Psalm 139:7, David had asked rhetorically, "Where can I go from Your Spirit? Or where can I flee from Your presence?" Jonah himself later exclaimed that God reigns over heaven and earth (Jonah 1:9). Though the prophet comprehended this theological truth, he denied it in practice, hoping geographical distance would be enough to thwart God's plans. Jonah's mad-dash escape was as foolish as it was futile. No matter how far away he tried to hide, Jonah knew that "even there Your hand will lead me, and Your right hand will lay hold of me" (Ps 139:10). Though aware of God's character, Jonah ran anyway, illustrating just how obtuse and offensive disobedience can be (cf. 2 Kgs 19:28; Pss 50:16–21; 51:4; Rom 1:20–21).

In departing for Tarshish, Jonah **went down,** a verb repeated numerous times in the next few verses (Jonah 1:3, 5). The prophet's repeated descent illustrated his determination to escape from Yahweh. The prophet first went down to **Joppa,** a town just south of modern Tel Aviv. It was the only city in Israel with a natural harbor, thus providing the fastest way to reach Tarshish. The people of Israel were not a seafaring people like those of Tyre (cf. Ezek 27:28–36). They viewed such ventures as risky and perilous (cf. Acts 27:14–44). But in his determination to disobey, Jonah prioritized speed over safety. He preferred to face the dangers of the open sea rather than follow God's command.[3]

At Joppa, the prophet **found a ship which was going to Tarshish.** Instead of obediently journeying northeast over land to Nineveh, Jonah attempted to head west over water. A **ship going to Tarshish** would most likely be a trade vessel carrying cargo (cf. Jonah 1:5), not passengers. So, Jonah's fare was probably very expensive, since he would have taken up space normally reserved for goods. It is even possible that Jonah chartered the entire ship, since the wording in Hebrew is literally "its [the ship's] wages." While Jonah may have paid only for a berth on the vessel, it is possible that he actually financed the entire expedition. Rapidly pulling together the large amount of money, bringing it to the port, and negotiating

3 Allen, *The Books of Joel, Obadiah, Jonah, and Micah,* 205.

passage on a cargo ship was no small task. Jonah went to great lengths not to obey God.

Having secured transport, the fugitive prophet **went down into it to go with them to Tarshish from the presence of Yahweh.** Jonah again **went down,** this time **into** the ship. In his continual descent, he attempted to hide himself further from God, again displaying both stubbornness and stupidity (cf. Gen 3:8, 10). As the Lord declared in Jeremiah, "'Am I a God who is near,' declares Yahweh, 'and not a God far off? Can a man hide himself in hiding places so I do not see him?' declares Yahweh. 'Do I not fill the heavens and the earth?' declares Yahweh" (Jer 23:23–24). No matter how far Jonah tried to go **down,** he could not descend beyond God's reach. The defiant prophet arrogantly assumed he could flee **from the presence of Yahweh.** That phrase is found at the beginning and the end of verse 3, emphasizing the irrational nature of Jonah's antics.

Jonah was acting as if God reigned in just one place and over only one people. He evidently wished that were the case, since he did not want the Lord to extend His compassion to anyone beyond the borders of Israel. As he later confessed, he feared that God would show mercy to the Gentiles. He exclaimed to the Lord, "You are a gracious and compassionate God, slow to anger and abundant in lovingkindness, and one who relents concerning evil" (Jonah 4:2). Significantly, Jonah was not afraid of the Ninevites themselves, but of the possibility that God would show them mercy.[4] Jonah knew that the Lord would be compassionate if the Ninevites repented, and he did not want to give them that opportunity.

Jonah's story thus began with an amazing directive from God and an equally astounding act of disobedience on the part of His prophet. Though Jonah's defiance was deeply disappointing, God had a purpose for it, not only in regard to ancient Israel but also in the grand scope of redemptive history. Jonah went to Joppa to avoid taking God's message to those outside of Israel. But

4 Smith and Page, *Amos, Obadiah, Jonah,* 223

nearly 800 years later, Peter Bar-Jonah arrived at Joppa to fulfill his God-given mission to the Gentiles (Acts 9:39; 10:9–16). Unlike Jonah, the Apostle Peter obeyed the Lord's command, travelling from Joppa to Caesarea to the house of a Gentile named Cornelius (10:17–33). There, Peter declared the truth that Jonah sought to suppress. As Peter declared, "I most truly comprehend *now* that God is not one to show partiality, but in every nation the one who fears Him and does righteousness is welcome to Him" (10:34–35). For Jonah, Joppa represented an egregious act of defiance against God's mission to the nations; for Peter and the early church, it signified the inclusion of believing Gentiles into the people of God (cf. 11:18).

The Lord's Discipline

But Yahweh hurled a great wind on the sea, and there was a great storm on the sea so that the ship gave thought to breaking apart. (1:4)

Though Jonah thought he could escape God's presence, the Lord did not allow it. As the ship was in transit, **Yahweh hurled a great wind on the sea.** The wind and subsequent storm were not the result of predictable weather patterns but the effect of God's direct intervention. The verb **hurled** vividly describes the ferocity with which the Lord launched this storm. The same word was used when Saul threw his javelin at David, attempting to pin him to the wall (1 Sam 18:11). In the case of Jonah, this divine act of hurling produced a chain reaction. Because God **hurled** the storm, the sailors hurled their cargo over the side of the ship (Jonah 1:5). Jonah subsequently instructed them to hurl him into the sea (1:12), which is what they ultimately did (1:15). As the repetition of the word **hurled** demonstrates, the Lord not only orchestrated the storm but also sovereignly directed every part of the ensuing action.

The name **Yahweh** stresses God's commitment to His elect, both to chastise them when they disobey (Prov 3:11; Heb 12:4–17) and to bring to Himself those on whom He has set His love (John 6:44; 10:16; Rom 9:23–24). On this occasion, the Lord used the storm both to discipline Jonah and to draw the sailors to Himself. He hurled a **great wind** to incite **a great storm on the sea.** The Hebrew word for **storm** can encompass torrential downpours, hurricane-force winds, and flooding waters (cf. Ps 55:9). Because of their fierce intensity, storms served as a metaphor for battle and the breakout of God's wrath (Jer 23:19; 25:32; 30:23; Amos 1:4). Though any storm would be fearsome, this storm was far from typical. It was **great,** beyond what any of the seasoned crew members had experienced before, causing them to be overcome with terror (cf. Jonah 1:5, 10, 13). The tempest was so furious that the sailors knew it was not natural but supernatural (cf. 1:5).

With power and precision, the Lord whipped up **the sea** exactly where Jonah was located. The omnipresence of God comforts the saints with the reality that they will never be lost from His protective gaze (cf. Ps 139:7–12). But it also brings constant accountability (cf. Prov 15:3). No sin is secret from God, and no one can hide from His judgment (cf. Num 32:23; Eccl 12:14; Ezek 7:5–19; Hos 10:8; Luke 12:2; Heb 4:13; Rev 6:16). As Ruler of heaven and earth (cf. Pss 24:1–2; 50:12; 89:11; 98:7; Isa 42:10), the Lord moved sky and sea to usher judgment with pinpoint accuracy upon a solitary ship carrying a stubborn stowaway.

Even the boat recognized God's hand of discipline. The storm was so violent that the **ship gave thought to breaking apart.** Most English translations simply state that the ship was about to fall apart, emphasizing the severity of the gale as it eviscerated the wooden vessel. But the Hebrew text personifies the ship as if it contemplated breaking into pieces. This anthropomorphic description of the boat is in line with how other objects are depicted throughout the book. The stormy gale (Jonah 1:4), the sea (1:15), the fish (1:17; 2:10), the plant (4:6), the worm (4:7), and the scorching east wind (4:8) were all immediately submissive to the Lord. Everything in the book reacted properly to Yahweh's commands except for Jonah. The prophet's disobedience warranted divine discipline, which is why the Lord hurled such a sudden and severe storm upon the sea.

The Sailors' Dread

Then the sailors became fearful, and every man cried to his god, and they hurled the cargo which was in the ship into the sea to lighten *it* for them. (1:5a)

The Lord's primary purpose for the storm was to intervene in the life of His runaway prophet. But God also used it to work in the hearts of the **sailors** on the ship. With the storm surrounding them, the sailors **became fearful.** God employed the weather to arrest their full attention. The words of Psalm 107 describe such a scene:

> Those who go down to the sea in ships,
> Who do business on many waters;
> They have seen the works of Yahweh,
> And His wondrous deeds in the deep.
> He spoke and set up a stormy wind,
> Which raised up the waves of the sea.
> They went up to the heavens, they went down to the depths;
> Their soul melted away in *the* calamity.
> They staggered and swayed like a drunken man,
> And all their wisdom was swallowed up.
> Then they cried to Yahweh in their trouble,
> And He brought them out of their distresses.
> He caused the storm to stand still,
> So that its waves were hushed.
> Then they were glad because they were quiet,
> So He led them to their desired haven.
> Let them give thanks to Yahweh for His lovingkindness,
> And for His wondrous deeds to the sons of men! (Ps 107:23–31)

The events of Jonah 1 displayed the extent of Yahweh's compassion. His care extended not only to Gentiles living in great cities like Nineveh, but even to crusty sailors venturing on a boat in the middle of the sea.

The storm struck such fear into the crew that **every man cried to his god.** While these pagan Gentiles did not yet know the true God, the Lord used the storm to bring **every man** to consider his mortality and the need for divine intervention. The sailors frantically **hurled the cargo which was in the ship into the sea to lighten *it* for them. The cargo which was in the ship** included heavy equipment and the ship's payload—the goods that were being hauled for trade. The sailors took drastic measures to lighten the ship, incurring massive financial loss as a result. With life and death flashing before them, their priorities shifted from saving material goods to saving themselves (cf. Job 33:19–22; Ps 49:1–20; Eccl 12:6–7; Luke 7:1–9; Jas 1:2–4, 9–11; 1 Pet 5:10). As noted above, the verb "hurl" was also used of God hurling the great wind that incited the storm (Jonah 1:4). The Lord had hurled the wind that caused the sailors to hurl their cargo. He brought them to a point of despair so their eyes would turn from temporal concerns to spiritual realities.

The Prophet's Disregard

But Jonah had gone down *below* into the innermost part of the vessel, lain down, and fallen deep asleep. (1:5b)

While the sailors were overcome with fear, Jonah exhibited total disregard for the danger of those around him. He was overcome only by drowsiness. **Jonah had gone down *below* into the innermost part of the vessel, lain down, and fallen deep asleep.** For the third time, **Jonah had gone down.** He had gone down to Joppa (Jonah 1:3a), then down to the boat (1:3b), and now down **into the innermost part of the vessel.** He was still attempting to escape God's presence by hiding in the lowest place he could find. The prophet buried himself in the bowels of the ship to insulate himself from the Lord. While the sailors in their terror prayed to false gods, Jonah deliberately ignored the true God. In so doing, he engaged in an idolatry of his own, by treating Yahweh as though He were a God who is neither omnipresent nor omniscient (cf. Exod 20:4–5; Ps 50:21).

After descending below deck, Jonah demonstrated further audacity by laying himself down (cf. Judg 5:27), confidently silencing his conscience, and being at ease as he fell **deep asleep.** The same word described Adam's sleep when the Lord took one of his ribs to form Eve (Gen 2:21), or Sisera's slumber before he was killed by Jael (Judg 4:21). While the sailors panicked, Jonah slept soundly, oblivious to the peril surrounding him. The prophet's smug indifference illustrated the self-righteousness that characterized unrepentant Israel throughout the nation's history (cf. Isa 1:11–15; Jer 7:1–26; Matt 15:1–9; Luke 18:11–12).

The Captain's Desperation

So the captain came near to him and said to him, "How is it that you are deeply sleeping? Arise, call on your god. Perhaps *your* god will be concerned about us so that we will not perish." (1:6)

In verse 6, the **captain came near** to look for Jonah. The term **captain** designated the chief of those who pulled the ropes to steer the ship. Though unable to navigate the storm, this captain was used by God to steer Jonah. The Lord directed him to confront the disobedient prophet, asking incredulously, **"How is it that you are deeply sleeping?"** The captain was shocked that Jonah displayed such apathy in light of their dire circumstances. That a pagan sailor understood the situation better than an Israelite prophet was a severe indictment. At one point in Israel's history, God used a donkey to restrain a prophet's madness (Num 22:31–34; cf. 2 Pet 2:15–16); here, the Lord used the rebuke of a Gentile sea captain.

The bewildered sailor not only reproved Jonah but also exhorted him, saying, **"Arise, call on your god."** The captain commanded the sleeping prophet to **arise** and repent from his wicked indifference. Moreover, to the prophet who tried to escape the Lord's presence, the captain urged him to **call on your god.** In a strange way, this was a call from a pagan for genuine repentance—for Jonah to turn from rebellion to his God. In that call, the captain served as God's mouthpiece to Jonah. The commands to **arise** and **call** are the very commands the Lord used when He initially commissioned Jonah (cf. 1:2). God put His words in the captain's mouth to summon His wayward prophet to return to Him and fulfill what He had commissioned him to do.

Even while employing the captain to work on Jonah, God was also at work on the captain himself. The captain concluded his speech to Jonah, saying, **"Perhaps *your* god will be concerned about us so that we will not perish."** The captain was still spiritually blind, viewing Yahweh as merely a **god.** But the Lord was introducing him and the other crew members to Himself, using the storm to open their eyes to the true God (John 9:39; 2 Cor 4:4–6). The sailors had been calling on their gods, but to no avail (Jonah 1:5). The crisis revealed the impotence of their demonic pagan deities, who were neither **concerned** for them nor able to prevent them from perishing. Having exhausted all other options, the captain turned to Jonah. In saying **"perhaps,"** the captain indicated he was not certain that Yahweh would have compassion on him and his fellow shipmates. But he was desperate enough to acknowledge his helplessness and to turn to Jonah's God for deliverance. The Lord was bringing the captain to the point where he would realize that the God of Israel was his only hope. Every sinner, whether Jew or Gentile, must come to that same point of recognition in order to be saved (cf. Rom 10:13). The question was whether or not Yahweh would show compassion to him and his colleagues. The answer to that question lies at the heart of this book. It was the very reality

Jonah resisted—the willingness of the Lord to show grace and kindness to the nations.

This was not the last time a ship, a storm, and salvation figured into God's plan. Eight centuries after Jonah, the Lord Jesus, like Jonah, boarded a boat (Matt 8:23; Mark 4:36; Luke 8:22) and fell asleep (Matt 8:24b; Mark 4:38; Luke 8:23a) as the ship encountered a storm (Matt 8:24a; Mark 4:37; Luke 8:23b). But this time, unlike Jonah, Christ not only calmed the storm (Matt 8:26; Mark 4:39; Luke 8:24) but also went to the Gentiles in obedience to God's call (Matt 8:29; Mark 5:1; Luke 8:26; cf. Matt 28:18–20). About thirty years after that account from the life of Christ, another ship set sail only to be wrecked by a storm (Acts 27–28). This time, the Apostle Paul, sent by Christ, boarded that vessel (27:2) to journey to Rome (27:6), so that the gospel would go forth from Rome to the ends of the earth (28:28). Jonah's hard-hearted disobedience was not the final word on Yahweh's heart for the nations. The God who was drawing the sailors to Himself in the book of Jonah is the God who continues to draw sinners to Himself from every nation, tribe, and tongue.

A Great Fish and the Fishing of Men

2

JONAH 1:7–17

Then each man said to the other, "Come, let us have *the* lots fall so we may know on whose account this *calamitous* evil *has struck* us." So they had *the* lots fall, and the lot fell on Jonah. Then they said to him, "Tell us, now! On whose account *has* this *calamitous* evil *struck* us? What is your occupation? And where do you come from? What is your country? From what people are you?" And he said to them, "I am a Hebrew, and I fear Yahweh, the God of heaven, who made the sea and the dry land." Then the men became greatly fearful, and they said to him, "What is this you have done?" For the men knew that he was fleeing from the presence of Yahweh because he had told them. So they said to him, "What should we do to you that the sea may become quiet for us?"—for the sea was becoming increasingly stormy. So he said to them, "Lift me up and hurl me into the sea. Then the sea will become quiet for you, for I know that on account of me this great storm *has come* upon you." However, the men rowed *desperately* to return to dry land, but they could not, for the sea was becoming increasingly stormy against them. Then they called on Yahweh and said, "Ah! O Yahweh, we earnestly pray, do not let us perish on account of this man's life, and do

not put innocent blood on us; for You, O Yahweh, as You have pleased You have done." So they lifted Jonah up and hurled him into the sea, and the sea stood still from its raging. Then the men greatly feared Yahweh, and they offered a sacrifice to Yahweh and made vows. And Yahweh appointed a great fish to swallow Jonah, and Jonah was in the stomach of the fish three days and three nights.

Why do natural disasters and catastrophic events occur in this world? Scripture answers that question by pointing to mankind's fall into sin (Gen 3:1–7), when God placed a curse on creation as a result of Adam and Eve's disobedience (Gen 3:17–19; Rom 6:23; 8:22–23; Col 1:20). Ever since, calamities have occurred as a consequence of sin and its curse, including droughts (Job 24:19; Jer 14:1), floods (Matt 7:27), earthquakes (Ps 46:2–3; Amos 1:1), and wildfires (Isa 1:7). These deadly realities serve as painful reminders of what it means to live in a fallen world.

Though every natural disaster represents divine judgment in a general sense, the Lord sometimes unleashes calamity in response to particularly egregious sin. Because of humanity's exceeding wickedness, God sent a global flood to destroy the world, preserving only those on the ark (cf. Gen 6:5). In Genesis 19, the Lord rained down fire and brimstone on the perverse cities of Sodom and Gomorrah. He later leveled Egypt with ten devastating plagues because Pharaoh refused to stop oppressing God's people (Exod 1–15). Because of Israel's grumbling in the wilderness, Yahweh sent poisonous serpents, causing many to die (Num 21; cf. 25:1–9). When David sinfully took a census, the Lord sent a pestilence that claimed the lives of 70,000 people (2 Sam 24:15; and see 1 Chr 21). Looking to the future, Jesus foretold that at the end of the age, "Nation will rise against nation and kingdom against kingdom, and there will be great earthquakes, and in various places famines and plagues; and there will be terrors and great signs from heaven" (Luke 21:10–11; cf. Matt 24:7; Mark 13:7–8). While natural disasters are not always indicative of God's specific condemnation (cf. Job 1; John 9:1–3), the Lord often uses catastrophic events to execute His wrath.

Whether due to the general effects of a fallen world or to a special act of divine wrath, all natural disasters punctuate a critical spiritual reality. Commenting on two deadly tragedies that occurred in Jerusalem (Luke 13:1, 4), Jesus warned His listeners, "Unless you repent, you will all likewise perish" (13:5). Catastrophic events serve as vivid reminders of the brevity of this life and the need for divine forgiveness. As Jesus explained, only by repenting from sin, and turning to the Lord in faith, can sinners be saved from God's judgment in both this life and the life to come (John 11:25–26; 1 Thess 4:13–18).

Any disaster should point people to the need for repentance and salvation, but God created this storm recorded in Jonah 1 specifically to draw the attention of both the desperate sailors and His disobedient servant to Himself. Building on the dramatic scene presented in verses 1–6, this passage (vv. 7–17) continues to describe all that God was accomplishing through the fierce tempest. Verses 7–8 recount the sailors' discovery that Jonah was the specific target of this deluge of divine discipline. Verse 9 records Jonah's declaration of Yahweh's sovereign power. Verses 10–13 depict the crew's subsequent dismay, culminating with their deliverance from the storm in verses 14–16. Finally, the chapter concludes with Jonah's detainment and miraculous deliverance by means of a great fish (v. 17). God's deep-sea rescue of His prophet was so spectacular that it foreshadowed the greatest deliverance of all—the salvation of sinners accomplished through the death and resurrection of the Lord Jesus Christ (cf. Matt 12:38–41). Though Jonah fled from God to counteract His mercy, God nevertheless used Jonah's actions to display the wonder of His grace.

The Sailors' Discovery

Then each man said to the other, "Come, let us have *the* lots fall so we may know on whose account this *calamitous* evil *has struck* us." So they had *the* lots fall, and the lot fell on Jonah. Then they said to him, "Tell us, now! On whose account *has* this *calamitous* evil *struck* us? What is your occupation? And where do you come from? What is your country? From what people are you?" (1:7–8)

The suddenness and severity of the storm convinced the sailors that it was no natural event. They believed that it was driven by a supernatural source, but they did not understand why it was being hurled against them. So, **each man said to the other, "Come, let us have *the* lots fall..."** In ancient times, **lots** could be anything from dice to little pieces of straw or small sticks. People would cast these items, believing that the way they fell provided a divine answer to the question asked. Though this primitive action may seem random and merely superstitious, it was not outside of God's sovereign control. As Solomon declared, "The lot is cast into the lap, but its every judgment is from Yahweh" (Prov 16:33). While no longer a valid means for discerning His will, God sometimes worked through the casting of lots in the past before the canon of Scripture was completed (cf. Josh 7:14; 1 Sam 14:36–45; Acts 1:26). The sailors were hoping for such a supernatural result, saying, **"so we may know on whose account this *calamitous* evil *has struck* us."** The crew assumed that someone in their midst was guilty of great evil against some powerful deity, and they believed that it was on his **account** that this god sent the ***calamitous*** **evil. So they had *the* lots fall, and the lot fell on Jonah.** In a single verse, the word **fall** is used three times as the sailors propose to make the lots **fall,** the lots then **fall,** and they **fall** on Jonah. The repetition of this word indicates that God providentially directed the seemingly random action of the sailors to uncover the culprit who knew the truth.

The sailors immediately barraged Jonah with an interrogation to confirm that he was the guilty party, asking, **"On whose account *has* this *calamitous* evil *struck* us?"** Wanting to gauge his credibility, they questioned, **"What is your occupation?"** Perhaps thinking Jonah had offended a regional deity, they inquired, **"And where do you come from?"** To gain more information about Jonah's God, they pressed him, **"What is your country?"** And further, **"From what people are you?"** Fear made the sailors eager to know the person whose offense had put them in such danger. They were not, however, prepared for the truth that Jonah was about to reveal.

The Prophet's Declaration

And he said to them, "I am a Hebrew, and I fear Yahweh, the God of heaven, who made the sea and the dry land." (1:9)

Jonah answered the sailors' questions with one terse sentence. First, by nationality, he was a **Hebrew.** The word was often used by foreigners to identify the people of Israel (Gen 39:14, 17; 40:15; 41:12; Exod 1:15–16), distinguishing the nation from all others in their appearance, practices, and ideology (Gen 43:32; Exod 3:18; 7:16). For example, the Philistines spoke of Israel as "the Hebrews" in recounting the plagues against Egypt (1 Sam 4:6–8). Like the term "Christian" associated Jesus' followers with Jesus in the New Testament (cf. Acts 11:26; 26:28), so the term "Hebrews" associated the Israelites with Yahweh and the practices related to the worship He prescribed. By identifying himself in this way, Jonah revealed to the sailors his homeland, heritage, history, and the distinctives of his people with regard to holiness, sin, and sacrifice.

Jonah then summarized the nature of his relationship with God by saying that he lived in the **fear** of **Yahweh,** denoting not only supreme reverence but also genuine terror. While the gods of the ancient Near East might have been respected, they were also exploited and even mocked by their followers. The God of Israel, Yahweh, however, was not like the demonic, capricious, and foolish deities of the surrounding nations, nor was He a projection of human imagination (cf. Ps 50:21). False demon-inspired gods could make their followers afraid, but Yahweh was the one to be truly feared (cf. Exod 14:31). As Jonah knew, the true God was perfectly holy (Lev 19:1–2). He refused to tolerate wickedness (Hab 1:13). His glory compelled angels to worship Him perpetually (Isa 6:3). His sovereignty caused the rise and fall of kingdoms (Dan 2:37–45). He created and destroyed with a word (Gen 1:1–2; Ps 33:6; Heb 1:3). And His righteous wrath devastated the disobedient (Lev 10:1–3; Ps 7:10–16). Such a God truly was fearsome (Pss 46:8; 76:7; 111:9). Ironically, while Jonah only claimed to fear the Lord, the pagan sailors, terrorized by the fierce storm, actually were gripped by fear (Jonah 1:5, 10), grasping in ignorance Yahweh's majestic power far better than the disobedient prophet who represented Him.

Jonah declared to the men that he served not just any god, but that he served **Yahweh.** By using God's personal and covenant name, the prophet pointed the sailors to the God of Israel. The name **Yahweh** refers back to God's self-disclosure to Moses in the revelation of "I AM WHO I AM" (Exod 3:14). As "I AM," God revealed that He is self-existent, since He always is, eternally existing and never having been created. He is also immutable since He constantly is and never becomes anything else. As "I AM," God is infinite, for He is not confined to time; He always is and forever will be (John 8:58; Heb 13:8). God is transcendent, so that, unlike false gods, He cannot be defined by any created thing in this world or fully described by human language. Nothing compares to Him (cf. Exod 15:11; Ps 113:5; Isa 44:7). God gave His people His personal name, Yahweh (cf. Exod 3:14), demonstrating that He is a God both of eternal preeminence and of boundless love and faithfulness (cf. Ps 89:8).

Jonah emphasized that Yahweh was the **God of heaven,** highlighting His supreme authority and lordship over the supernatural realm. God also had complete sovereignty over the natural realm, for He **made the sea and the dry land.** By identifying Yahweh as the Creator, Jonah highlighted both God's transcendence over and distinction from His creation. The doctrine of creation lays the foundation that God is the sovereign Sustainer and Judge of the world. Jonah, like the prophets and the apostles, began his declaration of the truth with creation and with God as the Creator of all (cf. Gen 1:1; Ps 95:5; Isa 51:13; Acts 17:24–26; Rom 1:19).

As Creator and sovereign God, Yahweh alone possesses definitive and comprehensive authority over everything. By referencing **the sea and the dry land,** Jonah made plain to the sailors that Yahweh was the One who caused the terrifying storm on **the sea** and that He alone would determine whether they returned to **the dry land** (cf. Jonah 1:13, 16). The prophet stressed not only that Yahweh reigned over the world in a general sense but also that He exercised specific and absolute control over the sailors' current situation.

For conversion to occur, sinners must hear the truth (cf. Rom 10:17) and turn from false idols to the one true God (cf. Acts 17:22–31; 1 Thess 1:9). In a short sentence, Jonah pointed the sailors away from their gods to recognize the one true God of Israel, Yahweh, the Creator, who exclusively rules over the natural and the supernatural. In an ironic twist, the prophet who fled God's presence to avoid telling a Gentile city about Yahweh found himself declaring the truth about the Lord to these Gentile sailors.

The Crew's Dismay

Then the men became greatly fearful, and they said to him, "What is this you have done?" For the men knew that he was fleeing from the presence of Yahweh because he had told them. So they said to him, "What should we do to you that the sea may become quiet for us?"—for the sea was becoming increasingly

stormy. So he said to them, "Lift me up and hurl me into the sea. Then the sea will become quiet for you, for I know that on account of me this great storm *has come* upon you." However, the men rowed *desperately* to return to dry land, but they could not, for the sea was becoming increasingly stormy against them. (1:10–13)

Upon hearing the truth, **the men became greatly fearful.** Literally, the text says in Hebrew, "the men became fearful *with* great fear." The repetition of the word "fear" along with "great" describes overwhelming dread. The sailors were already fearful (Jonah 1:5), but upon hearing about the one true God, who controlled His creation, they experienced terror that far surpassed their earlier misgivings. While Jonah claimed to fear God (1:9), the sailors actually did fear Him, fearing Him **greatly,** even more than the storm itself (1:5). Their fear indicated that they rightly grasped the awesome and majestic nature of the true God (Deut 10:12, 20; Phil 2:12; 1 Pet 1:17).

In dismay, the sailors exclaimed to the fugitive prophet, **"What is this you have done?"** Jonah's reckless rebellion had placed them in grave danger. The **men knew that he was fleeing from the presence of Yahweh** and expressed their disbelief at what Jonah had cavalierly **told them.** Horrified by the prophet's defiant insubordination, the sailors expressed shock at Jonah's audacity. At that point, the pagan idolaters manifested a clearer understanding of the one true God than Jonah did.

Having conveyed their alarm, the panicked sailors sought a remedy, pleading, **"What should we do to you that the sea may become quiet for us?"** Those who fear God and discern the seriousness of sin, sincerely inquire, "What should we do?" (Acts 2:37; 16:30), and the sailors demonstrated such concern. They recognized that **the sea** would **become quiet** only after God's wrath was appeased. Unlike Jonah, these men comprehended the gravity of sin and its consequences, so they were fully preoccupied with how they might placate Yahweh.

The urgency of the sailors' question reflected the dire nature of their circumstances, as **the sea was becoming increasingly stormy.** The storm had already overwhelmed the ship and its crew, and it was growing more dangerous and deadly.

Strangely, Jonah remained arrogant, unrepentant, and resigned to divine judgment. Responding to the sailors' questions, Jonah said, **"Lift me up and hurl me into the sea. Then the sea will become quiet for you, for I know that on account of me this great storm *has come* upon you."** While Jonah's answer may have appeared pious—giving a pretense of taking responsibility for his sin to save others—it was far from righteous. Stubbornly unwilling to repent of his sin and to agree to go to Nineveh, he preferred death by drowning over obedience to God. He said to the sailors, **"Lift me up and hurl me into the sea"** in an attempt to coerce them to end his life. Only then, he insisted, **"the sea will become quiet for you."** The stiff-necked prophet knew his sin, acknowledging **that on account of** him **this great storm** had ***come* upon** the crew. But he made clear that he would rather perish in the sea under God's judgment than submit and see the Ninevites repent.

Hurl is used in verse 4 to describe God hurling the wind to instigate the storm. Yahweh had hurled the storm to orchestrate a set of circumstances that would compel His impenitent prophet to request being hurled into the sea. God still had a plan for Jonah, even if Jonah had not yet repented of his rebellion.

Responding to Jonah's words and fearing His God, **the men rowed *desperately* to return to dry land. Rowed** can refer to digging into or breaking through a great wall (cf. Ezek 8:8; 12:5, 7, 12). The sailors were vigorously digging their oars into the water, attempting to **return to dry land.** Though Jonah's disobedience had placed them in great danger, they nonetheless showed Jonah mercy, seeking to return to shore without tossing him overboard. Such an action would have constituted murder, and the men did not want to be guilty of taking a life. Incredibly, Jonah was not willing to show compassion to the Gentiles in Nineveh, but these

Gentile sailors were further endangering their lives by showing compassion to him.

Though the sailors made extended efforts to row to shore, **they could not, for the sea was becoming increasingly stormy against them.** The violent weather (Jonah 1:11) became **increasingly stormy,** actively preventing any progress. God directed the tempest to counter the sailors' efforts. In the face of such immense power, the men understood the truth of what Jonah had declared, that Yahweh was indeed over "the sea and the dry land" (1:9). Try as they might, the sailors could not resist His sovereign power. The Lord had hurled the storm on the sea (1:4) so that Jonah would be hurled off the ship (1:12, 15), and God's purpose would be accomplished.

The Gentiles' Deliverance

Then they called on Yahweh and said, "Ah! O Yahweh, we earnestly pray, do not let us perish on account of this man's life, and do not put innocent blood on us; for You, O Yahweh, as You have pleased You have done." So they lifted Jonah up and hurled him into the sea, and the sea stood still from its raging. Then the men greatly feared Yahweh, and they offered a sacrifice to Yahweh and made vows. (1:14–16)

Having become exhausted with every effort, the sailors acknowledged their inability and **called on Yahweh.** Having heard Jonah's declaration in verse 9, they no longer appealed to their native gods nor to a generic supernatural power. Rather, they directed their petitions to Yahweh, the Creator of the sea and the land. In this way, the sailors turned from their idols to beseech deliverance from the one true God (cf. Acts 14:15; Gal 4:8–9).

The crew's attitude reflected their new religious focus—the fear of Yahweh. They pleaded, saying, **"Ah! O Yahweh, we earnestly pray."** The Hebrew original expresses deep emotion, conveying the humility and desperation of their entreaty. Their prayer consisted of two requests. First, regarding their immediate situation, they begged the Lord, **"Do not let us perish on account of this man's life."** The sailors appealed to God not to kill them for participating in His punishment of the disobedient prophet. They assumed God to be an impartial (Deut 10:17) and righteous Judge (Ps 96:13) who does not overlook wicked means in accomplishing righteous ends. Accordingly, the sailors made a second request, **"Do not put innocent blood on us."** Though Jonah was far from **innocent,** the sailors did not want to be held guilty for killing a prophet of Yahweh. The shedding of **innocent blood** was a heinous crime, even in pagan culture. Any murderer usurps God's authority as judge and executioner by taking the life of another person (cf. Deut 19:10; 21:8; Jer 26:15). Fearful of Yahweh, the sailors did not merely want to avoid divine retribution, but they also wanted to avoid sinning against the one true God. So they begged for the Lord's mercy even as they considered killing Jonah.

The sailors' appeals were predicated on a recognition of Yahweh's power and sovereignty. They confessed, **"for You, O Yahweh, as You have pleased You have done."** By directly addressing the Lord with the words **"for You, O Yahweh,"** the sailors acknowledged the true and living God. They also declared the theological truth that, **"as You have pleased You have done,"** a reality that distinguishes Yahweh from all others (cf. Pss 115:1–3; 135:5–6). Unlike inanimate and lifeless idols, Yahweh is **pleased** to act, taking delight to select one matter over another (cf. Num 14:8; 1 Kgs 10:9; Hos 6:6). No one determines, influences, or counsels God on His decisions (Isa 40:14; Rom 11:34). He determines everything based on the counsel of His will (Eph 1:11). Recognizing this (**for**), the sailors understood what they needed to do. Yielding to God's will, the men reluctantly did what Jonah had initially told them was necessary. **They lifted Jonah up and hurled him into the sea** (cf. Jonah 1:12), so that God's sovereign purpose was executed.

Once the sailors had thrown the prophet overboard, **the sea stood still from its raging.** The chaotic scene became instantly calm just as Jonah had predicted (cf. v. 12). Yahweh irrefutably demonstrated Himself to be everything that Jonah had declared about Him. As the sailors experienced firsthand, the Lord was indeed sovereign over the sea. Therefore, the water **stood still from its raging** because unlike the prophet, the sea fully submitted to God (cf. Mark 4:41).

This undeniable miracle escalated the sailors' fear. **The men greatly feared Yahweh**—not the storm or the sea, but **Yahweh.** This exact language was used earlier to describe the highest reverence toward the one true God (cf. v. 10). Accordingly, **they offered a sacrifice to Yahweh,** evidencing their sincere worship to the Lord (Gen 46:1; Exod 24:5; Lev 17:5; 1 Sam 6:15). They also **made vows,** or solemn promises, to Yahweh because He had answered their prayers (cf. 1 Sam 1:11; Ps 116:17; Isa 19:21). They committed themselves to honor Him (Deut 23:22; Eccl 5:1–7), demonstrating true devotion to the Lord (cf. Ps 116:17; Isa 19:21; John 4:23–24; 17:3). That the name **Yahweh** is mentioned twice in this verse emphasizes the sailors' exclusive focus on and faith in the only God because He had extended grace to them. Though Jonah did all he could to prevent the message of salvation from going to the Gentiles, God turned Jonah's rebellion into an evangelistic opportunity in order to bring these Gentile sailors to Himself (cf. Gen 50:20).

Jonah's Detainment

And Yahweh appointed a great fish to swallow Jonah, and Jonah was in the stomach of the fish three days and three nights. (1:17)

When Jonah was hurled into the sea, he undoubtedly assumed he would die. It seems that was what he desired. But that was not what the Lord had purposed. Instead, to save Jonah's life, **Yahweh appointed a great fish to swallow Jonah.** The use of God's covenant name **Yahweh** again emphasized the Lord's faithfulness as He continued His sanctifying work in the life of His wayward prophet. To that end, the Lord **appointed a great fish** to swallow Jonah and prevent him from drowning. The word **appointed** can mean to count or apportion something valuable, whether that be food (Dan 1:5) or one's days (Job 7:3). Yahweh sovereignly **appointed** the fish by carefully selecting and assigning a particular sea creature to be at the predetermined place at precisely the right time. Throughout the book, the Lord would also employ other objects from nature to instruct and refine Jonah—including a plant (Jonah 4:6), a worm (4:7), and the wind (4:8). God's appointing came as a repeated reminder to the stubborn prophet that his life and ministry depended fully on the Lord's sovereign mercy (cf. Rom 9:16; Eph 2:1–10).

Because this account of the **great fish** is so incredible, skeptics have been critical of this miracle. Some have proposed that Jonah was simply thrown overboard, landed on the top of a dead whale, and floated along for a few days. Others have claimed that Jonah's ship actually found a port where the sailors removed Jonah from the ship and put him in an inn called "The Whale." Still others have proposed that the ship had a small dinghy tethered to it, which was named "The Great Fish." Explanations like these attempt to strip the event of its supernatural character and, quite clearly, are in no way supported by the text.

Rather, God chose a creature He had created—**a great fish**—to miraculously detain and deliver His servant. **Fish** in Hebrew is generic and can include a whale; and **great** indicates, in this case, that it was large enough to swallow a man whole. The Lord not only sent this colossal creature to ingest His prophet, but He also preserved Jonah's life inside the fish for three days and three nights. In some way, the Lord miraculously enabled Jonah to breathe while also protecting him from being digested by the fish.

The fish was not the only **great** object delineated in Jonah 1. There was a great city (1:2), a great storm (1:4), and now a great fish (1:17), all of which demonstrated both Yahweh's great power and His great mercy. Jonah had no right to begrudge God's compassion toward the Ninevites in a great city nor toward the sailors in a great storm if he himself was delivered by God through a great fish.

Though Jonah wanted to be done with obedience and perhaps even life, God had much more for him in fulfilling the original mission. The prophet who repeatedly went down to escape from God (Jonah 1:3, 5) now found himself in the darkest depths of the sea, imprisoned in **the stomach of the fish** (cf. 2 Sam 20:10; Isa 16:11; 63:15; Jer 4:19; Ezek 3:3). **Stomach** is not the typical Hebrew term for the human digestive organ (cf. Jonah 2:2) but a word that often refers to the womb of a woman (cf. Gen 25:23; Num 5:22; Isa 49:1). God brought Jonah to this low place not only to discipline him, but also to show him compassion by bringing him to repentance and granting him another opportunity to obey.

This unique preservation miracle lasted **three days and three nights.** The expression does not mean that the length of time was exactly seventy-two hours, but that it was a general period of time that touched three separate days (cf. Esth 4:16; 5:1). This phrase was idiomatic and often associated with death and even resurrection. In ancient Near Eastern culture, a deceased person was not officially considered dead until the third day. This is why Jesus waited for Lazarus to be in the tomb four days before raising him from the dead (John 11:17); and this is why Hosea declared that God "will raise us [Israel] up on the third day" (Hos 6:2). To raise someone on or after the third day was to demonstrate undeniable power over death. In like manner, Jonah was hidden away in the fish for three days and yet he lived. Though the prophet did not die in the belly of the fish (cf. Jonah 2:7), his experience served to illustrate God's sovereign power over death (cf. Hos 13:14; 1 Cor 15:55), and His ability to deliver those whom He chooses to save.

Jonah's detainment in the **great fish,** and his subsequent deliverance, served to authenticate his ministry to the Ninevites. Located right by the Tigris River, evidence suggests that the name Nineveh was associated with the Sumerian word for "fish" and with the river-goddess Nina (see "Historical Context" in the Introduction). The Lord providentially arranged for a man spewed out by a fish to bring His truth to the idolatrous worshipers of a demonic fish-god. When they heard Jonah's incredible story—that the God whom he served rescued him from the stomach of a great fish—the Ninevites would have paid close attention to his message. The reluctant prophet had done all he could to prevent the Gentiles from hearing the divine call to repentance, but Yahweh turned Jonah's efforts on their head, orchestrating everything he experienced to prepare the Ninevites to receive the truth.

Jonah's deliverance was so powerful that Christ appealed to it to validate His ministry, calling it "the sign of Jonah" (Matt 12:39). Just as God miraculously rescued Jonah from certain death to confirm him as a prophet, so God miraculously raised Jesus from actual death to confirm Him as the Messiah (Matt 12:40). Yahweh's powerful work in Jonah's life not only served as a sign to the Ninevites but also pointed to the resurrection of Christ on the third day. God used Jonah, despite the prophet's resistance, to put His sovereign grace on display. By delivering Jonah after three days in the depths, and subsequently sending him to fulfill his mission to Nineveh, Yahweh demonstrated His compassionate commitment to save the lost, whether Jew or Gentile.

The Marks of a Penitent Prayer, Part I

3

JONAH 2:1–4

Then Jonah prayed to Yahweh his God from the stomach of the fish, and he said,

> **"I called out of my distress to Yahweh,**
> **And He answered me.**
> **I cried for help from the belly of Sheol;**
> **You heard my voice.**
> **For You had cast me into the deep,**
> **Into the heart of the seas,**
> **And the current surrounded me.**
> **All Your breakers and waves passed over me.**
> **So I said, 'I have been driven away from Your sight.**
> **Nevertheless I will look again toward Your holy temple.'"**

Throughout church history, believers have often kept journals to record their progress through this life. From David Brainerd to Jonathan Edwards to Jim Elliot, the diaries of faithful missionaries, pastors, and theologians provide a treasure chest of wisdom for subsequent generations. Their experiences provide real-life insight into the sanctification process, including times of high spiritual joy and victory as well as low seasons of dryness and defeat. With honesty and grit, the personal testimonies of saints now in heaven serve as a compelling encouragement to those who follow in their footsteps (cf. Heb 12:1–2).

The second chapter of Jonah essentially serves as the prophet's spiritual journal, depicting the depths of divine discipline that prompted Jonah's impassioned prayer of contrition. In the first chapter, Jonah defied the Lord's commission and ran the opposite way, seeking to escape God's presence. After boarding a ship bound for Tarshish, he fell into a deep sleep, only to awaken to the raging reality of God's fierce displeasure. He was confronted for his slumber, exposed as the guilty party, and cast into the stormy sea where certain death awaited. But the Lord spared the life of His prodigal prophet. Entombed in the stomach of a fish, Jonah came to his senses as he reflected on the recklessness of his rebellion. His prayer of contrition recorded in Jonah 2 uses the language of the Psalms to express genuine penitence before the Lord.

In the utter darkness of the deep, incarcerated in a monstrous fish, Jonah exhibited five hallmarks of a penitent prayer. First, he recognized his humble condition (Jonah 2:1). Second, he expressed a heartfelt cry for mercy (2:2). Third, he made an honest confession regarding the consequences of his sin, acknowledging that his sin distanced him from Yahweh (2:3–4). Fourth, he prayed with hope-filled confidence in God alone to rescue and restore him (2:5–7). Finally, he responded with a heart of consecration, eager to turn from idols to worship and serve Yahweh without equivocation (2:8–9). The first three hallmarks of Jonah's prayer will be considered in this chapter. The remaining two will be discussed in the subsequent chapter. Though Jonah was far from a model prophet—marked at times by petulance, prejudice, and pride (cf. 4:1–2)—his penitent prayer from the belly of the fish serves as a template for any sinner seeking forgiveness and restoration from God.

A Humble Condition

Then Jonah prayed to Yahweh his God from the stomach of the fish... (2:1)

For the first time in the book, **Jonah prayed,** a term referring not only to general communication with God but also specifically to making intercession (cf. Num 21:7; Deut 9:20; 1 Kgs 13:6; Jer 7:16), whether for another (cf. Gen 20:7) or for oneself (cf. 1 Sam 1:26; 1 Kgs 8:33; Isa 45:20). With such a prayer, Jonah acknowledged personal weakness and dependence on God, looking to the Lord alone to act (cf. Pss 5:3; 32:6). The prophet had ample opportunities to pray. He could have prayed about his concerns to the Lord right after he was commissioned to go to Nineveh (Jonah 1:1–2), especially since he does so later in the book (cf. 4:2). He could have petitioned the Lord from the boat in the storm (1:4–5), especially since the sailors fervently exhorted him to cry out to his God (1:6). But blinded by pride (cf. Josh 9:14; 2 Chr 16:12; Pss 10:4; 107:11; Zeph 1:6), he had refused to do so. In response, God humbled His servant by casting him into the deep, so that the one who had rebelliously refused to pray would pray in extreme desperation and dependence.

Jonah prayed to **Yahweh,** the God of heaven, Creator of land and sea, and the One who made a covenant with His people. The use of God's covenant name is a reminder that prayer is both personal and particular. Jonah did not merely engage in a spiritual exercise or religious ritual (cf. Zech 7:5; Matt 6:7; Luke 18:11). Rather, he earnestly entreated God for deliverance. That Jonah felt he could entreat the Lord after defying Him so blatantly revealed his knowledge of Yahweh's gracious character. As the Lord revealed to Moses, His lovingkindness endures forever, which is evidenced by His willingness to pardon those who repent (cf. Exod 34:6–8; Jonah 4:2). Genuine repentance requires turning wholeheartedly to the Lord (cf. Acts 14:13–18; 17:23–34; 1 Thess 1:9; Heb 11:6) and away from any idolatrous competitor to Him (cf. Ps 50:21; 1 John 5:21). From the belly of the fish, Jonah turned to the Lord, fully convinced that Yahweh was his only hope.

Previously (and even subsequently, cf. Jonah 4:2), the prophet had resented Yahweh's gracious disposition toward sinners. But in this moment, he eagerly embraced it, pleading with the Lord for deliverance (2:9b). Thus, Jonah prayed to **his God,** clinging to his relationship with the Lord, both as His prophet and as part of His covenant people. To this point, Jonah had talked *about* God (1:9), declaring to others truths about the Lord's sovereignty, power, and omnipresence. Yet, he repeatedly acted in ways that contradicted his understanding of those attributes. But here, for the first time in the book, the text implies that Jonah not only feared the Lord (1:9) but also recognized Yahweh as **his God.**

Jonah offered this prayer of desperation and devotion to God **from the stomach of the fish,** a precarious position that would have been incomprehensibly terrifying and nauseating. Jonah could not have known that God had brought him through the waters to the womb of the fish only for a short time in order to refine him and then restore his life (see discussion on Jonah 1:17). The belly of the fish was the place of God's severe discipline, so that from that aquatic prison, Jonah would be profoundly humbled. As dramatically illustrated by Jonah's unparalleled experience, the Lord regularly allows His children to face severe hardship (including the immediate consequences of their sinful actions), in order to break them of their sin and pride (cf. Dan 4:37) and to produce spiritual life and growth in them (cf. Heb 12:4–13). The fact that the prophet turned to Yahweh his God in prayer demonstrated that such divine discipline was accomplishing its intended effect.

A Heartfelt Cry

...and he said,

> **"I called out of my distress to Yahweh,**
> **And He answered me.**
> **I cried for help from the belly of Sheol;**
> **You heard my voice."** (2:2)

Recognizing his desperate condition, Jonah cried out to God for mercy and deliverance. **And he said, "I called out of my distress to Yahweh, and He answered me."** In the Psalms, such expressions are used to emphasize the undeserved kindness and compassion of God toward His people (cf. Pss 4:1; 17:6–7; 27:7). The biblical writers acknowledged that Yahweh was under no obligation to answer the requests of those who cried out to Him (e.g., 22:2), especially those who had been flagrantly disobedient (cf. Ps 18:41; Isa 1:15; Jer 11:11; Mic 3:4, 7). Hence, they marveled at the wonder of God's abundant grace, that He would hear the penitent prayers of His people and respond in mercy (Ps 99:6).

Having experienced such mercy from God, Jonah echoed the same wonder as he stated that he too **called out,** giving voice to his desperate need. Earlier, the sailors called out to their gods (Jonah 1:5) and subsequently to Yahweh (1:14) because their lives were in imminent danger (vv. 5b, 14). By contrast, Jonah refused to call out to the Lord while on the ship. But after being hurled into the sea, and humbled in the belly of the fish, the prophet acknowledged his desperate situation. This was a critical step in Jonah's repentance, since God's grace is given to those who recognize their great need (cf. Matt 5:3; 18:23–24; Luke 18:13; Eph 2:1–4) and call on the Lord for help (cf. Rom 10:13).

Jonah acknowledged not only his urgent need but also his inability, as he spoke of his (**my**) **distress. Distress** has the notion of a tight space, in which a person is trapped and unable to escape. This certainly was Jonah's physical experience. Though the ocean is broad, Jonah was confined, constricted, and cut off.

He had no options and no ability to save himself. He knew that only the Lord could deliver him. Jonah's helpless state illustrates the hopeless condition of every sinner. In salvation, sinners are unable to come to God on their own (cf. Ps 31:1–2; John 6:44; Rom 1–3; 2 Cor 4:3–6; Eph 2:1–9; Titus 3:3–5). Like Jonah, their only hope is to call out to God for mercy. By crying out to **Yahweh,** Jonah showed that he understood that God alone had the power (cf. Exod 14:13–14; 15:2–3; Isa 40:10; 42:13; Zech 4:6) and the prerogative to save (cf. Exod 34:6–8; Hos 11:8).

Despite Jonah's previous disobedience, the Lord graciously heard the heartfelt cry of the sinner. As Jonah exclaimed, **"He answered me."** With these words, the prophet expressed his wonder at God's lavish mercy, that the Lord would answer the petition of His sinful servant. First in the deepest part of the furious sea, and then in the vile den of the fish's stomach, Jonah knew he should have been dead. Yet he was alive, and only because God's grace abounded more than Jonah's iniquity (cf. Rom 5:20).

In formulating his prayer, the penitent prophet used the language of the Psalms (cf. Pss 4:1; 81:7; 86:7; 91:15; 120:1), some of which anticipated the hope of resurrection (cf. Ps 17:6, 15; cf. Isa 26:19; Dan 12:2). Though Jonah's circumstances were extraordinary, he joined with believers from every age of redemptive history by resting in the truth of God's marvelous grace (cf. Matt 5:7; Rom 11:31; Eph 2:4; 3:14–21; 2 Cor 4:1; 1 Pet 2:10). Jonah's reflection also served as a powerful reminder that, even though he was a divinely commissioned prophet, he needed mercy just as any other sinner does. He should have never considered himself as spiritually superior to the Ninevites. In the same way that they needed divine grace, so did he. As the Apostle Paul reminded his fellow Israelites, "Where then is boasting? It is excluded" (Rom 3:27). The Lord manifested to Jonah His grace by rescuing him from the sea, even as He prepared Jonah to proclaim that same grace to the Gentiles (Jonah 3:1).

Having begged the Lord for mercy, Jonah also acknowledged God's power, as he **cried for help** to the only One mighty enough to save him. The verb **cried** implies a successive series of screams, being used elsewhere to describe the desperate shrieks of someone starving (Job 38:41), the panicked outbursts of a person terrified (Ps 31:22), or the agonizing groanings of one in deep affliction (Job 35:9). Knowing that only God could hear him, Jonah shouted out to Him for help.

The prophet described his circumstances of distress as being in **the belly of Sheol.** This phrase depicts the deep darkness of the churning sea as the grave of the dead at the very bottom of the ocean. While he had not drowned, deliverance required a miraculous escape from the bowels of his aquatic tomb.

At the bottom of the ocean floor, Jonah understood that his situation meant certain death. Many have died at sea (Rev 20:13), and that was undoubtedly Jonah's expectation (Jonah 1:14). For that reason, he compared his experience to being in **Sheol.** While the word can refer to the place where unbelievers are held in judgment (cf. Isa 14:15; Ezek 31:16; 32:27; Rev 20:13), the term fundamentally signifies the grave and, by extension, the afterlife (cf. Gen 37:35; Num 16:30; Pss 16:10; 116:3, 9; Ezek 32:27). Jonah knew that in the depths of the sea, he was as good as dead, about to depart from the land of the living (cf. Pss 88:10; 115:17; 116:3, 9; Ezek 32:23). In crying out to the Lord, he understood that only divine power could overcome death and save him.

Yahweh **heard** Jonah's **voice** and responded with supernatural power on behalf of His servant. By sending a fish to rescue Jonah from drowning in the sea, the Lord provided the vehicle to miraculously transport him to the shore (Jonah 2:10). Death is a mighty foe (1 Cor 15:26), an inevitable reality (Heb 9:27), and mankind's greatest fear (2:14–15). But God's power supersedes the threat of death (cf. Ps 23:4; 1 Cor 15:54–57), as illustrated by His extraordinary deliverance of Jonah. Though still in the fish, Jonah understood that because God had rescued him from the depths of the sea, He would also deliver him from the stomach of the fish.

In recounting the power of divine deliverance, Jonah acknowledged that such salvation was not for him alone. By continuing to quote the Psalms, he joined the ranks of those before him whom God had also rescued from Sheol. David, for example, wrote that Sheol had entangled him (Ps 18:5), but that the Lord had heard his cry for help (18:6). The author of Psalm 116 stated that the terrors of Sheol had come upon him, but that God had rescued him (116:3, 8). The writers of the New Testament likewise declared that God preserved His people from death (cf. 2 Cor 1:9; 4:7–10; 6:4–10; 11:23–33; 1 Pet 1:5–9). However, as Jonah poetically described God's might in his salvation, his words pointed to the ultimate deliverance from death: the resurrection from the dead (cf. Rom 6:3–4; 1 Cor 15:1–5; 1 Pet 1:3–4), the hope of the saints in every age (cf. Job 19:25; Pss 16:10; 17:15; Isa 26:19; Dan 12:2; 1 Thess 4:13–18). The reality of that hope was made certain by the Lord Jesus Christ, the One who fulfilled the sign of Jonah (Matt 12:40). Those who cry out for mercy and trust in the Lord, like Jonah did, will one day be raised by the power of God (cf. Rom 8:11; 1 Cor 15:20–23). They will overcome the threat of death and enjoy the blessings of eternal life (cf. John 11:25–26; 1 Cor 15:55–57). Thus, God unveiled the glories of His salvation not only *to* Jonah but also *through* Jonah to all His people. Jonah was in awe that he lived, though he should have died. Such wonder is shared by all the saints, for all the redeemed deserved death but received life in Christ and will be raised on the last day to eternal glory (cf. Job 19:25–26; Eph 2:1–10; Rom 6:1–4; 8:18–39; 1 Cor 15).

An Honest Confession

"For You had cast me into the deep,
Into the heart of the seas,
And the current surrounded me.
All Your breakers and waves passed over me.

> **So I said, 'I have been driven away from Your sight. Nevertheless I will look again toward Your holy temple.'"** (2:3–4)

In recollecting his deliverance (Jonah 2:1–2), the prophet acknowledged that he was under God's discipline and that it was his guilt that put him under judgment. Though the sailors hurled Jonah into the ocean, the prophet understood that it was God (**You**) who had taken action against Jonah and that the sailors were simply carrying out His will (cf. 1:4). The verb **cast** conveys the idea of throwing forcibly (cf. Ps 60:10), emphasizing the purpose and power with which the Lord took action. The verb also implies God's discipline, since it is used elsewhere to describe being thrown out of divine favor (cf. Pss 51:11; 71:9; 102:10). This is especially the case in this context since Jonah was cast **into the deep,** a place both distant and remote. The **deep** is where God casts sins so that they are gone forever (Mic 7:19) and where He drowned the Egyptian army so that they vanished from sight (Neh 9:11). So when Jonah exclaimed that God had **cast** him **into the deep,** he expressed the isolation of being completely cut off from everything, surrounded only by suffocating darkness in **the heart of the seas.** When he fled down to Joppa, Jonah wanted to escape from God. Here, in the murky depths, he had seemingly received his wish. While not escaping God's omnipresence, he had distanced himself from God's blessing. The Lord's discipline often grants sinners what they selfishly desire (cf. Num 14:28–30; Rom 1:24–32; Gal 6:8), which never satisfies and only further distances them from God (cf. Ps 107:10–12).

As Jonah recounted his watery descent, he recalled how **the current surrounded** him, dragging him further and further under the surface. The prophet described that **all Your breakers and waves passed over me. Breakers** crash on top of people, beating them down, while **waves** roll over people making them unable to stand (cf. Ps 42:7). In a deadly combination, these torrents **passed over** the prophet, beating him down, knocking him over, and overwhelming him completely. The Lord used the raging sea to chastise His rebellious servant. God's discipline served its good purpose in the life of Jonah, for in suffering such unique isolation and peril, God's prophet acknowledged that his condition was the Lord's work in his life. He confessed that the breakers and waves that passed over him were God's (**Your**) chastening instruments, wielded by His sovereign hand. Thus, though Jonah was cut off from God's blessing, he had not eluded God Himself. The Lord was not absent from Jonah's trial but working in and through it (cf. Jas 1:2–5; 1 Pet 1:6).

In assessing his dire situation, Jonah acknowledged not only the physical consequences of his sin but also its spiritual ramifications, saying, **"I have been driven away from Your sight."** The verb **driven away** is elsewhere associated with God's hand of punishment. The Lord drove Adam and Eve from the garden (Gen 3:24), Cain from his place of habitation (4:14), the Canaanites from the Promised Land (Josh 24:18), the Philistines from their cities (Zeph 2:4), and the unrepentant people of Israel from their homeland (Hos 9:15). With the same forceful power and displeasure, Jonah was **driven away** from God's favor. The prophet's exclamation acknowledged that he was the object of the most severe, and bizarre, chastisement for his sin. He also understood that his plight was directly from God, exclaiming that he **had been** driven away. The passive voice of the verb implies that God Himself drove the prophet away **from** His **sight** on account of Jonah's rebellion. That is not to say that God was not present (cf. Jonah 1:3); rather, Jonah was out of God's benevolent focus (cf. Pss 26:3; 31:22; 36:2; 101:3). The prophet lamented that he was no longer under God's gaze of protection and blessing, but that he had forfeited the benefits David described in Psalm 34:15: "The eyes of Yahweh are toward the righteous and His ears are *open* to their cry for help" (cf. Ezek 5:11; Zech 12:4). So, in the depths of the sea, Jonah turned his thoughts toward God, recognizing the Lord's chastening hand upon him. It took sinking to the ocean floor, and then being swallowed alive, but Jonah finally grasped the weight of the divine discipline his disobedience had brought upon him.

Jonah knew he deserved to die, yet he displayed amazing confidence in God. Having acknowledged honestly the consequences of his sin, he prayed to the Lord in faith, **"Nevertheless I will look again toward Your holy temple."** Some commentators have suggested that this may simply mean that Jonah desired to pray in the direction of the temple. However, the phrase **look again toward** indicates that Jonah believed he would see the temple again with his physical eyes (cf. Exod 3:6; Num 21:9; 1 Sam 16:7; Isa 8:22). Thus, the prophet expressed his hope that he would once again visit the **temple** in Jerusalem. Having been broken by the hand of God's discipline, Jonah trusted in the Lord to rescue him. He understood that his sin was monstrous and his situation hopeless; **nevertheless,** he fixed his hope on **Yahweh.** Knowing that God is faithful to His own (cf. Matt 28:20; Heb 13:5), Jonah placed his trust in the Lord.

Up to this point in his prayer, Jonah recognized his humble condition (Jonah 2:1), issued a heartfelt cry for mercy (2:2), and honestly confessed the reality that he had put himself at odds with the Lord, for which he was suffering the repercussions (2:3–4). These same attitudes and actions mark the response of every penitent sinner. A prayer of true repentance begins with humility; it cries out to God with heartfelt sincerity; and it honestly assesses the gravity and consequences of sin. But it does not stop there. The truly repentant moves from tears to triumph, finding hope and joy in the Lord and His grace. With that in view, the remaining characteristics of Jonah's penitent prayer are examined in the next chapter of this volume.

The Marks of a Penitent Prayer, Part II

4

JONAH 2:5–10

"Water encompassed me to *my very* soul.
The great deep surrounded me,
Weeds were wrapped around my head.
I went down to the base of the mountains.
The earth with its bars *closed* behind me forever,
But You have brought up my life from the pit, O Yahweh my God.
While my soul was fainting within me,
I remembered Yahweh,
And my prayer came to You,
To Your holy temple.
Those who regard worthless idols
Forsake their lovingkindness,
But as for me, I will sacrifice to You
With the voice of thanksgiving.
That which I have vowed I will pay.
Salvation belongs to Yahweh."

Then Yahweh spoke to the fish, and it vomited Jonah up onto the dry land.

When believers disobey the Lord and continue in sin, God disciplines them to bring them to repentance. The author of Hebrews wrote, "FOR THOSE WHOM THE LORD LOVES HE DISCIPLINES, AND HE FLOGS EVERY SON WHOM HE RECEIVES" (Heb 12:6). Believers who persist in disobedience suffer God's chastisement, which He inflicts to bring them back to Himself. When David committed adultery with Bathsheba, God chastened him until he repented (Ps 51:4, 8). In Psalm 32:3–4, David wrote, "When I kept silent *about my sin,* my bones wasted away through my groaning all day long. For day and night Your hand was heavy upon me; my vitality was drained away as with the heat of summer." God's hand of discipline drew David to suffering, sorrow, and penitence, and so he wrote: "I said, 'I will confess my transgressions to Yahweh'; and You forgave the iniquity of my sin" (32:5).

The Apostle Paul similarly explained that God's purpose for chastening was to bring wayward believers to recognize their sin and to turn from it. In 1 Corinthians 11:30, he wrote to the Corinthian church that those who participated in the Lord's table in an unworthy manner were severely chastened so that they became "weak and sick, and a number sleep." The Lord ended the earthly life of some of them, taking them to heaven, so that their evil influence would no longer stain His church (cf. Acts 5:1–11; 1 Cor 5:5; Jas 5:15; 1 John 5:16–17). Paul explained that the intention behind such discipline and its consequent sorrow was to compel the disobedient to repent and return to the righteousness that brings blessing (1 Cor 11:32; cf. Ps 32:3–5). Concerning this sorrow, Paul wrote in 2 Corinthians 7:9–10: "I now rejoice, not that you were made sorrowful, but that you were made sorrowful to repentance. For you were made to have godly sorrow, so that you might not suffer loss in anything through us. For godly sorrow produces a repentance without regret, *leading* to salvation, but the sorrow of the world brings about death."

The Lord disciplined Jonah for those same reasons—to bring him to repentance, to sanctify him, and to make him useful for service. In Jonah 2:5–9, the prophet concluded his prayer of contrition and repentance from the stomach of the fish. In the first part of the chapter, Jonah had recognized his humble condition (Jonah 2:1), issued a heartfelt cry for mercy (2:2), and made an honest confession of how his sin had distanced him from Yahweh (2:3–4). (For a discussion of those elements of Jonah's prayer, see the previous chapter in this volume.) Here, in verses 5–7, Jonah moved from desperation to dependence as he expressed hope-filled confidence in God's saving grace. In verses 8–9, he concluded his prayer by presenting a heart of consecration and by offering praise to the Lord. Finally, the narrative of Jonah 2 ends with God's response to Jonah's petition. The Lord answered His penitent prophet by removing His hand of discipline and extending instead His hand of compassion (2:10).

A Hope-filled Confidence

"Water encompassed me to *my very* soul.
The great deep surrounded me,
Weeds were wrapped around my head.
I went down to the base of the mountains.
The earth with its bars *closed* behind me forever,
But You have brought up my life from the pit, O Yahweh my God.
While my soul was fainting within me,
I remembered Yahweh,
And my prayer came to You,
To Your holy temple." (2:5–7)

To magnify the depth of his dependence on God, and the certainty of his hope in the Lord, Jonah expounded upon the extreme danger he faced. The prophet again took his words from the Psalms (cf. Ps 18:4 and 2 Sam 22:5; Pss 40:12; 116:3). While the Psalms used such language metaphorically to depict being overwhelmed by calamity, Jonah was describing the terrifying reality of drowning. As water flooded Jonah's lungs and brought him to the point of suffocation, Yahweh intervened to rescue His servant.

The currents of the waters (cf. Jonah 2:3) had dragged Jonah to **the great deep** which **surrounded** him. Far below the surface, in the cold darkness of the deep, he became entangled in kelp as the **weeds were wrapped around** his **head.** It was as if the plants of the ocean floor were reaching out to shackle him and force him to the bottom. Descending ever deeper, Jonah exclaimed, **"I went down to the base of the mountains. The earth with its bars *closed* behind me forever."** Death seemed inevitable. The prophet stated that he **went down,** employing the same word he had used to describe how he had gone down to Joppa (1:3), down to the boat (1:3), and down inside that vessel (1:5) in his efforts to run away from God. Jonah recognized that the wages of sin is death (Rom 6:23) as his disobedience now led him down to the bottom of the sea, the **base of the mountains.** Jonah's description expressed the tormenting experience of nearly drowning. The prophet had entered death's door as **the earth with its bars *closed* behind** him **forever.** It was as if he was imprisoned, and the bars that held him were permanently locked **behind** him, leaving no escape. But the Lord was with Jonah in that aquatic valley of the shadow of death (cf. Ps 23:4).

As Jonah's lungs were filled with sea water and he had no hope for life, God intervened to save him. Jonah recalled that moment with the exclamation **"but You,"** a phrase capturing the essence of so many divine interventions (cf. Pss 44:7; 49:15; Eph 2:4). When there was no hope, Jonah fixed his hope on the only One who could deliver him (cf. Jonah 2:3). The prophet who had tried to hide from God's presence now cried out to the Lord to not be hidden from Him (cf. Pss 27:9; 69:17). And Yahweh, in His grace, answered that prayer.

Jonah described God's intervention by saying, **"You have brought up my life from the pit."** The expression **brought up** reversed all the statements of going down (cf. Jonah 1:3, 5; 2:6a), which marked Jonah's destructive spiral of disobedience. For Jonah to be **brought up** signaled a divine reversal of his downward direction, as if God had raised him from the dead. The pit referred to the grave and was a common euphemism for physical death and entrance into the afterlife. The notion of coming up **from the pit** carried overtones of resurrection (cf. Job 33:30). In fact, this language closely parallels the anticipation of Christ's resurrection found in Psalm 16:10 (cf. Acts 13:35). Throughout this book (see discussion on Jonah 1:17; 2:2, 3, 5), Jonah alluded to other Old Testament passages about the hope of resurrection and the future work of the Messiah. Though Jonah, like the Apostle Paul, had the "sentence of death" in himself, he also, like Paul, had confidence in the "God who raised the dead" (2 Cor 1:9). The deadly and impossible nature of his circumstances put God's power of resurrection on vivid display.

Jonah then identified the object of his hope when he exclaimed, **"O Yahweh my God."** The penitent prophet knew that, while he had fled from God on the sea, the Lord had come to him in the sea. He responded by exclaiming the covenant name **Yahweh,** acknowledging God's perfect faithfulness (cf. Exod 34:6–7; Lam 3:22–23; 2 Tim 2:11–13; 1 John 1:9), eternal lovingkindness (cf. Exod 34:6–7; Pss 36:5; 136), unchanging nature (cf. Heb 13:8; Rev 1:4–5), and unwavering commitment to His promises (cf. Gen 12:1–3, 7; 15:5, 18–21; 17:4–8; 22:17–18; 26:24; 28:13–14; 35:11–12; Mic 7:18–20). The prophet understood from the rescue that Yahweh was truly his **God,** and he responded by expressing his love for Yahweh and his submission to Yahweh's divine authority. By experiencing God's discipline and deliverance, the prophet who had feared God in name only (Jonah 1:9) now responded with genuine reverence and affection.

In verse 7, Jonah focused on the precise moment of his repentance, recalling, **"While my soul was fainting within me."** This language suggests that Jonah did not actually die but was on the verge of losing consciousness (cf. Pss 77:3; 107:5; 142:3; 143:4; Lam 2:12). In that instant, with death imminent, Jonah

remembered Yahweh. To remember God is not merely to have mental recollection about Him, but to return to the Lord with full attention and renewed affection that leads to action (cf. Gen 8:1; 40:14; Deut 5:15). The prophet's thoughts raced to the Lord, as he fixed his heart and hope on Him (cf. 2 Tim 2:8; Heb 12:2).

With no indication of panic or hysteria, but rather an attitude of worship, the prophet uttered, **"And my prayer came to You, to Your holy temple."** Jonah's **prayer,** the same term as in verse 1, was a prayer of petition before God (**You**). Jonah declared his total dependence on God and God's sovereign ability to rescue him.

In referring to God's **holy** temple, Jonah acknowledged God's holiness in contrast to his own sinfulness. And since Yahweh was both graciously willing and powerfully present to answer Jonah's prayer from the depths, Jonah knew that his prayer had gone up to God in His holy **temple.** While there was a temple in Jerusalem, symbolic of God's presence on earth, Jonah believed that his prayer in fact came to God's throne in heaven—**to You, to Your holy temple** (cf. 2 Sam 22:7; Pss 11:4; 18:6; 102:19; Isa 66:1; Hab 2:20; Heb 4:16; Rev 11:19). Yet, Jonah also understood that though God's abode is in heaven, God is omnipresent and He dwells in holiness everywhere. Through this monumental drama, the Lord showed Jonah that the truth he tried to ignore (by seeking to outrun God's presence) was the truth he needed to depend on for deliverance.

Moreover, the Lord had been demonstrating to Jonah that He is not only present at all times and in all places, but that He is also sovereign over all peoples. That is why He sent Jonah to Nineveh to preach to the Gentiles in the first place. Jonah's words in this prayer acknowledged that he understood this lesson. God's presence is not confined to Jerusalem or Israel but extends to the depths of the sea and the ends of the earth. Accordingly, He is Lord not only of Jews but also of Gentiles (cf. Mal 1:5, 11; Rom 3:29; 10:12–13).

A Heart of Consecration

"Those who regard worthless idols
Forsake their lovingkindness,
But as for me, I will sacrifice to You
With the voice of thanksgiving.
That which I have vowed I will pay.
Salvation belongs to Yahweh." (2:8–9)

In response to God's mighty power (Jonah 2:1–2) and merciful presence (2:3–7), Jonah expressed a heart of grateful consecration to the Lord. He had formerly rebelled against the Lord's command, but now he committed himself to honor God with offerings of praise and acts of obedience (2:9). The prophet's words reflected a change of heart, indicating the reality of his repentance—transformation that produces fruits of worship and obedience (cf. Matt 3:8; Gal 5:22).

Jonah's repentance included a denunciation of false religion, as expressed by his attitude toward idols (cf. 1 Thess 1:9). Jonah exclaimed, **"Those who regard worthless idols forsake their lovingkindness."** Distancing himself from those who chase after false gods (cf. Pss 115:3–8; 135:15–18; Isa 44:9–20; 46:5–7; Jer 10:3–16; Rom 1:21–25), Jonah rejected the worship of **worthless idols.** Literally, the phrase in Hebrew means "vanities of worthlessness." As Jonah pointed out, pagan deities are as useless as they are powerless, being nothing more than demonic figments of imagination (cf. Isa 44:9–20; 46:6–7; Acts 19:26; 1 Cor 8:4; 10:19–20; Gal 4:8). Jonah's experience, both in the storm and in the sea, proved the impotence of false gods in contrast to the powerful presence of the true God. It was Yahweh alone who sent the wind, sparked the storm, controlled the sea, spared the sailors, directed the fish, and answered Jonah's prayer for deliverance.

Jonah rightly perceived that those devoted to false gods **forsake their lovingkindness.** To forsake God is to forfeit the **lovingkindness** that He alone provides. **Lovingkindness** refers to the loyal and enduring dedication that describes God's faithfulness to His people, backed by His power and presence, which no force of this world can thwart (cf. Rom 8:38–39), whether on land or in the sea (cf. Ps 107:1–32). The Lord's **lovingkindness** overcomes every form of affliction, whether it be a violent storm or death itself (cf. Pss 43; 107:13–14, 17–18; 1 Cor 15:26). Yahweh generously extends such triumphant grace to all His people (cf. Exod 20:6). But those in false religion have turned away from God, cutting themselves off from the only Source of grace and spiritual life. Thus, they have forfeited **their lovingkindness** from God. In Psalm 32:10, David wrote: "Many are the sorrows of the wicked, but he who trusts in Yahweh, lovingkindness shall surround him." False religion and idolatry involve not only trusting in that which cannot deliver but also forsaking the One who can (cf. Jer 2:5–13, 17, 19).

As in the case of many phrases in this chapter, the expression **"those who regard worthless idols"** also came from the Psalms, specifically Psalm 31:6. There, David wrote, "I hate those who regard worthless idols." While David reacted to idol-worshipers with righteous indignation, Jonah emphasized particularly the tragedy of forfeiting God's lovingkindness, for he himself had experienced this. Though he distanced himself from **those** who practiced idolatry, in his disobedience, the prophet had acted contrary to what he knew about God. He had suppressed the truth of God's omnipresence and omniscience, and in essence, he attempted to create a **worthless idol** for himself (cf. 1 John 5:21). Consequently, he also forsook God's **lovingkindness.** Recognizing his own idolatrous rebellion and then turning away from it, Jonah demonstrated a heart of repentance and a desire to consecrate himself fully to the Lord.

In full rejection of idolatry, Jonah exclaimed, **"But as for me."** He thereby declared his intention to stand in contrast to the unbelieving world (cf. Rom 12:1–2; Jas 4:4; 1 Pet 4:1–6). In so doing, Jonah articulated three resolutions for his life as he consecrated himself to Yahweh. First, he resolved to respond with worship and thanksgiving. Jonah said, **"I will sacrifice to You,"** reflecting his hope-filled expectation that he would participate in temple worship again (cf. Jonah 2:4). **Sacrifice** is a generic word describing various kinds of offerings to God, including burnt offerings of dedication, grain offerings of gratitude, and peace offerings to signify fellowship (Lev 1–3). These sacrifices all express worship, a priority for all of God's people (cf. John 4:24; Rom 12:1–2). Jonah purposed to live such a life of worship **with the voice of thanksgiving.** While the unredeemed are characterized by thanklessness (cf. Rom 1:21), believers are called to live in constant gratitude (cf. Eph 5:20; Col 3:16). They know and appreciate what God has done for them (cf. Rom 7:25; 1 Tim 1:12). In response to his deliverance, Jonah determined to cultivate a heart of gratitude that manifested itself in thanksgiving as the core of his worship.

Second, Jonah resolved to renew his commitments to the Lord, saying, **"that which I have vowed I will pay."** Although people make vows rashly or with wrong motives (cf. Gen 28:20; Judg 11:30), true vows express one's dedication to the Lord in light of His mighty work (cf. Num 6:2, 21; 30:3; Deut 12:17; 23:22). By making such a solemn promise to God, Jonah pledged not to forget God's lovingkindness but to live in light of it (cf. 1 Sam 1:11; Ps 132:2). He resolved to be a man of faithful action, not empty words (cf. Jas 1:22; 1 John 3:18; 4:20). Paying a vow can refer to a range of activities, such as offering a certain kind of sacrifice (Deut 12:6), setting aside something for special service (1 Sam 1:11), or even giving up one's own life for a certain purpose (Lev 27; Num 6:2). In Jonah's prayer, the vow likely centered around Jonah's duties as a prophet, including the Lord's commission for him to go to Nineveh (cf. Jonah 3:1). By announcing that he would pay his vows, Jonah declared his intention to obey God and submit to His will.

Interestingly, Jonah's response was the same as that of the sailors, who also offered a sacrifice and made vows to Yahweh (cf. 1:16). Therefore, Jonah was not to think of himself as better than the Gentiles. His sin was equally severe (see discussion on 2:8), his deliverance equally undeserved (see discussion on 2:10 below), and his repentance equally accepted by God. The rest of Scripture reiterates those realities. All people (whether Jew or Gentile) have sinned (Rom 3:23); all who believe are saved by grace apart from works (Rom 3:27; Eph 2:8–9; 2 Tim 1:9); and all the redeemed are empowered by God to walk in obedience (cf. Eph 2:10; Phil 2:12–13; 1 Pet 1:1–2). The gifts of justification and sanctification are given by God to Jew and Gentile alike (cf. Rom 1:16; 3:22; 1 Cor 12:13; Gal 3:28; Col 3:11). For this reason, no one ought to consider himself more highly than another (cf. Rom 12:10; Phil 2:3–4).

Third, having been delivered by God from the gates of death, Jonah resolved to rejoice in the truth of salvation. At the end of his prayer, he proclaimed, **"Salvation belongs to Yahweh."** The word **salvation** refers to God's entire work of rescuing and redeeming sinners (cf. Rom 8:28–30). The prophet recognized that salvation in its totality **belongs to Yahweh** (cf. Ps 3:8; Prov 21:31; Rev 7:10). Salvation is from Him, through Him, and to Him (cf. Eph 1:7–12; Rom 11:36). No man can take credit for his salvation (cf. Rom 3:20; Gal 2:16, 21; Eph 2:8–9), and Jonah's experience made this truth clear. Jonah had no ability to save himself or anyone else (cf. Jonah 2:2, 6, 9). It was Yahweh who appointed the fish to rescue the drowning prophet and deliver him onto the shore (cf. 1:17; 2:9).

Through this experience, Jonah grew to understand God's absolute sovereignty over all of salvation. The Lord reminded His prophet that He retains the right to save whomever He wills, including the Ninevites (cf. Rom 9:18). In fact, one day, a great multitude "from every nation and *all* tribes and peoples and tongues" will declare, "Salvation *belongs* to our God" (Rev 7:9–10), echoing the words Jonah himself had declared (Jonah 2:9). In response to Jonah's obstinate rebellion, God intervened in Jonah's life to sanctify him and teach him about the salvation that must reach the ends of the earth (Isa 49:6).

The culmination of Jonah's penitent prayer moved from contrition and confession to a heart of consecration. Because his heart had been changed, he eagerly rejected any form of idolatry and determined to follow God fully. The fruit of that repentance was seen in an attitude of praise and thanksgiving, in actions of submission and obedience, and in the articulation of God's grace toward sinners. In this way, Jonah exemplified the kind of heart-change that takes place in the life of any sinner who truly repents.

God's Hand of Compassion

Then Yahweh spoke to the fish, and it vomited Jonah up onto the dry land. (2:10)

In response to Jonah's prayer, **Yahweh spoke to the fish, and it vomited Jonah up onto the dry land.** As the covenant-keeping God, **Yahweh** demonstrated His faithfulness, even when Jonah was unfaithful (Jonah 1:3). Accordingly, the Lord hurled a storm to draw the sailors to Himself (1:4, 14), sent a fish to deliver His wayward prophet (1:17; 2:6), and then gave heed to Jonah's prayer from the depths of the sea (2:1). Having heard the prophet's penitent plea, **Yahweh** continued His faithful work in the life of His servant.

To deliver Jonah, Yahweh **spoke to the fish,** further displaying His control over every living thing. In the same way that God **spoke** and created (cf. Gen 1:20–21; Ps 148:1–5), so His speech to the fish demonstrated His absolute mastery over all creation (cf. Job 39:1–30; Ps 104:21). Just as Jonah spoke his prayer to Yahweh (Jonah 2:2), so God in turn **spoke** to the sea creature, showing that He heard and accepted Jonah's supplication. How well the prophet learned his lesson was yet to be seen, but God's response indicated that Jonah's contrition was genuine and that he had submitted himself to the Lord's directive.

God spoke to the fish, and it immediately obeyed as it **vomited Jonah up.** While this act of vomiting resulted in Jonah's return to dry land, in Scripture, vomiting is generally associated with evil. The Lord threatened that Israel would be vomited out of the land (Lev 18:25). Christ said of Laodicea, "I will spit [or vomit] you out of My mouth" because their love for Him was lukewarm (Rev 3:16). Job 20:15 describes a scene in which God caused a rich man who swallowed riches to vomit them up. Peter wrote that false teachers are like a dog returning to its own vomit (2 Pet 2:22). In Jeremiah 25:27, vomiting is associated with drunkenness. Every other time the word "vomit" appears in Scripture, it is used negatively. That same connotation applies to Jonah as well: the fish **vomited Jonah up** as a final and unforgettable reminder of the despicable nature of Jonah's disobedience.

At the same time, this act of vomiting brought about Jonah's rescue. It can therefore be viewed as the only time in Scripture where vomiting had a positive outcome. The fish **vomited Jonah up** not only as a reminder of the prophet's repugnant rebellion but also as the means of his deliverance. The Lord chose the strangest method to recover this unwilling missionary as an answer to his prayer (cf. Jonah 2:4, 9). In the regurgitation of Jonah up from the belly of the fish, the hand of God's discipline was met by the hand of His compassion.

The fish vomited Jonah onto **dry land,** fully delivering the prophet from the perilous sea. In this act, God displayed that He is "the God of heaven, who made the sea and the dry land," just as Jonah had declared to the sailors (1:9). By bringing both the sailors (1:13, 15–17) and Jonah back to the shore, the Lord demonstrated His prerogative to save both Gentiles and Jews (see discussion on 2:9). To that end, as most commentators rightly observe, Jonah was likely spewed out on the shores of Israel, probably near Joppa. This was the **dry land** the sailors were rowing to reach (1:13) and presumably the **dry land** to which the Lord directed the fish. God returned Jonah to the very place where he began, giving him another opportunity to carry out his prophetic commission and head to Nineveh.

Though the prophet's voyage went nowhere, with Jonah ending where he began, God had a specific purpose for Jonah's roundtrip journey. Through the storm, the sea, and the stomach of the fish, the Lord broke Jonah's pride and showed him the greatness of salvation. The Lord's aim was not merely to transport Jonah physically but more importantly to transform him spiritually. Before Jonah declared the message of salvation to the Ninevites, God first intended for His prophet to experience the wonder of that reality himself. Having imparted these vital lessons to Jonah, faithful Yahweh sent His prophet back to where he had begun. This time, Jonah was ready to obey God by going to Nineveh to fulfill the commission.

The Grace of Repentance, Part I

5

JONAH 3:1–5

Now the word of Yahweh came to Jonah the second time, saying, "Arise, go to Nineveh, the great city, and call out to it this *very* call which I am going to speak to you." So Jonah arose and went to Nineveh according to the word of Yahweh. Now Nineveh was an exceedingly great city, a three days' walk. Then Jonah began to go into the city, one day's walk; and he called out and said, "Yet forty days and Nineveh will be overthrown." And the people of Nineveh believed in God; and they called a fast and put on sackcloth, from the greatest to the least of them.

The opportunity for sinners to repent is available only because the Lord is gracious. God would be right to destroy the wicked immediately and without warning. Yet, He patiently offers them the opportunity to turn from sin and to turn to Him in order to receive forgiveness. Divine grace is so extensive that Paul wrote, "Where sin increased, grace abounded all the more" (Rom 5:20; cf. 6:1; 1 Tim 1:14). As the record of human history reveals, rather than executing instant and total judgment on sinners, God has repeatedly extended mercy and grace to the undeserving by calling them to repentance (cf. 2 Pet 3:9).

The pages of Scripture are filled with examples of sinners who repented and received God's abundant grace. After Israel sinned by worshiping a golden calf, Moses interceded, and the Lord did not destroy the people (Exod 32–34). David committed adultery with Bathsheba, but God forgave him when he confessed his sin in genuine contrition (2 Sam 11–12; Pss 32; 51). Though the Lord punished Israel by sending the people into exile, He spared the nation from extinction and brought the remnant back to the land (Ezra 1:1–4). When Zacchaeus, the chief tax collector, responded in repentance, Jesus forgave him (Luke 19:1–10). Though Peter denied his Master three times, the Lord restored him to fellowship and ministry usefulness (John 18:25–27 and 21:15–17; and see Matt 26:71–75; Mark 14:69–72; Luke 22:58–62). Paul violently persecuted the church, but God transformed him and commissioned him to take the gospel throughout the Roman empire (Acts 9:1–22; 22:3–16; 26:9–18). As examples like these illustrate, God's grace is so great that He is willing both to save the foremost of sinners (like Paul) and to restore disobedient disciples (like Peter). Those who repent are forgiven, reconciled, and restored to full fellowship with God.

Such grace upon grace does not give anyone a license to sin. Paul addressed that issue in Romans 6:1 by asking, "What shall we say then? Are we to continue in sin so that grace may increase?" He emphatically answered: "May it never be! How shall we who died to sin still live in it?" (Rom 6:2). God's grace never condones sinful conduct, but rather transforms the wicked heart into one that is eager to worship the Lord and walk in obedience to His Word (cf. 6:2–4). When Zacchaeus turned to follow Christ, his change of heart was immediately manifested in a change of life. He exclaimed, "Behold, half of my possessions, Lord, I will give to the poor, and if I have extorted anyone of anything, I will give back four times as much" (Luke 19:8). After Peter was restored, he professed his love for Jesus with these words: "Lord, You know all things; You know that I love You" (John 21:17). Paul was transformed from being a persecutor to being a preacher whose life was defined by his allegiance to the Lord Jesus: "For to me, to live is Christ and to die is gain" (Phil 1:21). In Ephesians 2:10, Paul explained that God's gracious work of salvation, which is received through faith apart from works, inevitably results in His equally gracious work of sanctification, in which the reality of saving faith is evidenced by the fruit of good works. Paul wrote: "For we are His workmanship, created in Christ Jesus for good works, which God prepared beforehand so that we would walk in them" (Eph 2:10). The Lord demonstrates His grace toward sinners by calling them to turn from sin and turn to Him, so that they might be forgiven and walk in newness of life (cf. Rom 6:4–5; 1 Thess 1:9).

The prophet Jonah is one of the clearest examples in Scripture of a wayward sinner who repented and was graciously delivered by God and restored to service. Jonah 3 reveals that God issued a second commission for His prophet to go and preach to Nineveh. While Jonah could not undo his act of disobedience (cf. Jonah 1), God mercifully granted him a second opportunity to obey. Though initially rebellious, the repentant prophet was, by unparalleled chastisement, made willing to comply with his Master's command (cf. Matt 21:28–30). In His grace, the Lord recommissioned Jonah to serve as His missionary (Jonah 3:1–3a), to proclaim His message (3:3b–4), and to reach the great multitude who lived in Nineveh (3:5).

A Restored Missionary

Now the word of Yahweh came to Jonah the second time, saying, "Arise, go to Nineveh, the great city, and call out to it this *very* call which I am going to speak to you." So Jonah arose and went to Nineveh according to the word of Yahweh. (3:1–3a)

With Jonah back where he started, likely on the shores of Israel (cf. Jonah 2:10), **the word of Yahweh came to Jonah the second time.** This opening statement is nearly identical to the one in Jonah 1:1. As in the first instance, **the word of**

Yahweh came to Jonah. Despite Jonah's initial disobedience, the Lord called the same prophet **Jonah** to be His messenger. To this point, the text of Jonah 3:1 corresponds word for word with the beginning of Jonah 1:1. The repetition in these two commissions is intentional—producing a sense of *déjà vu* that highlights the grace of God in giving His runaway prophet a second opportunity to serve.

To emphatically punctuate that reality, the text of Jonah 3:1 adds the phrase **"the second time."** This second commission reflected the patience and mercy of the Lord toward Jonah. Instead of replacing him with another, more worthy messenger (cf. 1 Sam 15:26–28), the Lord forgave Jonah and restored him to the rare privilege of being God's instrument in the repentance of an entire city of idolaters (cf. Ps 103:12).

Yahweh's command to Jonah on this second occasion was a repeat of His previous commission: **"Arise, go to Nineveh, the great city, and call out to it this *very* call which I am going to speak to you."** That God gave the same commission with the same commands (**arise, go**) further demonstrated His kindness to Jonah, even though he had failed in a colossal way the first time.

In this re-commission, the Lord still referred to **Nineveh** as **the great city,** reaffirming its importance in the Gentile world and highlighting His interest in saving that city (see discussion on Jonah 1:2). To that end, while originally the Lord declared that Jonah was to "call out against" the city (1:2), here He instructed Jonah to **call out to it.** Calling *against* the city stressed judgment, but calling *to* the city indicated that there was also a benevolent purpose behind God's warning—to prompt the Ninevites to repent. In this way, the prophet's message was to proclaim judgment and mercy. As He had done at the outset of the book, the Lord demonstrated His compassion toward the people of Nineveh, and directed His prophet to align with that divine perspective (cf. 1 Sam 13:14; Acts 13:22).

The Lord specified that Jonah was to declare to the Ninevites **"this *very* call which I am going to speak to you."**

The repetition of the word **call** reinforced the idea that Jonah's speech was fully prescribed by the Lord. Every word he was instructed to proclaim was that **"which I** [Yahweh] **am going to speak to you."** Because this message was from the Lord, Jonah could not alter or manipulate its content. He was obligated to preach the very words God had revealed to him.

In response to God's commission, **Jonah arose.** He had done this before (cf. Jonah 1:3), though only to flee in defiant disobedience. This time, however, the prophet moved in the right direction—he **went to Nineveh.** Previously, the prophet boarded a westbound ship for Tarshish in his effort to run from God's will. This time, he **went** where the Lord commanded him to go, traveling east toward Nineveh. The difficult journey of nearly five hundred miles, assuming the fish ejected Jonah somewhere in Israel, would have taken at least a month to complete.[1] The fact that Jonah went to Nineveh demonstrated the sincerity of his repentance and the reality of God's grace at work in his life. Repentance restores usefulness, as God forgives and enables His servants.

That Jonah obeyed God fully is indicated in the phrase **according to the word of Yahweh,** which describes full conformity to what God demands (cf. 1 Kgs 17:5, 16; 2 Kgs 10:17). In other words, Jonah journeyed to Nineveh not primarily because he was afraid of the consequences of disobedience but out of genuine and heartfelt submission to the Lord. In acting **according to the word of Yahweh,** the prophet moved beyond honoring God's command to honoring **Yahweh** Himself. True obedience not only does what God commands, but, more than that, it seeks to glorify the One who issues such commands (cf. Deut 6:4–6; Isa 58:1–19; Zech 7:5; 1 Cor 10:31; Col 3:17; Heb 13:15). While Jonah defied the presence of God at the outset (cf. Jonah 1:3), in response to the second commission, he honored the Lord from the heart, as demonstrated by his actions.

1 Smith and Page, *Amos, Obadiah, Jonah*, 256.

A Rebuking Message

Now Nineveh was an exceedingly great city, a three days' walk. Then Jonah began to go into the city, one day's walk; and he called out and said, "Yet forty days and Nineveh will be overthrown." (3:3b–4)

Arriving at his destination, Jonah was struck by the size of the city: **"Now Nineveh was an exceedingly great city, a three days' walk."** As noted earlier (see discussion on Jonah 1:2), Nineveh was a city of significant size by ancient standards. The walls of Nineveh were magnificent, in both the strength of their fortifications and the beauty of their construction.[2] The inner city was surrounded by eight miles of walls, and the rest of the city had a circumference that extended to fifty-five miles around.[3] Such a sprawling metropolis housed approximately 600,000 residents, including some 120,000 infants and children (cf. 4:11). One ancient writer remarked, "No one afterward built a city of such compass or with walls so magnificent."[4] With Nineveh being such an **exceedingly great city,** the journey through Nineveh would have amounted to **a three days' walk.** So, for Jonah to preach repentance through the entire city would have been a formidable challenge.

In describing Nineveh as an **exceedingly** great city, the Hebrew indicates that Nineveh was "God-sized," bringing forth its exceptional grandeur and magnitude. The Hebrew literally reads "a great city to God" (cf. Gen 23:6; Josh 10:2; Ps 36:6). Such greatness foreshadowed the greatness of Nineveh's repentance, and also highlighted the importance of this city to God. By declaring that He had a unique interest in and plan for the people of Nineveh, the Lord demonstrated that even Israel's worst pagan enemies were not beyond the reach of His mercy.

2 Allen, *The Books of Joel, Obadiah, Jonah, and Micah*, 221.

3 Smith and Page, *Amos, Obadiah, Jonah*, 260.

4 Allen, *The Books of Joel, Obadiah, Jonah, and Micah*, 221.

He had chosen to give mercy to them, and that was the reason He had sent Jonah to Nineveh. Because God chose these Gentile people, He reached down to save them. Nothing like this had ever happened to another Gentile city. Repentance always comes from God (cf. Deut 30:1–6; Acts 5:31; 11:18; 2 Tim 2:25), and He purposed to bestow this gift on the Ninevites not because the city was exceedingly great, but because He is exceedingly gracious.

Having arrived at Assyria's capital, **Jonah began to go into the city, one day's walk.** This detail highlights the swiftness with which the message swept through Nineveh. Before Jonah even reached the midpoint of the city, having completed only one-third of his journey, his warning of judgment and call for repentance had spread throughout the entire metropolis (Jonah 3:4–5). What should have necessitated at least three days was accomplished in a single day. The speed of Nineveh's surrender to the Lord testified to the sincerity of their repentance and to God's mighty work in the hearts of the people.

While the timing demonstrates how swiftly the city responded to the prophet's message, it equally indicates that Nineveh's repentance did not depend on the skill of the preacher. Jonah spent hardly any time with the Ninevites. He only **began to go into the city** before revival broke out. Having gone only a third of the way through Nineveh's metropolitan area, the prophet was still outside the city center. Yet, the entire city responded. Clearly, this turning from sin could never be attributed to Jonah—especially since the prophet, though obedient, did not want the Ninevites to repent (cf. 4:1–3). Rather, the speed and scope of Nineveh's repentance was entirely and exclusively the work of God, as the preacher's message spread by word of mouth (cf. 3:3).

Jonah's mission was to proclaim God's pending judgment to the people of Nineveh. The prophet **called out and said, "Yet forty days and Nineveh will be overthrown."** This message clearly expressed God's words of warning. The term **overthrow** denotes total upheaval, to uproot an object, flip it upside down, and smash it to the ground. This act of overthrowing describes thorough destruction, making something completely unusable (cf. Judg 7:13). This was the very judgment the Lord leveled against Sodom and Gomorrah (Gen 19:25), and Jonah was declaring that Nineveh was about to meet the same end. Jonah's doomsday message, as given to him by Yahweh (Jonah 1:2), flew through the city. It was utterly distinct from the usual lies of the false prophets who cried out "peace and safety" (cf. Ezek 13:10; Jer 28:11–17; 1 Thess 5:3).

The reality of divine judgment has always been a crucial part of God's message. The ministries of Enoch (Jude 14–15), Noah (cf. Heb 11:7; 1 Pet 1:20; 2 Pet 2:5), Moses (Exod 4:23), Joshua (Josh 24:19–20), the prophets (e.g., Isa 1:1–7; Jer 1:11–14; Joel 2:1–11), the apostles (Acts 2:40; 17:31; Rom 1–3; 2 Pet 2:20–22; Jude 4), and Jesus (Matt 11:20–24; 23:1–28; Luke 11:37–54) all included urgent warnings of God's pending wrath against the wicked. Faithful preaching is the work of a dutiful watchman who does not tickle ears (2 Tim 4:3) but warns the wicked (Ezek 3:17–27). This was precisely what Jonah did in Nineveh.

The prophet's message was that the destruction would take place in **forty days.** By giving the people time to repent, God demonstrated not only His righteousness but also His grace and compassion. The Lord could have annihilated the city immediately and without warning, as He destroyed Sodom and Gomorrah centuries earlier (cf. Gen 19:1–17; 2 Pet 2:6). Any delay of judgment against Nineveh was an expression of divine patience. The delay of **forty days** paralleled the amount of time God gave Moses to intercede for Israel's sin after the golden calf incident (cf. Exod 34:28; Deut 9:25; 10:10). The Lord extended to Nineveh the same mercy He had given to His own people in the wilderness. God gave the Ninevites **forty days** to repent and be spared from the devastation of divine wrath.

At the onset of Nineveh's repentance, Jonah gave no detailed record of his preaching. He simply declared the message given to him by the Lord. But that divine word did not and could not return empty (Isa 55:11). As illustrated by the response of the Ninevites, the gift of repentance is the result of God's work, as He powerfully sends His Word to convict and convert the heart of the sinner (cf. 1 Cor 1:18–2:5).

A Repentant Multitude

And the people of Nineveh believed in God; and they called a fast and put on sackcloth, from the greatest to the least of them. (3:5)

In a remarkable understatement, Jonah recounted that **the people of Nineveh believed in God.** After hearing the dire message of coming judgment, the Ninevites turned from their arrogance and iniquity and **believed in God.** Salvation is always by grace through faith (Eph 2:8–9), and without faith no one can please the Lord (Heb 11:1–6). Such faith is never limited to mere intellectual assent or agreement (cf. Jas 2:19) but includes complete trust and reliance on God Himself. Considering the simple brevity of Jonah's message and the repugnant reputation of the Ninevites, who were known for their savage brutality (see "Historical Context" in the Introduction), such repentant faith was clearly a miraculous work of God (cf. Acts 16:14; Eph 2:10; 2 Cor 4:1–6; 2 Pet 1:1). Just as Abraham believed God and was justified (Gen 15:6), so the Ninevites believed God and were saved. The Lord gave them the same faith He had bestowed on Abraham and all other believers throughout redemptive history (cf. Rom 4:3–5). Given the scale of the response, with hundreds of thousands of the **people of Nineveh** repenting, the salvation sparked by Jonah's preaching has no equal in redemptive history.

The Ninevites' response was characterized by a living faith (cf. Jas 2:17–20), which evidenced itself in acts of repentance. Immediately, **they called a fast,** refusing to eat because they recognized the urgency of the situation (cf. 2 Sam 12:16; Ps 35:13; Esth 4:3). The prophet Joel similarly called for a fast in light of the severity of Israel's sin and their dire need for repentance (Joel 1:14). Nineveh's fast (cf. Jonah 3:6–9), therefore, demonstrated an important parallel between Joel's message to Israel and Jonah's message to the Gentiles—the need for repentance (cf. Jonah 3:9 and Joel 2:14; Jonah 4:2 and Joel 2:13). However, Nineveh was more responsive to the words of Jonah than Israel was to all their prophets. That the Ninevites went without food revealed that they were fully consumed with repentance and righteousness, and that their belief in God was sincere.

The people also **put on sackcloth,** which was done to express the deepest state of distress and sorrow, whether for someone's death (cf. Gen 37:34; 2 Sam 3:31; 21:10) or during times of deep desperation (cf. 2 Kgs 19:1). In putting on these garments of woe, the Ninevites expressed self-loathing and mourning. The people sought to display their newly-attained hatred for sin, renouncing and despising the atrocities they had once celebrated. In this way, they dramatically depicted the sincerity of their contrition (cf. Ps 32:3–5; Matt 5:4; 2 Cor 7:9–12).

God's gift of repentance was bestowed on the citizens **from the greatest to the least of them.** From the rich and powerful to the poor and destitute—all repented. No matter their economic class or social status, all were brought to recognize their unworthiness and need to humble themselves before God. Their sincerity resembled the attitude later described by James: "Draw near to God and He will draw near to you. Cleanse your hands, you sinners, and purify your hearts, you double-minded. Be miserable and mourn and cry. Let your laughter be turned into mourning and your joy to gloom. Humble yourselves in the presence of the Lord, and He will exalt you" (Jas 4:8–10). At the preaching of divine truth, the inhabitants of Nineveh displayed this manner of desperate and penitent faith, which could only be the result of God's grace toward them.

Thus, the grace of God was repeatedly revealed throughout this passage (Jonah 3:1–5). The Lord showed grace to Jonah, not only by rescuing him from certain death in the sea but also by restoring him to service. Yahweh again demonstrated His mercy and grace by sending His prophet a second time to warn the wicked city of Nineveh. Finally, God put His grace on display by bestowing on the Ninevites the gift of repentance and faith (cf. 2 Tim 2:25), so that they believed in Him. By definition, such grace was completely undeserved. Yet, by extending such unmerited favor to His creatures, the Lord demonstrated His saving nature and redemptive power (cf. Eph 2:1–10). As Paul exclaimed in Romans 9:23–24, God has purposed to do this "in order that He might make known the riches of His glory upon vessels of mercy, which He prepared beforehand for glory—*even* us, whom He also called, not from among Jews only, but also from among Gentiles."

6

The Grace of Repentance, Part II

JONAH 3:6–10

Then the word reached the king of Nineveh, and he arose from his throne, laid aside his mantle from him, covered *himself* with sackcloth, and sat on the ashes. And he cried out and said, "In Nineveh by the decree of the king and his nobles: Do not let man, animal, herd, or flock taste a thing. Do not let them eat, and do not let them drink water. But both man and animal must be covered with sackcloth; and let men call on God with *their* strength that each may turn from his evil way and from the violence which is in his hands. Who knows, God may turn and relent and turn away from His burning anger so that we will not perish." Then God saw their works, that they turned from their evil way, so God relented concerning the evil which He had spoken He would bring upon them. And He did not bring it *upon them*.

The salvation of any sinner is a miracle. For conversion to occur, God must impart new life to a heart that was spiritually dead (cf. Eph 2:1–4). He grants sight to those who were blinded by sin and brings home those who were lost in darkness (2 Cor 4:6). He bestows the gift of faith (Eph 2:8) and the gift of repentance

(2 Tim 2:25), regenerating the heart of the sinner so that it beats with love for Him. When just one sinner is born again, the hosts of heaven respond with joy. As the Lord Jesus explained, "I tell you, there is joy in the presence of the angels of God over one sinner who repents" (Luke 15:10).

There are times also when the Lord multiplies this miracle by bringing many to saving faith. The pages of Scripture record such occasions, when God acted powerfully to bring large numbers of people to repentance. During the reign of King Josiah, for example, the nation of Judah experienced a widespread revival. The people repented by repudiating idolatry and restoring the worship of Yahweh (2 Chr 34–35). After the exile, when a group of Israelites returned to the land of Judah, "a very large assembly, men, women, and children, gathered" and "the people wept bitterly" in repentance before God (Ezra 10:1). When Peter preached at Pentecost, some 3,000 people embraced the Lord Jesus in repentant faith (Acts 2:41). After Paul evangelized the Jewish population in Berea, "many of them believed, along with not a few prominent Greek women and men" (17:12). God also told Paul to remain in Corinth and preach to the Corinthians, explaining that He had "many people in this city" (18:10). Significant seasons of salvation have also occurred in church history, including the sixteenth-century Reformation and the eighteenth-century Great Awakening. During those periods, large numbers of people repented and embraced the Lord Jesus in saving faith. Looking to the end of the age, God has also promised that the nation of Israel will repent and be saved (Zech 12:10–13:1; Rom 11:26).

Any list of history's largest collection of repentant sinners would be incomplete without including Nineveh in the days of Jonah. By saving the Gentile inhabitants of Assyria's capital city, God put His grace on vivid display. The Lord not only restored His repentant prophet (Jonah 3:1–2) but also sent him to Nineveh to proclaim a dire warning (3:3–4) in order to prompt the people to repent (3:5). In this passage (3:6–10), the prophet continued his description of Nineveh's remarkable conversion by recounting four key details: the remorse of Nineveh's monarch (3:6), the royal mandate he issued (3:7–8), the reliant meekness of the people (3:9), and the relenting mercy of God (3:10). Though this Gentile city was exceedingly wicked, God's grace was far greater than the people's sin. The salvation of Nineveh vividly demonstrated that God's grace revealed fully in the gospel "is the power of God for salvation to everyone who believes, to the Jew first and also to the Greek [Gentile]" (Rom 1:16).

A Remorseful Monarch

Then the word reached the king of Nineveh, and he arose from his throne, laid aside his mantle from him, covered *himself* with sackcloth, and sat on the ashes. (3:6)

As news of Jonah's message reverberated through the city, **the word reached the king of Nineveh,** possibly either Adad-nirari III or Ashur-dan III (see Introduction for discussion).[1] Jonah did not need to seek an audience with the king; rather, his judgment message traveled by word of mouth and **reached** (literally, "touched, struck") **the king,** both in his ears and in his heart. Though removed from the mundane activities of his subjects, the king soon heard about the Hebrew prophet whom God had miraculously delivered from the sea and subsequently deployed to Nineveh with the **word** of destruction.

When the message God gave Jonah to preach broke through to the courts of the palace, it struck the king and he immediately carried out four actions. First, **he arose from his throne.** Rising up conveys urgency to respond in a swift and decisive way. For the king to rise **from his throne** was significant. Sitting on a throne represented a posture of dominance and control, unthreatened by any challenge and poised to give

1 See Stuart, *Hosea-Jonah,* 492; John H. Walton, "Jonah," in *The Expositor's Bible Commentary: Daniel-Malachi,* revised edition, (Grand Rapids: Zondervan, 2008), 454–55.

judgments and orders (cf. Deut 17:18; 1 Kgs 1:17, 35; 2 Kgs 11:19; 13:13; Ps 47:8). But the warning from God so gripped the king's mind that he physically stood up to take action. The Lord had earlier commanded Jonah to arise and go to Nineveh (Jonah 1:2; 3:2). Ironically, while Jonah initially arose to disobey the message from God, this Gentile monarch immediately arose to obey God, displaying submission to Him.

Second, the king **laid aside his mantle from him.** Similar to a modern-day uniform, the **mantle** was an outer garment that depicted a person's role or job. For example, Elijah wore a mantle that designated him as a prophet (1 Kgs 19:19). In casting aside his mantle, a symbol of royalty, the king denounced his own position, signaling his full surrender to Yahweh (cf. Ezek 26:16). His actions acknowledged that he was no better than his subjects; together, they were all subjects before the holy Judge of heaven. Such abject humility reflected a profound recognition of God's threatening power and supremacy.

Third, the king **covered *himself* with sackcloth.** Like the rest of the city (Jonah 3:5), the king donned **sackcloth** to express sorrow and mourning over his transgressions (cf. 1 Chr 21:16; Neh 9:1; Esth 4:1–9). He did not cling to his royal status and his royal robes. Instead, in humiliation he acknowledged the severity of his sin symbolized by the sackcloth. To display the extent of his remorse, the king did not merely clothe himself with a few small pieces of sackcloth (cf. Jonah 3:5) but completely **covered** himself with it, layering this coarse and scratchy goat-hair over his entire body. By that open act of repentance, he acknowledged his sin (cf. Pss 32:3–7; 51:1–9; Joel 2:12–17; Jas 4:8–10), demonstrating the fruit of repentance (cf. Jonah 3:8; Matt 3:8).

In a final display of humiliation, the king **sat on the ashes.** These **ashes** would have been outside the city in a garbage dump where waste was burned—a place full of filthy refuse and foul odors. Though he had been seated on a royal throne, the king chose to sit in a heap of garbage, trading the highest honor for the lowest degradation. Like Job (cf. Job 2:8), Nineveh's ruler placed himself on these ashes to illustrate that he saw himself as condemned and unworthy before God (cf. Phil 3:8). He acknowledged that he had no standing in the sight of the Lord, being void of merit and under judgment, and he thus depicted the contriteness of the chief of sinners (cf. Luke 18:13; 1 Tim 1:15).

With the condescension of the king, truly the entire city was impacted by Jonah's message—"from the greatest to the least of them" (Jonah 3:5). The immediate, humble, remorseful, and destitute repentance of the king embodied the words of Job, "Therefore I reject *myself,* and I repent in dust and ashes" (Job 42:6; cf. Dan 9:3–6; Matt 11:21; Luke 10:13; Heb 9:13–14). The radical transformation of Nineveh's ruler stands as a remarkable testimony to the power of God's work in salvation. The Lord demonstrated in this act of conversion that He loves all kinds of sinners, and that even a wicked king is not outside the reach of His mercy (cf. 2 Chr 33:12–15; Dan 4:34–35; Phil 1:13; 4:22).

A Royal Mandate

And he cried out and said, "In Nineveh by the decree of the king and his nobles: Do not let man, animal, herd, or flock taste a thing. Do not let them eat, and do not let them drink water. But both man and animal must be covered with sackcloth; and let men call on God with *their* strength that each may turn from his evil way and from the violence which is in his hands." (3:7–8)

Under the weight of divine conviction, the king **cried out** with a loud shout as one alarmed by the threat of imminent death. The sailors expressed this same kind of outburst when they encountered the severe storm (Jonah 1:5). Ironically, the Gentile king and the Gentile sailors responded to the prospect of divine judgment with far more urgency than Jonah had done on the ship.

The king immediately issued a desperate decree, beginning with, **"In Nineveh by the decree of the king and**

his nobles." The king understood that drastic measures were necessary, involving everyone **in Nineveh.** No one was exempt from this royal mandate. Because this command was so sweeping, it was backed **by the decree of the king and his nobles.** The word **decree** is actually the Hebrew word for "taste," the same word in the command for man and animal not to "taste" any food (see below). This association reinforced that the king's taste (i.e., his decree concerning repentance) dictated what others could or could not taste (i.e., the food prohibited during a fast to demonstrate repentance). Such an edict came not only from the **king,** the highest authority in the land, but also **the nobles,** the officials who would execute the decree. The term **nobles** is literally "great ones," reinforcing that truly those "from the greatest to the least of them" turned from their wickedness to God (Jonah 3:5). With the backing of all those in authority, no one would dare defy the king's order, lest they face fearsome punishment.

The king then issued a series of prohibitions: **"Do not let man, animal, herd, or flock taste a thing. Do not let them eat, and do not let them drink water."** Three times he repeated the phrase **do not,** emphatically demanding complete abstinence from food and drink. No **man, animal, herd, or flock** was to **taste a thing.** The mention of **man** and **animal** shows that the command pertained to any living creature, and the reference to **herd** and **flock** included every domestic animal. The edict was all-inclusive.

The king further specified, **"Do not let them eat."** The word for **eat** refers to the grazing of cattle. People were already instructed not to taste a morsel of food or feed their animals. But this command went further than that. The king demanded that no animal was even allowed to graze in the countryside. In effect, the Ninevites would have had to lock up their animals to prevent them from finding food on their own. Such a command would have both suspended business operations and disrupted the economy. Life in the city was brought to a halt so that everyone could focus on repentance. Nineveh's monarch also added,

"Do not let them drink water." Fasts often abstain from food but not always from water. While people may survive a number of weeks without food, they cannot survive beyond a few days without water. Such restrictions elevated the severity of the fast to an extreme and dangerous level to display an attitude of spiritual desperation.

In addition to his prohibitions, the king also prescribed three requirements. First, he decreed that **both man and animal must be covered with sackcloth,** just as he had covered himself (Jonah 3:6). He demanded that even the **animal** population participate. Animals, of course, cannot repent, but covering them with sackcloth demonstrated that their owners had included everything in their repentance before the Lord. This was akin to Israel removing leaven from their homes during the Feast of Unleavened Bread (Exod 12:15). Just as the Israelites removed leaven from every crevice of their homes, showing their complete renunciation of sin, so the Ninevites would cover everything that breathed with sackcloth to display their contrition to God. Their actions served as an expression of the profound sorrow that filled their hearts (cf. Ps 32:3–5; Luke 19:8; 2 Cor 7:9–10).

Second, the king decreed, **"Let men call on God with *their* strength."** In turning to Yahweh and imploring His mercy, the sailors had also **called** on the Lord earlier (Jonah 1:14). The king exhorted his people to respond in the same way. He understood that sackcloth was not enough, but that true repentance included an earnest appeal to the Lord from every heart (cf. Rom 10:9–10; Eph 2:8–9; 2 Pet 1:1–2). The king summoned his subjects to call specifically and exclusively **on God with *their* strength,** a phrase that describes one's full might and effort (cf. Judg 8:1; 1 Sam 2:16). They were to pray to God for deliverance with wholehearted fervency.

Third, the king directed each Ninevite to **turn from his evil way and from the violence which is in his hands.** This was a call to demonstrate the inner reality of their repentance through the outer reality of a changed life. To **turn** denotes a complete change of direction. A life that experiences such a **turn** puts an end to an old way of conduct and establishes a new pattern of living. The people needed to repudiate both their **evil way,** that is their personal sins and actions, as well as their cruelty toward others, the **violence which** was **in** their **hands.** The king commanded his citizens to turn away from every form of iniquity. A momentary act of repentance or prayer was not sufficient; true repentance always results in transformed behavior (cf. Rom 12:1–2; 2 Cor 7:10–11; 1 Thess 1:9). Like John the Baptist, the king exhorted his people to bear fruit in keeping with repentance (Matt 3:8).

With these instructions, Nineveh's ruler directed his people to exhibit the righteousness that characterizes genuine repentance. Like descriptions earlier in the chapter (cf. Jonah 3:5), the king's exhortations to Nineveh continued to mirror the prophet Joel, who called Israel to true repentance: to cease from their daily tasks (cf. Joel 2:16–17), to fast, and to dedicate themselves to the Lord with all their heart (cf. 2:12–13). The parallel demonstrates that God's requirements of repentance are the same for both Jew and Gentile. That the Gentiles in Nineveh repented, unlike the Israelites in Joel's day, is both an indictment on Israel and a reminder that God sincerely offers repentance to undeserving sinners.

A Reliant Meekness

"Who knows, God may turn and relent and turn away from His burning anger so that we will not perish." (3:9)

In light of Nineveh's repentance, the king expressed a level of hope for himself and his people. He said, **"Who knows, God may turn and relent and turn away from His burning anger so that we will not perish."** With the words **"who knows,"** the king acknowledged his utter reliance on divine mercy, since he had no ability to control or manipulate God's response. Nineveh's ruler could not know if God would relent, since Jonah's preaching did not explicitly provide any such assurance. Nevertheless, the king still urged his people to repent, in the hope that God would show them mercy in the place of judgment.

While acknowledging his uncertainty about God's response, the king had come to believe that God could **turn and relent and turn away from His burning anger.** He understood that Yahweh had the prerogative to **turn** and mitigate the course of judgment. In doing so, God would not only **relent,** lessening the consequences of His fury, but also fully **turn away from His burning anger,** abandoning His wrathful disposition against the city (Jer 18:7–10; 26:3, 13). Altogether, the phrase describes a reversal of divine condemnation and judgment, an act of astounding compassion and mercy. The king's words underscored God's absolute sovereignty to withhold punishment and extend grace. As he acknowledged, only if God turned from His wrath would Nineveh not perish. The sailors had declared the same truth earlier (cf. Jonah 1:6). Like the sailors, the king understood that God alone had the power over life and death. Thus, he and his citizens surrendered themselves completely to God's will.

The king discerned, likely from Jonah's preaching, that unlike the pagan gods, Yahweh is a God of forgiveness and compassion who offers salvation to those who repent and call on Him. Scripture attests to the uniqueness of God's saving character. As Micah exclaimed, "Who is a God like You, who forgives iniquity?" (Mic 7:18). Yahweh is full of lovingkindness and truth, forgiving sin and showing lovingkindness to thousands (Exod 34:6–7). The Psalms repeatedly celebrate this truth about God, declaring that Yahweh's lovingkindness endures forever (cf. Pss 100:5; 106:1; 107:1; 118:1; 136:1). Jonah himself experienced such compassion inasmuch as he should have died in judgment but lived on account of God's grace (cf. Jonah 2:3–10). The prophet Joel had proclaimed this grace to Israel, calling Israel to repentance and saying of the Lord, "Who knows whether He will *not* turn and relent" (Joel 2:14). In God's providence, the king of Nineveh expressed the same words to his Gentile citizens. This, however, was not the only time the text of Jonah alluded to Joel's prophecy (cf. Jonah 3:5 and Joel 1:14; Jonah 4:2 and Joel 2:13). As these parallels demonstrate, God was offering the same grace to the Gentiles (through Jonah) that He had extended to the Israelites (through Joel). The hope of the Ninevite king was that if each citizen would "turn from his evil way" (Jonah 3:8), then God would **turn away from His burning anger** (3:9). While the king did not know whether God would act in mercy, the Lord used the king's words to indicate His benevolence and compassion toward the Gentiles. As God promised to forgive Israel, so the Lord also demonstrated His willingness to receive the genuine repentance of all sinners who turn to Him, including Gentiles.

Salvation swept through the city as the Ninevites obeyed the king's command. They responded to Jonah's message with meekness, contrition, and an acute awareness of their utter reliance on the mercy of God. In a single day (cf. 3:4), 600,000 people, from peasants to princes, joined together to loathe their sin and seek the Lord. Such widespread repentance can only be explained through the power of God. Unsurprisingly, skeptics and critics have attempted to ascribe this mass repentance to natural events (such as military defeats, earthquakes, or an eclipse) rather than to God.[2] But no natural cause can explain the supernatural reality of spiritual transformation. Only one explanation stands: God determined to save the entire population of that city in that generation, and He used a once rebellious prophet to draw a once rebellious people to Himself.

Every indication of the text suggests that this repentance was genuine. The Ninevites believed the message from God, as their works affirmed, and their hope centered on Him. The New Testament, moreover, provides a final confirmation of the genuineness of this repentance. In Matthew 12:41, the Lord Jesus used Nineveh as an illustration of true repentance, saying, "The men of Nineveh will stand up with this generation at the

2 See Simon, *Jonah*, xvii–xviii.

judgment, and will condemn it because they repented at the preaching of Jonah; and behold, something greater than Jonah is here." Jesus confirmed that Nineveh's repentance was true on every account.

Ultimately, the greatest miracle in the book of Jonah was not that the prophet was swallowed by a fish and survived. Though incredible, that deep sea miracle was far surpassed in number, power, and eternal consequence by the miracle on land—Nineveh's repentance and faith in God. God saved the entire population of Assyria's capital city, extending His grace and mercy to hundreds of thousands of Gentiles.

A Relenting Mercy

Then God saw their works, that they turned from their evil way, so God relented concerning the evil which He had spoken He would bring upon them. And He did not bring *it upon them.* (3:10)

As the city of Nineveh donned sackcloth and called on the Lord for mercy, **God saw their works** of contrition. Though Yahweh was not obligated to pay attention to their cries for mercy, as their king openly acknowledged (cf. Jonah 3:9), the Lord did not turn a blind eye to these penitent people. He had taken the initiative to warn them of His pending judgment. Here, He again took action by graciously recognizing the fruits of their repentance.

The Lord saw **that they turned from their evil way** (cf. 3:8). The king had hoped that as the city **turned** away from iniquity, so God would turn away His wrath from them (see discussion on 3:9). In acknowledging their turning from evil, the Lord demonstrated His grace to the undeserving king and his people by taking notice of the fruit of their repentance. Out of His abundant mercy, **God relented** and mitigated His wrath against Nineveh, showing them the same grace He promised to Israel through the prophet Joel (see discussion on 3:9). The Lord spared the city **concerning the evil which He had spoken He would bring upon them.** The Ninevites had been heading toward terrible divine punishment on account of their sin—punishment that would have involved an **evil** disaster befitting their evil deeds. This was the judgment of which God firmly **had spoken** in the message delivered by Jonah. Though His wrath was kindled and declared, God graciously relented. While He had revealed that **He would bring** such wrath **upon them,** in the end, **He did not bring *it upon them*,** a testimony that God's pardon is total and His grace is greater than sin (cf. Rom 5:18–21). Out of His grace, the Lord had warned the Ninevites that they would be destroyed if they did not repent. And out of His mercy, He withheld His hand of judgment when they heeded His warning. All of this, of course, took place according to His sovereign purposes, to save a city full of Gentiles and showcase His patience, compassion, and love toward the whole world.

To an undeserving people, God bestowed grace upon grace, a gift that went far beyond what the Ninevites could ever ask or think (cf. Eph 3:20). Jonah 3 stands as a remarkable testimony of God's saving benevolence, extended to both Jew and Gentile (cf. Rom 3:27–31; Eph 2:11–22). The conversion of Nineveh serves as a powerful demonstration of the mercy received by all redeemed sinners. Though deserving of divine punishment and eternal destruction, they have been pardoned by grace through faith and given the hope of eternal life, "and this not of [themselves], *it is* the gift of God" (Eph 2:8).

God's Forgiveness and Jonah's Fury

7

JONAH 4:1–4

But this was a great evil to Jonah, and he became angry. And he prayed to Yahweh and said, "Ah! O Yahweh, was not this my word *to myself* while I was still in my *own* land? Therefore I went ahead to flee to Tarshish, for I knew that You are a gracious and compassionate God, slow to anger and abundant in lovingkindness, and one who relents concerning evil. So now, O Yahweh, please take my life from me, for death is better to me than life." And Yahweh said, "Do you have good reason to be angry?"

The right response to God's salvation of sinners is to rejoice. The Lord Jesus explained that heaven's angels join around God's throne to celebrate the salvation of each individual sinner (Luke 15:10). When the prodigal son repented and returned home, the father (representing the Lord) joyfully prepared a feast to celebrate the occasion (15:22–24). On the Day of Pentecost, Peter gloried in the truth that God saves even those who are far off (Acts 2:39; cf. 11:18). Paul and Barnabas rejoiced as they recounted the conversion of the Gentiles (15:3). Heaven itself is a place of unending jubilation, as the redeemed from every tribe and tongue respond in wonder and worship at the reality of their salvation (Rev 4–5). As these examples illustrate, the only fitting reaction to God's work of redemption is to marvel at His grace and declare His praise (cf. Ps 96:1–2).

But that was not how Jonah reacted to Nineveh's repentance. Unlike the father who celebrated his prodigal son's repentance, Jonah despised God's mercy toward the Ninevites. The prophet demonstrated no compassion or grace toward his enemies. Like the prodigal's older brother (Luke 15:28–29), Jonah became angry and embittered. When Jesus came, He instructed His followers to "love your enemies and pray for those who persecute you" (Matt 5:44); but Jonah hated his enemies and hoped for their destruction. He foreshadowed the response of the Pharisees and the scribes who deplored Jesus' willingness to minister to sinners (Luke 15:1). Jonah did not share the heart of Yahweh for the lost. He preferred to be dead rather than to see the Gentiles converted. Having that deep seated prejudice, he opposed God when the Lord initially sent him to Nineveh; and the prophet again opposed God when the Lord extended salvation, grace, and mercy to the Ninevites.

When Jonah saw Yahweh restrain His hand of judgment against the Gentiles, he became angry (Jonah 4:1) and began making accusations against the Lord Himself (4:2–3). Yet, despite the prophet's wicked resentment, God responded with a gracious and forbearing answer (4:4) that simultaneously exposed Jonah's sin. The Lord answered his prophet with such longsuffering because, unlike Jonah, He is merciful and full of compassion, exhibiting patience and extending salvation to both Jews and Gentiles (cf. Acts 10:34–35; 1 Tim 2:3–4; 2 Pet 3:9).

A Fierce Anger

But this was a great evil to Jonah, and he became angry. (4:1)

The spiritual salvation of Nineveh under God's display of lavish mercy **was a great evil to Jonah.** While English translations often render this phrase as "but it greatly displeased Jonah," the Hebrew literally states that it was **evil** in his sight. Evil is clearly defined throughout the book—being identified with Nineveh's collective wickedness (Jonah 1:2; cf. 4:2), the people's individual acts of violence (3:8, 10), and the calamitous nature of divine judgment (3:10; cf. 4:6). But Jonah defined evil in a way that turned it on its head. He regarded the repentance of the Gentiles—the act of turning from evil to God—as itself being evil. For Jonah, the fact that God mercifully restrained His hand of judgment against Nineveh constituted divine injustice. In Jonah's view, God's salvation of Nineveh made God guilty of evil. The prophet's perspective was so distorted that he called what is good, evil (cf. Isa 5:20; Rom 1:32). The repetition of the word **evil** twice in Hebrew (literally, "it was evil to Jonah, a great evil") emphasizes the depth of his darkened thinking.

The prophet went so far as to conclude that Nineveh's salvation was not merely evil but a **great** evil. This response evidenced two blind spots in Jonah's perspective: he was blinded by his hatred for his enemies, and he was blinded to the magnitude of God's grace. Throughout the book, the Lord acted in great ways. He sent a prophet to a great city (Jonah 1:2); He hurled a great storm so that the sailors would fear Him (1:4, 10, 16); He appointed a great fish to rescue His servant (1:17); and He sparked a great revival, from the small to the great, in Nineveh (3:2–3). But Jonah viewed these marvelous acts of God's goodness through a negative lens. The Lord's great acts of grace were matched by Jonah's great act of animosity against all that Yahweh had done.

Because he so strongly resented God's grace toward the Ninevites, Jonah **became angry,** which, in Hebrew, includes the notion of becoming hot. The prophet was burning in his displeasure, his temper boiling within him. Soon, that anger would manifest itself in words of bitter accusation toward the Lord (Jonah 4:2–3; cf. Matt 12:34; Luke 6:45). Jonah's sin had not only twisted his mind but also taken control of his emotions, manifesting itself in words and actions that constituted an assault on God's character.

A Flagrant Accusation

And he prayed to Yahweh and said, "Ah! O Yahweh, was not this my word *to myself* while I was still in my *own* land? Therefore I went ahead to flee to Tarshish, for I knew that You are a gracious and compassionate God, slow to anger and abundant in lovingkindness, and one who relents concerning evil. So now, O Yahweh, please take my life from me, for death is better to me than life." (4:2–3)

Overcome by anger, Jonah **prayed to Yahweh and said, "Ah! O Yahweh."** Previously, the prophet prayed because he was grateful for God's grace (Jonah 2:1), but at this point he **prayed** out of derision for divine mercy (see discussion on 4:1). Rather than calling out **to Yahweh** for salvation as he had done earlier (2:1), Jonah vented his anger toward the Lord. Though Jonah began his prayer with the emotional expression **"Ah,"** just as the repentant sailors (1:14), the prophet was far from contrite; his tone was caustic and his heart calloused. Instead of worshiping God for His mercy as he had done previously (2:6), Jonah cried out **"O Yahweh"** in protest of God's saving character.

Jonah then bitterly complained, **"Was not this my word *to myself* while I was still in my own land?"** Jonah was, in essence, saying that he had believed from the outset that God would be gracious to the Ninevites. Yet, the prophet's words evidenced his self-centeredness and pride. He had prioritized his own (**my**) **word,** though Yahweh had sent him to speak God's Word (cf. Jonah 1:1–2; 3:1–2). Jonah's references to Israel as **my *own* land** emphasized his attitude that the land belonged to him and the Israelites rather than to the outsiders or even to God. Rather than expressing gratitude for his homeland by recognizing that it was a gift from God (cf. Deut 4:40; 5:16; 11:9; 1 Kgs 8:34; 2 Kgs 21:8), the prophet expressed nothing but bitterness and vitriol. Reverting to his initial insubordination (Jonah 1:1), he again spoke with defiant disregard for the Lord's gracious prerogative. Consumed with self-interest, he was glad to embrace God's grace for himself but unwilling to see that same grace extended to pagan idolaters.

Jonah's selfishness and long cultivated hatred had driven him in his initial disobedience. As he admitted, **"Therefore I went ahead to flee to Tarshish."** The statement **"I went ahead"** denotes getting in front of something to redirect or prevent it. The prophet acknowledged that he understood what God had intended, yet he deeply resented God's sovereign purpose. In a foolish attempt to hinder the Lord's will, he headed **to Tarshish,** an endeavor that required careful planning, extensive travel, and significant expense (see discussion on Jonah 1:3). That the prophet confessed his hateful contempt for the Gentiles and disappointment in God reflected the severity and stubbornness of his anger. Instead of responding in worship and love to the Lord, as he ought to have done (cf. Jer 18:6; Rom 9:20), Jonah addressed Yahweh with contempt.

Still seeking to justify his earlier rebellion, the prophet explained the rationale behind his disobedience, saying, **"for I knew that You are a gracious and compassionate God, slow to anger and abundant in lovingkindness, and one who relents concerning evil."** Jonah first described God as **gracious,** a word conveying that God is lavish and generous. The Lord is always inclined to act with favor, to do good above and beyond what is required (cf. Pss 46:1; 103:1–5; 107:39–43; Eph 3:20–21;

Heb 4:14–16). Jonah further described the Lord as **compassionate,** a term derived from the Hebrew word "womb" and used to describe the love a mother has toward her children. Because of His compassion, God shows great interest in and sympathy toward others. The prophet continued by noting that Yahweh is **slow to anger,** meaning that God is longsuffering. His wrath is not quickly kindled (cf. Gen 15:16; Exod 34:6; Joel 2:13; Rom 9:22; 2 Pet 3:9, 15). Jonah noted that God is also **abundant in lovingkindness** toward others. **Lovingkindness** refers to a compelling loyalty, one that faithfully keeps a covenant without fluctuation or failure. God's lovingkindness speaks of His grace (John 1:17; cf. Exod 34:6–8), which saves (Rom 6:23), transforms (Rom 12:1–2; Phil 1:6; 2:12–13), and empowers (Phil 4:13) according to His sovereign will. God implements this loyalty in **abundance,** surpassing the need of any situation. Out of the abundance of His lovingkindness, God shows mercy to those whom He wills (Rom 9:23), as He **relents concerning evil.** He does this in keeping with both His gracious character and predetermined purposes. Though He is never obligated to do so, God delights in showing mercy toward sinners, restraining His wrath and refraining from bringing catastrophic judgment on those who deserve it. This was what He did for Nineveh (cf. Jonah 3:9). Jonah recognized that the reason the city was spared was entirely because of God's magnanimous saving character, which he described accurately. It would have been worship if Jonah had praised God for those attributes; but, instead, he shockingly responded with disdain and disgust.

Though it came from an embittered heart, Jonah's articulation of God's saving character was theologically accurate. It reflected the Lord's self-description in Exodus 34:6–7, when He showed His glory to Moses. The Lord declared of Himself:

> Yahweh, Yahweh God, compassionate and gracious, slow to anger, and abounding in lovingkindness and truth; who keeps lovingkindness for thousands, who forgives iniquity,

> transgression, and sin; yet He will by no means leave *the guilty* unpunished, visiting the iniquity of fathers on the children and on the grandchildren to the third and fourth generations.

Israel should have died for worshiping the golden calf (Exod 32). However, out of His infinite mercy, the Lord spared and restored the nation. Accordingly, God's people joyfully repeated this declaration throughout the Old Testament (Neh 9:17; Pss 86:15; 103:8; 111:4; 112:4; 116:5; 145:8). In referring to God as the **one who relents concerning evil,** Jonah's specific phrasing not only reflected these earlier texts but specifically drew from Joel 2:13. The prophet Joel declared to Israel that if they would repent, they would receive mercy because God faithfully extends grace to His people Israel. Jonah's prayer summarized an entire history of Yahweh's forbearance, forgiveness, and faithfulness toward His people. This truth about God's kindness to Israel exposed Jonah's hypocrisy, revealing that he fully accepted God's grace when it was extended to undeserving Israel, yet he rejected it when it was given to any other people.

Incredibly, Jonah disobeyed the Lord's command while being fully aware of God's compassionate character. As he confessed, **"for I knew."** The prophet grasped God's lavish mercy and patience, both to Israel historically and to him personally. But instead of allowing those truths to prompt him to desire mercy for others (cf. Eph 4:32), he attempted to prevent the Ninevites from experiencing that same grace (cf. Matt 18:32–33).

Jonah ended his complaint by saying, **"So now, O Yahweh, please take my life from me."** The pouting prophet's concluding request (**so now**) was the culmination of his hateful prejudice. He appealed to **Yahweh** with a manipulative and melodramatic demand, insisting that the Giver of life **take** his **life.** As previously, in asking to die, Jonah was driven by his selfish desires, not the honor of Yahweh. The prophet's response was sensational and childish, asking God to kill him if he could not have his way. Earlier, he had told the sailors to throw him overboard (Jonah 1:12), preferring to die at that time as well. Jonah stubbornly maintained this bitter attitude throughout the rest of the chapter (4:3, 8, 9). While the prophet expressed joy when God extended grace to him (2:9), he hated that the Lord would show grace to the Gentiles. He would rather experience death than see the Ninevites experience life.

The prophet continued by declaring the rationale for his death wish, saying, **"For death is better to me than life."** Jonah did not merely have a warped view of the nature of evil and the saving purposes of God (see discussion above); his understanding of life and death was also distorted. Jonah viewed his **life** as no longer worth living because the Ninevites were spared from divine judgment. In making this claim, the prophet demonstrated his ingratitude for the fact that God had rescued him from certain death in the sea (Jonah 2:6–10). Though the psalmist once declared that God's "lovingkindness is better than life" (Ps 63:3), Jonah's animosity toward the Gentiles was so formidable—apparently, the dominating passion of his life—that God's lovingkindness toward them would rob him of his reason to live. With this twisted perspective, Jonah declared, **"Death is better to me than life."**

A Forbearing Answer

And Yahweh said, "Do you have good reason to be angry?" (4:4)

In response to Jonah's misguided and outlandish ultimatum, **Yahweh said,** which is a reaction that demonstrates His grace and patience. God did not strike Jonah dead for his profane impertinence or thunderously denounce His insubordinate servant. Instead, He asked Jonah a direct question, displaying longsuffering toward the angry prophet with a response that was strikingly antithetical to Jonah's foolish blasphemy. Again, God's grace stood in stark contrast to Jonah's heart of hatred. The Lord could have killed Jonah at any point, and He certainly had every right to do so. But the Lord showed patience and mercy, traits Jonah did not possess. The prophet saw a wicked people and desired their annihilation. God encountered a wicked prophet and showed him ongoing care and patience.

While continuing to show grace, the Lord posed a question that was designed to expose the fullness of Jonah's warped perspective. God asked, **"Do you have good reason to be angry?"** As evidenced by his prayer, Jonah had a distorted understanding of reality, including God's saving purposes (4:2), life and death (4:3), and the nature of evil (4:1). The Lord asked Jonah if he had a legitimate **reason to be angry,** one that could be genuinely considered **good.** Though there are valid reasons to have righteous anger, especially at that which offends God (cf. John 2:13–17; Eph 4:26), Jonah's anger was evil on its face and even more so because it was directed at God. Jonah's temper flared not in response to Nineveh's sin, but in response to the city's repentance and God's mercy. Jonah's fury was directed toward God Himself. The prophet did not have any **good reason** to be upset, revealing that he had distorted the very meaning of what was good. In viewing life and death as well as good and evil through such a warped lens, Jonah's understanding of Yahweh was severely distorted. The Lord's question unveiled the twisted person Jonah had become because of his prejudice.

Throughout this passage (Jonah 4:1–4), the prophet's repugnant reaction serves as a dramatic foil to magnify the marvelous grace of God. The natural response of fallen human beings is a desire to see their enemies suffer, while selfishly seeking mercy for themselves. That was Jonah's arrogant attitude. What a contrast to the benevolent response of the Lord. Unlike His sinful servant, God displayed patience, love, kindness, and mercy—not only toward the Ninevites, but also toward Jonah. In this way, the glorious Person and saving purposes of Yahweh are vividly displayed, shining brightly in contrast to the depraved darkness of Jonah's self-centeredness and pride.

A Prophet, a Plant, and a People

8

JONAH 4:5–11

Then Jonah went out from the city and sat east of the city. And there he made a booth for himself and sat under it in the shade until he could see what would happen in the city. So Yahweh God appointed a plant, and it came up over Jonah to be a shade over his head to deliver him from his *miserable* evil. And Jonah was extremely glad about the plant. But God appointed a worm at the breaking of dawn the next day, and it struck the plant, and it dried up. Then it happened that as the sun rose up, God appointed a scorching east wind, and the sun struck down on Jonah's head so that he became faint and asked with *all* his soul to die and said, "Death is better to me than life." Then God said to Jonah, "Do you have good reason to be angry about the plant?" And he said, "I have good reason to be angry, even to death." Then Yahweh said, "You had pity on the plant for which you did not work and *which* you did not cause to grow, which came to be overnight and perished overnight. So should I not have pity on Nineveh, the great city, in which there are more than 120,000 persons who do not know *the difference* between their right and left hand, as well as many animals?"

The glorious theme of God's abundant grace permeates the book of Jonah. In His grace, the Lord commissioned His prophet to warn the Ninevites about His pending wrath. In His grace, He delivered the sailors from the storm, and rescued Jonah from the depths of the sea. In His grace, He restored His wayward prophet to service, and deployed him a second time to Nineveh. In His grace, Yahweh prompted the Ninevites to repent when they heard the sobering message; and in His grace, He restrained His hand of judgment against them. When Jonah reacted in anger to God's mercy toward Nineveh, the Lord again demonstrated grace by responding to Jonah with forbearance. Repeatedly, God put His benevolent lovingkindness on display—with Jonah, the sailors, and the Ninevites. If not for divine mercy and unmerited favor, the stubborn prophet, the pagan seafarers, and the fearsome Assyrians would all have perished. The lesson is clear. Every sinner stands in equal need of divine grace, whether Jew or Gentile. Moreover, the Lord generously extends His mercy and kindness to all who call on Him in repentant faith (cf. Rom 10:13).

Though Jonah had personally benefited from God's unmerited favor, he failed to appreciate the scope of God's saving purposes. Instead of celebrating the salvation of an entire city, the indignant prophet considered the extension of grace toward the Ninevites to be evil. This backward understanding of good and evil reflected the same confusion for which God had condemned the nation of Israel (cf. Isa 1:4; 5:20, 24). Even so, the Lord responded to Jonah with patient instruction. In this final response to His prophet, God delivered one last object lesson about the wonder of His grace. It was instruction designed to pierce Jonah's calloused heart.

The final section of the book (Jonah 4:5–11) begins with the prophet's flawed anticipation (4:5) that Nineveh would yet be destroyed by Yahweh. Instead, the Lord used a short-lived plant as a fitting analogy (4:6–8) to illustrate the hypocrisy of Jonah's anger regarding the Ninevites. The book concludes with a final admonition (4:9–11) from the Lord to His prophet. That closing rebuke came in the form of a rhetorical question to Jonah: If the prophet had pity on a passing plant, should God not show mercy to a perishing people?

A Flawed Anticipation

Then Jonah went out from the city and sat east of the city. And there he made a booth for himself and sat under it in the shade until he could see what would happen in the city. (4:5)

In reaction to God's question (in 4:4), Jonah **went out from the city.** Clearly unhappy with the Lord's response, and having completed his preaching assignment, Jonah departed and in a sour sulk **sat east of the city.** While east identified Jonah's physical location, it also signaled his judgmental disposition toward the Ninevites, evoking other passages where the east is associated with divine judgment (cf. Gen 3:24; 13:11; Isa 9:11–12; 46:11; Ezek 43:2; and cf. Gen 16:12; 25:18). Rather than rejoicing in God's saving power and purpose, Jonah insisted on waiting for divine wrath to fall on Nineveh in keeping with his warning (Jonah 3:4). So, he positioned himself where he could see the city, hoping God would still unleash just judgment on the population. That Jonah **sat** demonstrated his resolve to watch there until Nineveh was destroyed.

Intent on seeing his enemies suffer and determined to wait until God struck them, the bitter prophet **made a booth for himself and sat under it in the shade.** This was a temporary structure typically made from twigs or tree branches to provide some shelter from the natural elements, such as the heat of the sun (cf. Gen 33:17; Job 27:18; Isa 1:8; 4:6; Amos 9:11). Motivated by hatred and hostility, Jonah labored to set up a shelter for himself so that he could have a front-row seat to enjoy Nineveh's demise. That he built **a booth** further revealed his hypocrisy and hardness of heart. The prophet was familiar with such a shelter from the Feast of Booths (Lev 23:40–44), which was a festival celebrating God's grace toward Israel. During this feast, the Israelites constructed booths and showed hospitality to foreign sojourners (Deut 16:14). The celebration commemorated God's gracious and faithful sustaining of His people when the Israelites were sojourners in a land not their own (Lev 23:43). For Jonah, a **booth** that should have symbolized compassion, thanksgiving, and hospitality instead represented hatred, bitterness, and hostility. The booth assembled by the prophet truly was **for himself,** serving the prophets' selfish antagonism toward souls on the brink of divine judgment.

After completing his makeshift shelter, Jonah **sat under it in the shade.** Though the sun beat down with its heat, the booth provided some **shade** for Jonah to wait in anticipation of Nineveh's destruction. While God extended grace to the city (cf. Jonah 3:10), Jonah persisted in protesting the Lord's mercy, hoping calamity would yet befall the Ninevites.

The prophet intended to stay **until** the end of the forty-day period, so **he could see what would happen in the city.** With a wicked hope that Nineveh's repentance was not genuine, or that God would heed the prophet's protest and reject the people's repentance, Jonah positioned himself to watch Nineveh's downfall. To accentuate the prophet's eagerness for the city's demise, the text repeats the word **city** three times in this verse. The prophet went out from **the city,** sat against **the city,** and looked to see what God would do with **the city.** In the previous verse (4:4), the Lord asked Jonah if he thought he had a righteous reason to be angry. The prophet clearly had none. Nevertheless, consumed with disdain and hope for the destruction of his Gentile enemies, Jonah waited and watched.

A Fitting Analogy

So Yahweh God appointed a plant, and it came up over Jonah to be a shade over his head to deliver him from his *miserable* evil. And Jonah was extremely glad about the plant. But God appointed a worm at the breaking of dawn the next day, and it struck the plant, and it dried up. Then it happened that as the sun rose up, God appointed a scorching east wind, and the sun struck down on Jonah's head so that he became faint and asked with *all* his soul to die and said, "Death is better to me than life." (4:6–8)

In response to Jonah's warped perspective, the Lord provided His prophet with an object lesson about divine grace. To do so, **Yahweh God appointed a plant.** This was not the first time the Lord appointed something in the book. In Jonah 1:17, God "appointed" a fish to rescue the prophet, sovereignly ordaining this merciful miracle. But Jonah clearly did not learn from that monumental act of divine mercy, and so God once again **appointed,** this time a plant to sprout up as a display of His lovingkindness. The name **Yahweh** identifies the Lord as the Giver of unbending loyalty and grace (cf. Exod 3:14–16; 34:6–7), while the title **God** declares His supreme power and creative might (cf. Gen 1:1). Because He is both supremely powerful and immeasurably gracious, the Lord intervened in the life of His sulking servant, providing unforgettable instruction that grace comes solely from His sovereign hand (cf. Eph 2:1–10; 2 Tim 1:9; Titus 3:5–6).

The plant, likely a castor oil plant with bushy leaves providing ample shade, **came up over Jonah,** growing at a miraculous speed and sprouting in the very place where Jonah sat. Jonah did not have to move to receive the comforting benefits of its cover. The Lord graciously caused the bush to shield Jonah, with no work on the prophet's part (cf. Gal 3:10–14; Eph 2:8–10; 1 Pet 1:21).

Thus, God created the plant to provide immediate **shade over** Jonah's **head** and the makeshift shelter (cf. Jonah 4:5), which was clearly inadequate to furnish full protection from the sun. This plant offered shade in a way that Jonah's booth failed to do. Again, God's grace bestowed on Jonah what the prophet needed but was unable to provide for himself.

Yahweh graciously created this protection for Jonah **to deliver him from his *miserable* evil.** The phrase ***miserable* evil** is rendered in different ways by English translations, often having the idea of misery or discomfort. However, the Hebrew word itself is the specific word for **evil,** the very same term used to describe Jonah's assessment of Nineveh's repentance (Jonah 4:1). While the prophet had a completely warped view of evil (see discussion on 4:1), God was working on Jonah to show him the true nature of evil. The repentance of Nineveh's people was not **evil;** but Jonah's stubborn misery was, as he brooded selfishly because of God's saving grace. To **deliver** someone (whether Nineveh or Jonah) from evil was not evil; rather, it was the highest good. As Jonah sat comfortably, sheltered from the ***miserable* evil** of the scorching sun, the Lord was making the point unmistakably that the grace Jonah resented when it was given to others was actually what he welcomed for himself—and it was very good!

Additionally, the Lord demonstrated that the expressions of grace should produce rejoicing and not resentment. Anything less is evil! When God delivered Jonah from the intense heat, **Jonah was extremely glad about the plant.** The idea of gladness is not merely an external act of shallow happiness but an internal attitude of deep rejoicing and bliss. The plant and the protection it offered caused Jonah to respond with delight and joy. In Hebrew, the text states that "Jonah was glad...with great gladness," mirroring the structure of Jonah's evaluation of Nineveh's repentance when "it was evil to Jonah...a great evil" (Jonah 4:1). God provided the prophet a taste of His goodness to show him that grace was the opposite of the great evil he claimed it was. At the same time, Jonah's response revealed how deep-seated his hatred was, as he expressed elation **about the plant** while exhibiting only contempt for the grace that offered salvation to Nineveh. God used this plant to expose Jonah's self-centeredness and hypocrisy. Though the prophet received God's grace for himself with joy, he responded to God's grace toward others with anger.

The Lord's object lesson took an unexpected and dramatic turn as **God appointed a worm.** Yahweh had appointed a fish (Jonah 1:17) and a plant (4:6) to deliver. This time, He appointed a **worm** to destroy. While the exact species of this worm is unknown, worms were well known to attack and kill plants (cf. Deut 28:39) and to spoil food (cf. Exod 16:20). In this instance, God ordained the worm to remove the protection He had graciously provided through the plant.

God sent the worm **at the breaking of dawn,** literally "when the dawn came up." Just as the plant "came up" to provide deliverance (Jonah 4:6), so the plant disappeared and deliverance was removed when the dawn "came up." God suddenly removed the experience of the goodness He had supernaturally bestowed on Jonah, assuring that the prophet felt the loss. The Lord ordained the worm to kill the plant at **dawn,** so that the prophet would feel the full torment of exposure to the rising of the scorching sun. The Lord also allowed Jonah to enjoy the shade of the plant for only one day to take it away **the next day,** maximizing his discomfort.

So, the worm that the Lord appointed **struck the plant** such that the plant **dried up** and withered away. The God who showed grace by bringing the sailors and Jonah to dry land (1:9; 2:10) is the same One who removed His grace by drying up the plant. As the sun increasingly beat down on Jonah's head, Jonah was feeling the effect of God's grace being removed.

Following the destructive work of the worm, **then it happened that as the sun rose up, God appointed a scorching east wind.** Just as God had sovereignly appointed a fish (1:17) and a plant (4:6) for Jonah's benefit, He also **appointed** a worm and then **a scorching east wind** to inflict suffering on Jonah. The **scorching east wind,** a Sirocco, came across the arid desert with a fury, collecting sand and dust to blast everything in its path. Like other items in the book of Jonah—the storm, boat, sailors, Ninevites, and worm—this wind immediately and fully submitted to Yahweh's control. The Lord ensured that the Sirocco rushed in just **as the sun rose up** so that the prophet would find no relief, not even in the morning. God added to the beating heat of the sun the blistering wind, as it stung Jonah's skin with sand and filled his choking lungs with dust.

So, just as the worm struck the plant (4:7), the **sun struck** the prophet, intensifying his discipline. While the plant had previously shaded Jonah (4:6), the sun now beat **down on Jonah's head.** The blessing Jonah had lost and the misery he experienced in its place was to teach him what it meant to enjoy grace, to have grace removed, and to suffer judgment.

Because of the relentless heat under the blistering sun, Jonah **became faint.** The term translated **became faint** (*wayyitallaph*) is different than the word used earlier with Jonah "fainting" in the water (*behitatteph*; see Jonah 2:7). Previously, the term referred to the prophet losing consciousness, but here the term depicts collapsing from thirst and weariness (cf. Isa 51:20; Amos 8:13). Though different in nuance, the words are similar in sound and meaning, forging a parallel between the two moments in which Jonah became faint—previously, in the depths of the sea, and then in the desert heat. The Lord's choice of discipline was fitting. Jonah had been hot with anger (Jonah 4:1), having hoped to see the fiery destruction of the city (4:5). So, God exposed Jonah to the heat of His judgment, as the scathing wind and the searing heat tormented him.

Strangely, instead of asking God to relieve his suffering and spare his life, Jonah **asked with *all* his soul to die and said, "Death is better to me than life."** He still could not accept the grace of God to Gentile enemies. He would rather be dead! Throughout the book, the prophet in his twisted selfishness repeatedly asked to die, requesting the sailors to throw him overboard (1:12) and then asking God to take his life (4:3). This final instance was no different. Jonah exclaimed the same words he had uttered earlier, **"Death is better to me than life"** (cf. 4:3). He had reached an even deeper level of defiant intolerance, for in this case he made this request **with *all* his soul.**

Jonah's words also reveal an addition to his death wish. Earlier, the prophet had asked for death out of spite for God's grace. He pleaded to die when God spared the Ninevites (4:3). In that instance, Jonah believed that death was preferable to a life in which the Lord extended grace to Israel's enemies (see discussion on 4:3). But here, Jonah wished to die not only because God had extended grace to his enemies, but also because He had removed grace from him. By graciously providing a plant and then taking it away, the Lord gave Jonah a taste of both the goodness of His grace and the misery of its absence. The prophet here realized that **death is better...than life** without God's grace, since a life in which grace is removed leaves the sinner with nothing to experience except judgment and calamity. Though Jonah was still indignant, an important lesson began to break through to him: that the Lord's "lovingkindness is better than life" (Ps 63:3).

A Final Admonition

Then God said to Jonah, "Do you have good reason to be angry about the plant?" And he said, "I have good reason to be angry, even to death." Then Yahweh said, "You had pity on the plant for which you did not work and *which* you did not cause to grow, which came to be overnight and perished overnight. So should I not have pity on Nineveh, the great city, in which there are more than 120,000 persons who do not know *the difference* between their right and left hand, as well as many animals?" (4:9–11)

As the wind blew and the sun beat down on the beleaguered prophet, the Lord asked Jonah a piercing question: **"Do you have good reason to be angry about the plant?"** Earlier, God had asked a similar question to point out the prophet's distorted understanding of good and evil (see discussion on Jonah 4:4). Here, the question served to correct Jonah's errant understanding about grace. The question emphasized how perverted Jonah's thinking had been: the prophet was **angry** that God showed mercy to repentant Nineveh (cf. 3:10–4:3), and he was just as angry that God removed mercy from him (cf. 4:7–8). The prophet was irate that God killed **the plant,** and he was equally angry that God did not kill the people in Nineveh (cf. 4:3). The Lord questioned Jonah to expose his selfish and sinful priorities, and to demonstrate that he did not in fact have **good reason** for his anger. Previously, Jonah was enraged because God had extended His grace to hundreds of thousands of Ninevites, sparing them from judgment (cf. 4:1–3), but then he was angry because God had removed His grace from him by killing an insignificant plant. The point behind Yahweh's question was to compel Jonah to consider whether it was better for divine grace to be extended or removed.

In response to this question, the prophet replied frankly: **"I have good reason to be angry, even to death."** Previously, when God asked Jonah if he had good reason to be angry on account of His grace toward Nineveh, Jonah did not respond (4:4). In this case, Jonah openly claimed to have **good reason** for his anger. He had greatly needed the plant, and he was deeply incensed when the Lord took it away. Jonah assumed his anger was justifiable—both when God extended His grace (to Nineveh) and when God removed His grace (by destroying the plant). Blind to his inconsistency, the prophet was so convinced of his position that he boldly declared he had the right to be angry at the grace given to his enemies and the grace removed from him, **even to death.** As elsewhere in the book (cf. 1:12; 4:3), Jonah's desire to die evidenced his sinful folly.

Having heard these words from Jonah's mouth, the Lord proceeded to explain all that Jonah had acknowledged. The prophet not only confessed the goodness of God's grace (since he was angry when it was removed) but also revealed that he **had pity on the plant.** The term **pity** carries the notion of compassion and concern for another (cf. Neh 13:22), especially toward those who are needy or destitute (cf. Deut 7:16; Ezek 7:9; Joel 2:17). Although arising from selfish motives and a skewed mindset, Jonah felt sympathy for the wilted plant.

But God pointed out that the prophet's compassion for the plant was superficial and selfish. It was superficial because Jonah had not personally invested in the plant; he **did not work and did not cause** the plant **to grow.** The term **work** conveys the notion of toil, referring to the arduous labor required to cultivate agriculture. Jonah exerted no such effort to care for the plant, nor did he cause it to sprout up and flourish. Likewise, the plant touched very little of Jonah's life, for it **came to be overnight and perished overnight.** Though it came and went in a very short time, roughly twenty-four hours, Jonah was nonetheless furious that it **perished.** Incredibly, he did not care that the sailors (Jonah 1:6, 14) or the Ninevites (3:9) were about to perish, yet he cared deeply about a transitory sheltering bush. The irony exposed the nature of Jonah's selfishness and hardhearted hypocrisy.

Based on Jonah's pity for a passing plant, God declared, **"So should I not have pity on Nineveh?"** The expression **pity on Nineveh** captures the entire theme of the book—the great care of God for undeserving sinners who are perishing, including those outside of Israel. In familiar Hebrew fashion, God moved from the lesser to the greater. Since the prophet insisted that his pity for a fleeting bush was reasonable, he was compelled to acknowledge that God's pity on the immortal souls of people was far more significant. The Lord reinforced His indisputable case by providing five features that reveal His compassion on Nineveh as far superior to Jonah's pity for the plant.

First, the significance of the city far surpassed that of the plant. By reminding the prophet that Nineveh was **the great city,** God declared to Jonah that Nineveh had far greater value than any plant. Earlier in the book, the Lord described Nineveh as "the great city" to declare His intention to reach the Gentiles (1:2) and to assert the value He placed on the souls residing there (3:3). If Jonah, who did nothing to nurture the plant, could have pity on a piece of vegetation, then surely God who created the inhabitants of this great city was entitled to show pity for their eternal souls. Unlike Jonah's pity, which was based on what the plant had done for him, God took pity on the Ninevites despite their actions against Him.

Second, the size of Nineveh's population was numerically far greater than a solitary plant. Jonah was distressed over a single shrub, but God declared that **there are more than 120,000** people in the city. Since the 120,000 referred specifically to children (see below), the population of the city was actually far higher, likely around 600,000. In terms of sheer quantity, God had far more warrant to take pity on Nineveh than Jonah had to show sympathy for one plant.

Third, the eternal souls of the people made them inherently more valuable than a plant. The Hebrew word for **persons** is *adam,* which is the term for man and the name given by God to the first man, Adam. The word *adam* alludes back to creation when God uniquely made man in His image and according to His likeness as the crown of creation (Gen 1:26–28). As the Creator and Sustainer of every human life (cf. Acts 17:28), the Lord placed value on a city full of people whom He created in His image. Jonah was indicted for prioritizing a plant over immortal souls.

Fourth, the state of Nineveh's children elicited divine compassion. The Lord explained that 120,000 of the city's inhabitants **do not know *the difference* between their right and left hand.** This refers to the youngest children who could not differentiate between right and wrong. This language points back to Deuteronomy 1:39 and Isaiah 7:16 which describe moral authority and the ability to make reasoned ethical decisions (cf. Gen 3:22; Isa 5:20; Amos 5:14; Mic 3:2). Little children do not have such ability. Though not innocent of sin (Ps 51:5; Eccl 7:20; Rom 3:9–18), the children would not have committed the deliberate acts of violence and immorality for which God threatened to destroy the adults. Nahum later declared that God punished Assyria's capital for sins like harlotry and sorcery—evils that young children would not have knowingly committed (cf. Nah 3:1, 4). Certainly, such children were more in need of mercy than Jonah's plant. If the Lord had been willing to show mercy on Sodom and Gomorrah for as few as ten righteous people (Gen 18:16–33), it is not surprising that He chose to show mercy on Nineveh for the sake of 120,000 little children. God's love for Gentile sinners went far deeper than Jonah's superficial and selfish affection for a shade bush.

Fifth, the scores of animals in Nineveh made the city more valuable than Jonah's cherished plant. God pointed out that the city had **many animals.** Animals are obviously of higher value than plants. While this may refer to the way the Ninevites included their animals in their display of repentance (Jonah 3:7–8), the statement ought to be viewed in light of God's ordering of creation. In Genesis 1, God made animals superior to plants (Gen 1:30). If Jonah could justify his compassion on a plant, which was lower in the created order, he could not deny that God was justified in showing compassion toward creatures who were higher on that order. And if the Lord was right to have pity on the animals, how much more on the people of Nineveh.

In this way, God demonstrated that His pity for the city was reasonable while Jonah's pity for the plant was not. If the prophet appreciated the goodness of God's grace in providing a temporary shade bush, then he also had to acknowledge the goodness of God's grace in sparing a city full of eternal souls.

In the face of such an irrefutable argument, the prophet remained silent. The Lord's last words served as a final admonition to His prophet. God's rhetorical question left Jonah speechless in light of his flagrant hypocrisy. Jonah rejoiced when divine grace was applied to him, but he resented that same grace when it was extended to others, even though he was just as undeserving as they were.

Did Jonah ever learn his lesson? Throughout the book, the prophet often remained silent as his defiant actions spoke louder than his words (Jonah 1:3; 4:5). Though silent once again, this time he responded differently. Having been confronted by the Lord and shown his hypocrisy, the prophet returned to Israel where he was inspired by the Holy Spirit to write the book that bears his name, recounting his foolishness and offering his testimony as an object lesson to all. This book is Jonah's repentance. It not only recounts the great measures God took to draw the Ninevites to Himself but also testifies to the great work of God to restore His wayward prophet.

The story of Jonah is a marvelous revelation of God reaching down in His grace to save sinners, both Jew and Gentile. All those whom the Lord draws to Himself will come to Him in repentant faith (cf. John 6:44; 10:11–16; Rom 8:31–39; 11:1–36). In the end, the book of Jonah displays God's desire to save sinners who have egregiously transgressed His law. In His grace, He will forgive all who turn from sin and turn to Him (cf. 1 Thess 1:9). Because of His abundant grace, He offers forgiveness and eternal life to undeserving sinners through the One who fulfills the sign of Jonah—the Lord Jesus Christ who rose from the dead!

Matthew 12:38–41 states:

> Then some of the scribes and Pharisees answered and said to Him, "Teacher, we want to see a sign from You." But He answered and said to them, "An evil and adulterous generation eagerly seeks for a sign; and *yet* no sign will be given to it but the sign of Jonah the prophet; for just as JONAH WAS THREE DAYS AND THREE NIGHTS IN THE BELLY OF THE SEA MONSTER,

so will the Son of Man be three days and three nights in the heart of the earth. The men of Nineveh will stand up with this generation at the judgment, and will condemn it because they repented at the preaching of Jonah; and behold, something greater than Jonah is here.

NAHUM

Introduction to Nahum

More than a hundred years after Jonah preached to Nineveh, God raised up the prophet Nahum to pronounce judgment on the same city. Though the Assyrians repented in Jonah's day and received mercy, later generations presumed upon God's grace and returned to their wicked ways. So, Nahum prophesied woe against them, demonstrating that although God is merciful and gracious, He is also righteous and holy. In promising to pour out His wrath on wicked Nineveh, God also comforted His people by reminding them that He will bring evildoers to justice.

Nahum's message parallels that of his predecessor in at least eight ways. First, just as Jonah declared that God is longsuffering and gracious (Jonah 4:2), so Nahum acknowledged divine grace while affirming that the Lord is also jealous and avenging (Nah 1:3). Second, in Jonah God orchestrated a storm and then calmed the sea (Jonah 1:4, 15–16; 2:10–3:5), and in Nahum God directed the rivers to flood Nineveh in order to destroy the city (Nah 1:8; 2:6). Third, in Jonah God allowed the prophet to reach dry land (Jonah 2:10), and in Nahum God rebuked the sea and made it dry in judgment (Nah 1:4). Fourth, in Jonah the common people were spared (Jonah 3:5–10), but in Nahum all the people were scattered (Nah 1:2; 3:18). Fifth, in Jonah the message reached the king and he repented (Jonah 3:5–10), but in Nahum God addressed the king and described his demise

(Nah 3:18–19). Sixth, in Jonah both the sailors and the prophet offered vows to God (Jonah 1:16; 2:9), so Nahum called Israel to pay their vows and give praise to the Lord for His judgment (Nah 1:15). Seventh, the book of Jonah ended with a question (Jonah 4:11), so the book of Nahum ends with a question (Nah 3:19), the only two books in Scripture to do so. Finally, Nahum's description of the Ninevites mourning at the fall of their city intended to evoke the prophet Jonah and his ministry. Nahum expressed that the women moaned like doves (cf. 2:7), recalling the prophet Jonah since his name is the Hebrew word for "dove" (*jonah*).

These parallels demonstrate that the book of Nahum is the sequel to the book of Jonah, though with vastly different conclusions. The city that received divine grace became the city that was destroyed by divine wrath. Nineveh serves as a memorial to both the mercy and wrath of God. While the Lord gives grace to the worst of sinners who repent, He also executes judgment on those who refuse to turn from their sin (cf. 2 Pet 3:3–9; Jas 5:7–9). Nahum's prophecy demonstrates that God will avenge His people by punishing the wicked and preserving the righteous (Nah 1:15; cf. Isa 52:7).

Title

The book is titled after the name of the prophet Nahum (i.e., "comfort" or "comforter"), which is related to the name "Nehemiah" (i.e., "Yah[weh] comforts"). Despite the prophet's name, the message Nahum preached was one of judgment. This tension indicates that God intended Nahum's prophecy to communicate both comfort and judgment—comfort to Israel that the Lord was zealous for the protection of His people, and judgment against Nineveh that God would destroy the nation for her wickedness.

Author

The author of the book is God's prophet Nahum the Elkoshite (Nah 1:1). Nahum came from Elkosh, a town whose location is unknown. Three possible locations have been proposed: 1) Al Qosh, located in Northern Iraq, and potentially suggesting that Nahum came from a city taken captive by Assyria in 722 BC; 2) Capernaum (i.e., "Village of Nahum"), which is mentioned in the New Testament (e.g., Matt 4:13; 8:5; 11:23; 17:24); and 3) a general geographical location in Judah, important to the prophet since he mentioned it in Nahum 1:15.[1] The reference to Nahum as an Elkoshite indicates that Nahum was a specific historical figure, associated with his hometown, and therefore having a distinct identity. Scripture similarly refers to Amos of Tekoa (Amos 1:1), Jeremiah of Anathoth (Jer 1:1), and Joseph of Arimathea (Matt 27:57; Mark 15:43; Luke 23:51; John 19:38). By introducing himself with such specificity, Nahum demonstrated that he was willing to be held accountable for the message he preached (cf. Deut 18:22). His prophecy reveals that he was zealous to see the Lord's righteous justice prevail against the wickedness of God's enemies.

Date

The prophecy of Nahum is typically dated to a time between 663 BC and 627 BC.[2] Since the destruction of Thebes (No-amon) in 663 BC was fresh in Nahum's mind (cf. Nah 3:8–10), he must have received this prophecy not long after that date. Inasmuch as Nahum envisioned Assyria to be a prominent nation still, his message would have been most relevant prior to the weakening of the empire with the death of Ashurbanipal

1 See Yoshitaka Kobayashi, "Elkosh," *The Anchor Yale Bible Dictionary* (New York: Doubleday, 1992), 2:476; Kenneth L. Barker, *Micah, Nahum, Habakkuk, Zephaniah*, New American Commentary (Nashville: Broadman & Holman, 1999), 144.

2 See Daniel C. Timmer, *Nahum: The Divine Warrior as Avenger and Deliverer*, Zondervan Exegetical Commentary on the Old Testament (Grand Rapids: Zondervan Academic, 2020), 33; Barker, *Micah, Nahum, Habakkuk, Zephaniah*, 137–38; O. Palmer Robertson, *The Books of Nahum, Habakkuk and Zephaniah*, New International Commentary on the Old Testament (Grand Rapids: Eerdmans, 1990), 31.

around 627 BC. Most notably, because Nahum made no mention of the restoration of Thebes in 654 BC, he likely delivered the prophecy between 663 BC and 654 BC.[3] In light of this, Nahum would have preached long before the fall of Nineveh took place in 612 BC, which demonstrates that his prophecy was indisputably predictive.

Historical Context

Nahum delivered his prophecy concerning the destruction of Nineveh, the capital of Assyria, likely between 663 BC and 654 BC (see "Date" above). At this time, Assyria was still a powerful empire that dominated the ancient Near East under the reign of Ashurbanipal (ca. 669–633 BC). Northern Israel had been exiled by Assyria (722 BC; cf. 2 Kgs 17), while Judah, under King Manasseh (ca. 695–642 BC; cf. 2 Kgs 21), remained in a politically precarious situation, facing a constant threat from Assyria.

The Assyrian threat of cruel subjugation defined the ancient Near East for much of its history (see "Historical Context" in the Introduction to Jonah). The Black Obelisk depicts Shalmaneser III (ca. 859–824 BC) receiving tribute from Jehu, the defeated king of Israel (ca. 841 BC; cf. 2 Kgs 9–10; Hos 1:4). This Assyrian king is also pictured in various images surrounded by piles of dismembered heads, hands, and feet, along with bodies impaled on stakes.[4] An Assyrian relief from Sennacherib's campaigns (ca. 701 BC) likewise portrays a pile of heads at the feet of an Assyrian soldier, while another shows Assyrians skinning their enemies.[5] Known for its violent war practices, Assyria was infamous for bloodthirsty brutality.

Assyrian aggression and hostility temporarily subsided during the reign of Israel's king Jeroboam II (ca. 793–758 BC). During that time, Assyria turned its focus inward due to internal

3 See Timmer, *Nahum*, 34, n. 2; Klaas Spronk, *Nahum*, Historical Commentary on the Old Testament (Kampen: Kok Pharos, 1997), 13; Ralph L. Smith, *Micah–Malachi*, Word Biblical Commentary (Dallas: Word, 1984), 66.

4 JoAnna M. Hoyt, *Amos, Jonah, & Micah*, Evangelical Exegetical Commentary (Bellingham, WA: Lexham, 2018), 354.

5 Ibid., 354–55.

conflict and external pressure from an enemy nation Urartu.[6] In addition, the Assyrian generation of this time included the Ninevites who repented at the preaching of Jonah and turned to worship the God of Israel. However, Israel's reprieve from the Assyrian threat was short-lived. In the generations after Jonah, the Ninevites returned to their old ways. The Assyrian army conquered the northern kingdom of Israel in 722 BC and took the people into captivity.

After Shalmaneser V (ca. 727–722 BC; 2 Kgs 17:1–5; Hos 10:14) besieged the northern kingdom of Israel, Sargon II (cf. 722–705 BC; cf. 2 Kgs 17:6; Isa 20:1) completed the conquest and sent the nation into exile (722 BC). The focus of Assyria's wrath then shifted to the southern kingdom of Judah (ca. 701 BC; cf. 2 Kgs 18:13; 2 Chr 32:1; Isa 36:1–39:8). During the reign of Hezekiah over Judah (ca. 715–686 BC), Hezekiah rebelled against Assyria (cf. 2 Kgs 18:7), even though Judah had previously served the Assyrians during the reign of Ahaz (ca. 735–715 BC; cf. 16:7–9). Provoked by this rebellion, Sennacherib (ca. 705–681 BC) marched against Judah and conquered forty-six cities surrounding Jerusalem.[7] Even though Hezekiah subsequently sought to appease Sennacherib with tribute (cf. 18:13–16), the pagan king demanded unqualified surrender (cf. 18:17–24). Laying siege to Jerusalem, the Assyrian commander Rabshakeh threatened the people of Judah, even contending that Yahweh was not able to defend Jerusalem (cf. 18:13–19:13). This threat, however, was quelled when God sent the Angel of Yahweh to put to death 185,000 Assyrian soldiers in one night (cf. 2 Kgs 19:35–36; Isa 37:36).

The looming threat of Assyria continued as the empire sought to reinforce its power in the ancient Near East. A building inscription from the time of Esarhaddon (ca. 681–669 BC) records that the Judaean king Manasseh was summoned to provide

6 Daniel DeWitt Lowery, "Assyria," *The Lexham Bible Dictionary* (Bellingham, WA: Lexham, 2016); and Brian Neil Peterson, "Urartu," *The Lexham Bible Dictionary* (Bellingham, WA: Lexham, 2016).

7 James Bennett Pritchard, ed., *The Ancient Near Eastern Texts Relating to the Old Testament,* 3rd ed., with Supplement (Princeton: Princeton University Press, 1969), 287–89.

assistance to build an Assyrian palace, suggesting that Judah likely served as Assyria's vassal.[8] Later, when Manasseh rebelled against Assyria, Ashurbanipal (ca. 669–633 BC) took him captive and exiled him to Babylon (then under Assyrian rule; ca. 648 BC).[9] The author of 2 Chronicles described Assyria's gruesome tactics vividly, saying, "Yahweh brought the commanders of the army of the king of Assyria against them, and they captured Manasseh with hooks, bound him with bronze *chains*, and took him to Babylon" (2 Chr 33:11). The brutality of Assyria continued to define the empire as it had done throughout its history.

Beyond Judah, Ashurbanipal expanded his rule even down to Egypt. In 663 BC, he campaigned against Thebes (No-amon), the capital of Egypt, and decimated the city. Describing this conquest, Ashurbanipal boasted:

> From Thebes [I] carried away booty, heavy and beyond counting: silver, gold, precious stones, his entire personal possessions, linen garments with multicolored trimmings, fine horses, (certain) inhabitants, male and female. I pulled two high obelisks, cast of shining *zaḫalû*-bronze, the weight of which was 2,500 talents, standing at the door of the temple, out of their bases and took (them) to Assyria. (Thus) I carried off from Thebes heavy booty, beyond counting.[10]

This conquest left such an impression on Judah that Nahum referred to it and listed various horrors from the battle, as he prophesied the impending destruction of Nineveh (cf. Nah 3:8–10). Nahum's prophecy, in effect, announced that not only would Nineveh fall but that the Ninevites would experience the same violence their armies had inflicted on others.

The magnitude of Nineveh's demise was stunning given the city's historic significance. Among the first major cities in the history of the world, Nineveh is originally mentioned in

8 Ibid., 291; J. A. Thompson, *1, 2 Chronicles*, New American Commentary (Nashville: Broadman & Holman, 1994), 369; Eugene H. Merrill, *A Commentary on 1 & 2 Chronicles*, Kregel Exegetical Library (Grand Rapids: Kregel, 2015), 563–64.

9 Thompson, *1, 2 Chronicles*, 369.

10 Pritchard, ed., *The Ancient Near Eastern Texts Relating to the Old Testament*, 295.

Genesis 10:11–12, when Nimrod built "Nineveh and Rehoboth-Ir and Calah, and Resen between Nineveh and Calah." Nineveh's distinction endured as it boasted the glory of an ancient temple for Ishtar, the goddess of love and war (ca. 2300 BC).[11] Prominent kings such as Hammurabi (ca. 1792–1750 BC) and Tiglath-pileser I (ca. 1115–1071 BC) acknowledged the greatness of Nineveh and developed it into a grand metropolis.[12] Located on the east bank of the Tigris River (in modern-day Iraq), with ample water to cultivate plentiful crops, Nineveh enjoyed an abundance of trade and rich agriculture. Being the capital of Assyria, Nineveh was home to Assyria's royal houses, including the grand palace of Sennacherib (cf. 2 Kgs 19:36; Isa 37:37). Nineveh also became a major cultural center in which Ashurbanipal (ca. 669–633 BC) built an impressive library.[13] With the inner city being approximately three to four square miles, the outer city stretched to about fifty-five miles all around.[14] According to Jonah 4:11, with more than 120,000 children in Nineveh, the total population was likely about 600,000 people. God, therefore, appropriately referred to Nineveh as "the great city" (Jonah 1:2).

Nineveh's history was marked by both magnificence and brutality. So, God raised up Nahum to confront this formidable and vile capital. Though God had spared Nineveh in the time of Jonah as an expression of His surpassing grace, the Ninevites subsequently returned to their wicked ways. Therefore, Nahum pronounced judgment on them, and exactly as he prophesied, Nineveh was destroyed in 612 BC. Its destruction was so complete that the ruins of the city were not discovered for over 2,400 years, until the nineteenth century.

11 C. T. Fritsch, "Nineveh," *International Standard Bible Encyclopedia*, revised edition (Grand Rapids: Eerdmans, 1979–1988), 3:539.

12 Ibid., 3:539.

13 A. Kirk Grayson, "Nineveh," *The Anchor Yale Bible Dictionary* (New York: Doubleday, 1992), 4:1118.

14 Billy K. Smith and Frank S. Page, *Amos, Obadiah, Jonah*, New American Commentary (Nashville: Broadman & Holman, 1995), 260.

Themes

Various theological themes appear in the prophecy of Nahum, filling out the purpose of the book.

JUDGMENT ON SINNERS

The overarching focus of Nahum's prophecy is God's judgment against Nineveh for its unrepentant wickedness. Nahum opened the book by emphatically declaring that God would execute vengeance against His adversaries (Nah 1:2). The Lord stated that because Nineveh had devised evil against Him (1:9), He had taken His stand and was against Nineveh (2:13). The major part of the prophecy delivers a detailed description of the coming destruction of the city. While raging torrents would flood the city (1:8; 2:6), fire would also burn it to ashes (2:13; 3:13, 15). Though the Ninevites would prepare themselves for war (2:3–5; 3:12–17), they would ultimately flee in search of safety (2:8; 3:3, 7, 18). Just as the Assyrians had devastated other nations (3:8–10), Nineveh too would be conquered and decimated (3:7, 11). As a result, surrounding nations would rejoice and celebrate its demise (3:19).

As Nahum foretold Nineveh's imminent destruction, he also used language that alluded to end-time prophecies. For example, he portrayed Nineveh as a locust horde that assaulted Israel (Nah 3:16–17), just as Joel prophesied regarding Israel's enemies at the end of the age (cf. Joel 2). But Nahum also prophesied that Nineveh itself would be destroyed by an enemy that attacked like a locust swarm (Nah 3:15). In similar fashion, Joel predicted that God will afflict Israel's future enemies just as they afflict Israel (Joel 2:25; 3:1–21). By using similar language and imagery, Nahum indicated that his prophecy concerning Nineveh was the near prophecy that foreshadowed and guaranteed the distant prophecies given by Joel.

COMFORT FOR ISRAEL

While the focus of Nahum's prophecy was divine judgment on Nineveh, his message also intended to provide hope for God's people. The righteous are comforted by knowing that the Lord will hold the wicked accountable for their evil deeds. God's holy justice will prevail. Providing this comfort, Nahum declared that the Lord is good and a stronghold for those in need (Nah 1:7). Moreover, He knows those who take refuge in Him (1:7). While Israel's affliction was the result of their rebellion against the Lord (2 Kgs 17:6–17), God nonetheless promised that He would remove this affliction (Nah 1:12). He added that Nineveh's destruction would be good news for Israel (1:15). Similarly, describing the fall of Nineveh, God stated that the peoples will rejoice because the wicked will be eliminated (3:19). As his name indicates, Nahum brought comfort through his prophecy of God's judgment on Assyria. The Lord further promised that He would restore the majesty of Jacob and Israel (2:2).

As noted above, Nahum not only predicted events that would be fulfilled in the near future; he also used language that referenced end-time prophecies. When he stated, "Behold, on the mountains the feet of him who proclaims good news" (Nah 1:15), he alluded to the prophecy of Isaiah which anticipated the good news of God's eschatological triumph (cf. Isa 52:7). Nahum's description of Nineveh's demise was the near prophecy that foreshadowed and confirmed the distant prophecy given by Isaiah. In this way, Nahum offered comfort to God's people, not only regarding what the Lord would do to Assyria in the near-term, but what He will do for Israel in the end.

GRACE AND WRATH OF GOD

As Nahum began his prophecy, he explicitly stated that "Yahweh is slow to anger" (Nah 1:3), a practical expression of God's grace. The Lord's longsuffering was the exact attribute Jonah recounted in his complaint to God for delivering the Ninevites. Jonah exclaimed, "I knew that You are a gracious and compassionate God, slow to anger and abundant in lovingkindness, and one who relents concerning evil" (Jonah 4:2). Nineveh had experienced the blessing of divine grace in the days of Jonah (3:5–10), and Nahum recalled such mercy in his book. He declared that God is good and a strong defense on the day of distress (Nah 1:7).

However, a later generation of Ninevites returned to the wickedness that had historically characterized Assyria (cf. Nah 1:2, 9; 2:13). They assumed they could pursue idolatry, immorality, and brutality, without having to face divine judgment (cf. Zeph 2:15). Therefore, throughout Nahum's prophecy, beautiful descriptions of God's mercy are juxtaposed with somber reminders of His wrath. Nahum described the Lord as jealous, avenging, wrathful, and righteously indignant (1:2). He will not leave the guilty unpunished (1:3). God's anger is so fierce that no one can endure His judgment (Nah 1:6; cf. Heb 10:27, 31; 12:29). While the Ninevites thought they could withstand or escape divine punishment (cf. Zeph 2:15), Nahum declared that though God is slow to anger, He is also a righteous Judge who is great in power (Nah 1:3).

To illustrate God's power, Nahum first depicted Yahweh's supremacy over nature. He stated that when God pours out His wrath, the sea and the rivers become dry (1:4), the fertile regions of Bashan, Carmel, and Lebanon languish (1:4), the mountains and the hills quake and dissolve (1:5), the immovable rocks are torn down (1:6), and the entire world is thrown into upheaval (1:5). Focusing on the Ninevites, Nahum stated that God would flood them in judgment so that the city would be destroyed (1:8), pursue them into darkness (1:8), destroy all their wicked plans (1:9), consume them like fire scorches stubble (1:10; 2:13), cut them off irrevocably (1:11, 15; 2:13), and end their name forever (1:14; 2:13). To any who presume upon God's grace like Nineveh did, Nahum's prophecy serves as a sober reminder that though the Lord is abundant in grace and lovingkindness, He is also perfectly holy and righteous. As the author of Hebrews declares, "It is a terrifying thing to fall into the hands of the living God" (Heb 10:31).

IDOLATRY

In addition to God's clear opposition to Nineveh for her mistreatment of Israel, Nahum indicated that a primary reason the Lord would judge Nineveh was for her idolatry. God explicitly condemned the Ninevites for their graven images, molten idols, and the temple of their gods (Nah 1:14). The Assyrian king and the Ninevite people had centered their lives around pagan deities such as Ashur (the patron god), Ishtar (the patron goddess), Nabu (the god of writing), Nergal (the god of the underworld), Tiamat (the sea goddess), as well as Marduk, Enlil, Ninlil, Nisroch, and other false gods. In judging Nineveh, Yahweh declared that He would eradicate every expression of idolatry in the city.

God further condemned Nineveh for seducing the world with their "many harlotries of the harlot" (3:4). Assyria implemented both political propaganda and religious idolatry to conquer and subjugate nations. When Ahaz king of Judah made a political pact with Assyria, he built an Assyrian altar in the temple court in Jerusalem (2 Kgs 16; cf. Isa 7–8). As Rabshakeh besieged Jerusalem, he urged the people of Judah to forsake Yahweh and follow the Assyrian king (2 Kgs 18:22–25, 30–35; 19:4–6, 10–13, 36–37; Isa 36:7–8, 14–21). God loathed Assyria's sin of spiritual harlotry and therefore destroyed the nation. In His judgment of Nineveh, He demonstrated that He alone is God and He tolerates no other (cf. Deut 4:35, 39; Isa 42:8; 48:11).

VERACITY OF SCRIPTURE

In proclaiming the prophecy of Nineveh's destruction, Nahum sought to assure Israel that God's promises are certain. To this end, the prophet disclosed his precise identity as Nahum the Elkoshite, so that he could be held accountable for the predictions he made (see discussion on Nah 1:1; cf. Deut 18:22). With such forthrightness, Nahum recounted unique and specific details about Nineveh's impending demise, demonstrating that God fully knew and determined the future. The prophet reassured his readers that the decree of the Lord "stands fixed" (Nah 2:7) and would not be stopped. Most notably, Nahum indicated that the prophecy was not of his own invention but was the precise Word of Yahweh (Nah 2:13; 3:5; cf. 2 Pet 1:21).

After Nahum wrote down this revelation (Nah 1:1), God fulfilled His promise and brought every detail of this prophecy to pass. The Lord revealed that Nineveh would be destroyed in a flood (cf. 1:8; 2:6). That is exactly what occurred, with the city being leveled to the ground by a raging torrent (see discussion on 2:6). God also predicted that the city would be burned by fire (3:13, 15). That also took place, as Nineveh was reduced to ashes even while being flooded with water. The Lord further declared that Nineveh would be utterly devastated as though by locusts (3:7, 15–17). This too came to pass. The decimation of Nineveh was so thorough that the ruins of the city were not uncovered for more than two millennia.

Such precise predictions confirm the divine nature of Nahum's message and the rest of Scripture. The Lord's fulfillment of this near prophecy reassured His people Israel that He will fulfill every prophecy with the same level of exactness (see discussion on 1:15; 2:1–2). The destruction of Assyria, the mightiest nation of the ancient Near East, demonstrated that God is sovereign over history and that every event He has predicted will come to pass. Thus, the book of Nahum testifies both to the certainty of God's promises to Israel and to the veracity of all Scripture.

Purpose

As a sequel to the book of Jonah, Nahum is an oracle of judgment against Nineveh, a city that had once in the past received God's mercy. Nahum's prophecy serves both as an exhortation to evildoers never to presume on the Lord's patience, and also as an encouragement to God's people to rest in His love and care for them. By demonstrating the infallible nature of divine prophecy, Nahum's message provided hope to Israel and all God's people, reminding them that the Lord will keep His promises precisely as He has revealed them, both to preserve the righteous and to punish the wicked.

OUTLINE

9. Who God Is (1:1–8)
   a. The God of Irrevocable Condemnation (1:1)
   b. The God of Inevitable Vengeance (1:2–3a)
   c. The God of Irresistible Power (1:3b–6)
   d. The God of Impeccable Justice (1:7–8)
10. Comfort through Judgment (1:9–15)
    e. Judgment Affirms God's Plan (1:9–13)
    f. Judgment Affirms God's Promises (1:14)
    g. Judgment Affirms God's Prophecies (1:15)
11. A Prophetic Judgment (2:1–7)
    a. The Purpose of Judgment (2:1–2)
    b. The People under Judgment (2:3–5)
    c. The Place of Judgment (2:6)
    d. The Plight of Those under Judgment (2:7)
12. A Definitive Judgment (2:8–13)
    a. Destruction of Pride (2:8)
    b. Destruction of Prosperity (2:9)
    c. Destruction of Power (2:10)
    d. Destruction of Preeminence (2:11–12)
    e. Divine Prosecution (2:13)
13. An Avenging Judgment (3:1–7)
    a. Vengeance for Savage Brutality (3:1–3)
    b. Vengeance for Spiritual Harlotry (3:4–7)
14. A Certain Judgment (3:8–19)
    a. Inevitable Judgment (3:8–13)
    b. Inescapable Judgment (3:14–17)
    c. Irreversible Judgment (3:18–19)

Who God Is

NAHUM 1:1–8

The oracle of Nineveh. The book of the vision of Nahum the Elkoshite.

א ALEPH
A jealous and avenging God is Yahweh;
Yahweh is avenging and wrathful.
Yahweh is avenging against His adversaries,
And He keeps *His anger* for His enemies.
Yahweh is slow to anger and great in power,
And Yahweh will by no means leave *the guilty* unpunished.

ב BETH
In whirlwind and storm is His way,
And clouds are the dust beneath His feet.

ג GIMEL
He rebukes the sea and makes it dry;
He dries up all the rivers.
Bashan and Carmel languish;
The blossoms of Lebanon languish.

ה HE
Mountains quake because of Him,

ו VAV
And the hills melt;
Indeed the earth is upheaved by His presence,
The world and all the inhabitants in it.

ז ZAYIN
Who can stand before His indignation?
Who can endure the burning of His anger?

ח HETH
His wrath is poured out like fire,
And the rocks are torn down by Him.

ט TETH
Yahweh is good,
A strong defense in the day of distress,

י YODH
And He knows those who take refuge in Him.
But with an overflowing flood

כ KAPH
He will make a complete destruction of its place
And will pursue His enemies into darkness.

In his classic work, *The Knowledge of the Holy*, A. W. Tozer made this striking observation: "What comes into our minds when we think about God is the most important thing about us."[1] As Tozer understood, to have a wrong view of God is to worship a distorted version of who He is, which is idolatry. True worship, by contrast, is characterized by purity of both devotion and doctrine.

1 A. W. Tozer, *The Knowledge of the Holy* (San Francisco: HarperCollins, 1961), 1.

The Lord Jesus explained it this way in John 4:24: "God is spirit, and those who worship Him must worship in spirit and truth."

Scripture also warns against holding an incomplete and therefore inaccurate view of God. While He is certainly a God of grace and love (John 3:16; 1 John 4:8), He is also a God of righteousness and wrath (Exod 34:6–7), who will judge every form of sin (cf. Num 32:23; Rom 2:5; Rev 21:8). Though He is longsuffering toward sinners, the reason for His patience is that they might repent and turn to Him (cf. 1 Thess 1:9; 2 Pet 3:9). Unbelievers wrongly assume that God's forbearance means that His judgment will never fall (cf. Rom 2:3–4; 2 Pet 3:3–10). They wrongly conclude that God is like them (cf. Ps 50:21), when in fact He is holy and other (cf. Ps 51:4; Isa 6:3). Though He is patient and slow to anger, the Lord will certainly judge all wickedness with impartiality (cf. 1 Pet 1:15–17). Even believers sometimes assume that because they have received grace, they can live any way they please. Paul confronted such thinking with a series of rhetorical questions: "What shall we say then? Are we to continue in sin so that grace may increase? May it never be! How shall we who died to sin still live in it?" (Rom 6:1–2).

Nahum's prophecy delivers a corrective to the misconception that love and grace are God's only perfections. The prophet's message was addressed to Nineveh, which several generations earlier experienced the riches of divine mercy. Yahweh relented from destroying the people of Nineveh who repented at the preaching of Jonah. But subsequent generations of the Ninevites returned to Nineveh's former practices of wickedness, supposing that God would never judge them (cf. Zeph 2:15). So, more than a hundred years after Jonah, the Lord raised up another prophet to issue a message of pending judgment. In this way, the book of Nahum serves as a compelling complement to the book of Jonah. The truth revealed through these two prophets magnifies the character of God by focusing on both His grace and His justice (cf. Rom 9:22–23).

To confront Nineveh's distorted view of God, the prophet described the Lord in four ways: that He is the God of irrevocable condemnation (1:1), inevitable vengeance (1:2–3a), irresistible power (1:3b-6), and impeccable justice (1:7–8). Nahum's description not only corrected Nineveh's warped view of God, but also assured God's people that He remained zealous for Israel and would soon judge the wickedness of their oppressors (cf. Deut 6:15; 2 Pet 3:7).

The God of Irrevocable Condemnation

The oracle of Nineveh. The book of the vision of Nahum the Elkoshite. (1:1)

Conveying the weight of his message, Nahum introduced his prophecy as **the oracle of Nineveh.** The designation **oracle,** a specialized term for divine revelation, can also be translated "burden," indicating the difficulty and gravity of this message. In this case, the divine utterance of judgment was directed against **Nineveh,** the capital of Assyria and the greatest city of that time (cf. 2 Kgs 19:36; Isa 37:37; and see "Historical Context" in the Introduction).[2] **Nineveh** was not unfamiliar either to God's proclamations or to the people of Israel. Approximately one century prior to Nahum, Jonah preached God's Word to the Ninevites, which brought them to repentance (cf. Jonah 3:5–10). But since the time of that revival, a new generation had arisen that ignored the threat of God's judgment and returned to the sins of their fathers. They even attacked the people of God, taking the northern kingdom of Israel into captivity (cf. 2 Kgs 17). The fall of Nineveh, foretold by Nahum, serves as a warning not to forget God's past blessings or the reality of His judgment (cf. Deut 8:11–20; Ps 103:1–2). It also provides a vivid reminder that each generation is responsible for its own sin (Ezek 18:20).

Against the forgetful Ninevites, and for the benefit of His people Israel, God gave a prophetic message in **the book of the**

2 Thomas Renz, *The Books of Nahum, Habakkuk, and Zephaniah,* New International Commentary on the Old Testament (Grand Rapids: Eerdmans, 2021), 130.

vision of Nahum the Elkoshite. That this prophecy is referred to as **the book** indicates that the text was written down and meant to be preserved. The Lord went on record regarding what He would do to Nineveh, intending for later generations to read this **book** and observe that the judgment He promised came to pass in a precise way. The accuracy of these prophecies ought to instill confidence in God's people. In the same way that Nineveh's destruction was fulfilled, so every divine promise will be perfectly realized. Nahum's revelation was the near prophecy proving that more distant prophecies will also come to pass as promised (see discussion on Nah 1:15).

God's prophecy to Nahum came in the form of a **vision,** a supernatural revelation of realities (cf. 1 Sam 3:1; Isa 1:1; Hos 12:10). Though Israel could see only their own defeat and demise, Nahum's prophecy unveiled the coming of divine judgment against Israel's oppressors—the bloodthirsty Assyrians. The Lord revealed that He would avenge the suffering of His people and fulfill all His promises, remaining faithful to His character and His covenant.

The prophet to whom God gave this vision was **Nahum the Elkoshite,** whose name means "comfort" or "comforter." That name was fitting to the prophet's message, in that his prophecy of judgment brought comfort to Israel as they witnessed divine justice fulfilled. So, while this book is filled with descriptions of God's wrath against Nineveh, it is ultimately a book that brings great hope to God's people. Nahum introduced himself as an **Elkoshite,** and though the location of Elkosh is unknown, associating a person with his hometown was a common method of distinguishing one's identity (see "Author" in the Introduction). By presenting himself with such specificity, Nahum indicated that he was willing to stand accountable for the prophecy he wrote (cf. Deut 18:22).

Despite Nineveh's smug self-confidence and sense of security, Nahum's divine message revealed that God was not blind to Nineveh's presumption, pride, and aggression. He would judge the inhabitants of this city for their evil. In this prophecy, the Lord provided comfort to Israel both immediately and ultimately, assuring them that all His promises were true. While God had earlier commissioned Jonah with a message of merciful warning (Jonah 1:1), He then delivered an irrevocable decree of judgment against Nineveh through His prophet Nahum.

The God of Inevitable Vengeance

א ALEPH
A jealous and avenging God is Yahweh;
Yahweh is avenging and wrathful.
Yahweh is avenging against His adversaries,
And He keeps *His anger* for His enemies.
Yahweh is slow to anger and great in power,
And Yahweh will by no means leave *the guilty* unpunished.
(1:2–3a)

Nahum's prophecy began in the form of an acrostic, in which letters from the Hebrew alphabet introduce the various poetic stanzas. (For more on Nahum's use of this rhetorical structure, see the discussion on verse 8.) Each of these stanzas depicted Yahweh's holy justice, beginning with the declaration that God is **jealous.** While the term "jealous" can denote sinful envy, when applied to God it refers to His righteous zeal, His strong desire to protect that which is rightfully His. As a husband is justly jealous for his wife (Prov 6:34; Song 8:6; cf. Num 5:11–31), so God is jealous for His people and unwilling to tolerate any form of spiritual adultery (cf. Exod 20:5; Deut 4:24). The Lord is characterized by a holy zeal for His own, to the extent that His very name is Jealous (Exod 34:14). God's fervent affection for His people motivates His hand of discipline in response to their disobedience and also prompts His hand of grace to restore and protect them (cf. Joel 2:18). The Ninevites, like so many godless and wicked adversaries (cf. Pss 2:1–3; 10:1–6; 94:7), assumed they could severely mistreat God's people without suffering any consequences. However, Nahum declared that Yahweh was neither passive nor apathetic. The Lord was zealous for Israel and would not overlook the wickedness enacted against them (cf. Deut 6:15).

Because of God's great jealousy for His people, Nahum unequivocally declared that an **avenging God is Yahweh.** Out of His righteous zeal, the Lord would exact the precise punishment from the Ninevites that they deserved and that His holiness demanded (cf. Deut 32:41; Rom 12:19; Heb 10:30). The prophet repeated the word **avenging** three times in this verse, assuring Israel that such retribution would be intense, inescapable, and inevitable. Because **Yahweh** is a covenant-keeping God who is loyal to His people (cf. Gen 12:1–3), He would be diligent to fulfill this vengeance against Israel's enemies.

To convey the fullness of God's vengeance, Nahum provided a threefold explanation of such divine retribution. First, Yahweh's vengeance would be intense as **Yahweh is avenging and wrathful.** The term **wrathful** describes hot anger, one that explodes with destructive force (cf. Gen 27:44; Deut 9:19; 29:23). Ezekiel described such wrath in the following manner:

> "And it will be in that day, when Gog comes against the land of Israel," declares Lord Yahweh, "*that* My wrath will mount up in My anger. In My zeal and in My blazing fury I have spoken *that* on that day there will surely be a great earthquake in the land of Israel. And the fish of the sea, the birds of the sky, the beasts of the field, all the creeping things that creep on the ground, and all the men who are on the face of the earth will quake at My presence; the mountains also will be pulled down, the steep pathways will fall, and every wall will fall to the earth. And I will call for a sword against him on all My mountains," declares Lord Yahweh. "Every man's sword will be against his brother. With pestilence and with blood I will enter into judgment with him; and I will rain on him and on his troops, and on the numerous peoples who are with him, a torrential rain, with hailstones, fire, and brimstone." (Ezek 38:18–22)

As Ezekiel revealed about the end of the age, the Lord's wrath will destroy animals, devastate mankind, collapse mountains, and shake the earth. Through Nahum, God promised to unleash similar fury in His vengeance against Nineveh. The Hebrew term translated **wrathful** literally states that Yahweh is the "master of wrath," sovereignly deploying divine retribution in accordance with His justice. God had warned Nineveh through Jonah that He would overthrow the city if the people did not repent (Jonah 3:4). Subsequently, He declared through Nahum that Nineveh was about to face overwhelming judgment, much like that experienced by Sodom and Gomorrah (Gen 18:20–21).

Second, the Lord's vengeance would be inescapable as **Yahweh is avenging against His adversaries.** Though in the days of Jonah God had declared that Nineveh was a great city to Him and had shown the people mercy (cf. Jonah 3:2, 10), in the days of Nahum the city had become God's enemy. The Ninevites, by attacking and oppressing the people of God, proved to be His **adversaries.** In declaring them as such, the Lord pronounced that He was determined to unleash His wrath against them. He would not relent against those who refused to submit to Him and who persisted in their wickedness (cf. Exod 23:22; Num 24:8; Luke 19:27).

Third, Yahweh's vengeance would be inevitable as He **keeps *His anger* for His enemies.** To keep something is to watch over and guard it (cf. Song 1:6; Lev 19:18). In such a manner, God maintained and upheld His displeasure against His foes. The people of God recognized this, often asking whether He would keep His anger forever (cf. Pss 79:5; 85:5; 103:9; Jer 3:5, 12). In the case of Nineveh, Nahum proclaimed that God would not allow His intense wrath to rest until His vengeance was satisfied.

Having expounded on divine vengeance, Nahum also asserted that **Yahweh is slow to anger and great in power.** Israel knew that **Yahweh,** their loving and covenant-keeping God, **is slow to anger.** They had experienced His patience and forbearance many times throughout their history. In spite of their idolatry and rebellion in the wilderness (e.g., Exod 32; 34:6–8; Num 16; 21; 25) and their numerous sins in the Promised Land (e.g., Judg 3:15; 4:23; 8:28; 1 Kgs 11:11–13), the Lord had shown Israel mercy and longsuffering. The city of Nineveh had also experienced the patience of God when Yahweh previously spared its inhabitants. Jonah himself recognized this reality, saying, "I knew that You are a gracious and compassionate God, slow to anger and abundant in lovingkindness" (Jonah 4:2). Yet, in contrast to what Nineveh saw in Jonah's day, Nahum pointed out that God is not only great in patience but that He is also **great in power.** When the Lord does bring the wicked to justice, He wields infinite **power,** with which He subjugates every form of resistance. Therefore, being both righteous and omnipotent, **Yahweh will by no means leave *the guilty* unpunished.** He never turns a blind eye to sin (cf. Ps 7:11; Isa 59:12–15). Rather, as Nahum proclaimed to both Israel and Nineveh, the Lord will certainly judge every form of rebellion and wickedness (cf. Rom 2:5; Rev 21:8).

The God of Irresistible Power

ב BETH
In whirlwind and storm is His way,
And clouds are the dust beneath His feet.

ג GIMEL
He rebukes the sea and makes it dry;
He dries up all the rivers.
Bashan and Carmel languish;
The blossoms of Lebanon languish.

ה HE
Mountains quake because of Him,

ו VAV
And the hills melt;
Indeed the earth is upheaved by His presence,
The world and all the inhabitants in it.

ז ZAYIN
Who can stand before His indignation?
Who can endure the burning of His anger?

ח HETH
His wrath is poured out like fire,
And the rocks are torn down by Him. (1:3b–6)

Having described the vengeance and fury of God, Nahum proclaimed the power of God that carries out His judgment. The prophet declared that even the sky stands at the Lord's disposal to execute His wrath. He explained that **in whirlwind and storm is His way, and clouds are the dust beneath His feet.** The **whirlwind** refers to the violence of a tornado, blowing away anything in its path (cf. Job 21:18). Additionally, the **storm** describes a fierce downpour or tempest (cf. Job 9:17). Together, these terms depict God's comprehensive judgment in the form of a massive assault, so that whatever escapes being blown away by the whirlwind is overwhelmed by the storm (cf. Job 27:20–21; Ps 83:15; Isa 29:6; 66:15–16; Amos 1:14). Such is **His way** in judgment, as Yahweh stirs up the weather to bring calamity and destruction under His controlling hand (cf. Job 38:1; and Exod 19:9, 16; Ps 83:15; Isa 29:6). Nahum also wrote that the **clouds are the dust beneath His feet.** The military machinery of the Ninevite army, including chariots and horses, kicked up fine dust as it proceeded along its destructive course (cf. Isa 29:5; Ezek 26:10). But the transcendence of the Lord of hosts, the Captain of the armies of heaven, is such that large **clouds are the dust beneath His feet** (cf. Exod 16:10; Pss 99:5; 110:1; 132:7; Isa 66:1; Lam 2:1; Ezek 1:4; Dan 7:13). God can employ the weather to manifest His mighty presence, demonstrating that He is far more destructive than any horse, chariot, or man-made war machine. In His vengeance against Nineveh, the Lord declared that He would use even the elements of the heavens to bring down wrath upon the city (cf. Pss 29:3, 7; 102:26–27; Rev 6:12).

In addition to the sky, God directs the waters of the earth to execute His judgment. In stating that **He rebukes the sea and makes it dry,** Nahum alluded to the splitting of the Red Sea during the Exodus (cf. Exod 14). Declaring that God also **dries up all the rivers,** the prophet referred to the crossing of the Jordan River that took place in the days of Joshua and in the time of Elijah (cf. Josh 3; 2 Kgs 2:7–8). These historical events indicated that God's power is not merely metaphorical but literal, and that God exercises full control over nature and wields its forces to accomplish His purposes. All creation submits to God's command because He is the sovereign Creator who made the sea and the dry land (Gen 1:9–10; Job 38:8–11; Pss 33:7; 136:6; Jer 5:22; cf. Matt 8:23–27; Luke 8:22–25; cf. Rev 8:8–10 and 16:20). Nahum prophesied that Yahweh would wipe out Nineveh in a flood (cf. Nah 1:8), which is in keeping with God's total power over the waters. The Lord would leverage every element of creation to judge those who oppressed His people.

Just as the Lord is sovereign over the sky and the sea, so His power extends over the dry land. Nahum noted that **Bashan and Carmel languish; the blossoms of Lebanon languish.** Not only can the Lord divide the sea and dry up rivers, but He can also parch the ground so that it is no longer fruitful. **Bashan** (Mic 7:14), **Carmel** (Song 7:5), and **Lebanon** (Ps 72:16) refer to regions in or near Israel known for their fertile vegetation. Though typically lush, at God's rebuke these places would **languish,** a word that denotes dwindling, drying out, and withering away (Isa 16:8; 24:4; 33:9). Nahum's point was that the Lord can make any place, no matter its historic abundance, shrivel up and become a wasteland. This is precisely what He did to **Bashan** and **Carmel** and **Lebanon** when Assyria invaded Israel (2 Kgs 19:23). He promised to do the same to Assyria's capital city, Nineveh.

In God's providence, Israel's own destruction at the hand of Nineveh illustrated Nineveh's pending demise.

God's power over the earth extends beyond its vegetation, for Nahum prophesied that the **mountains quake because of Him.** In Scripture, **mountains** stand as symbols of immovable strength (cf. Ps 36:6). But God's might exceeds even the grandest natural monuments on earth, causing that which has stood firm since its formation to **quake because of Him** (Ps 18:7; Isa 64:1, 3; Jer 4:24; cf. Matt 17:20). Throughout redemptive history, God has displayed His power through earthquakes (Amos 1:1; Zech 14:5; Matt 27:51–54). The book of Revelation predicts a future earthquake that will shake the globe so fiercely that cities and nations will collapse and mountains will not be found (Rev 16:18–21). At the end of the age, the Lord will exert all His might to shake the world so that He will establish His unshakable kingdom (Hag 2:6–7, 21–23; Heb 12:26–29).

Since God's might is overwhelmingly sufficient to shake the mountains, for Him to cause **the hills** to **melt** is not difficult. In Scripture, the **hills** served as longstanding landmarks for boundaries between regions and cities. Because of their familiarity and permanence, these ridges were called the "everlasting" hills (Gen 49:26; Deut 33:15). At Christ's return, even these features, which have always defined the landscape of Israel, will **melt** away like wax (cf. Ps 97:5; and Mic 1:4; Ezek 21:15). Peter wrote that after Christ's millennial reign, all the elements of the world will melt away under the intense heat of God's wrath (2 Pet 3:12).

God's ability to strip the land bare and overturn mountains and hills is not limited to one region of the world, for **indeed the earth is upheaved by His presence. Upheaved** fundamentally means "to lift up," depicting an image of the land moving up and down. The power of God that topples mountains is also able to raise up the **earth** from one end of the horizon to the other. As a result, the **world and all the inhabitants in it** will melt before His presence. The **world,** which includes every place on the globe, as well as each of **the inhabitants** of those places, will be utterly devastated. This cataclysmic upheaval will take place at the appearance of **His presence.** The book of Revelation's description of what will take place at the Second Coming of Christ demonstrates that Nahum's description of God's power is not hyperbole (cf. Exod 19:18; Rev 16:18). When the Lord appears, the entire earth will toss and turn, rise and fall like the ocean, and its inhabitants will be thrown into unmitigated dread.

Thus, Nahum extolled Yahweh's power over the sky, the sea, and the land. In the days of Jonah, God provided a glimpse of this power for the benefit of the Ninevites. He exercised control over the sky and the sea, sending a storm that caused the sailors to fear Him and that compelled Jonah to go and preach to Nineveh (cf. Jonah 1:4, 15–16). God also displayed power over the land as He brought Jonah safely to the shore so that he would deliver the message of salvation to the Ninevites (2:10–3:5). But Nahum declared that, as God had controlled the sky, the sea, and the land for their benefit in Jonah's day, so would He now wield that creation power for the purpose of their destruction. The divine force previously exacted in their favor was now being summoned against them. Nahum's message to the Ninevites was that God's former kindness should have led them not to presumption but to repentance. They had taken the Lord's grace for granted and therefore He was preparing to judge them definitively (cf. Rom 2:4). And this onslaught of wrath would be just a taste of what God will do against the world when He returns to judge.

In light of God's vengeance and omnipotence, Nahum posed two rhetorical questions: **"Who can stand before His indignation? Who can endure the burning of His anger?"** The answer to both questions is obvious. No one **can stand before His indignation,** to survive His wrathful and destructive curse (cf. Isa 10:5; 13:5; Jer 10:10). No one **can endure the burning of His anger.** The word **endure** means "to rise up," and no one can rise up to resist **the burning of** God's **anger** when His fury is ignited and unleashed (cf. Exod 32:12; Ps 1:5). No one can stop or survive the wrath of God. Instead, people will hide in the face of His judgment, crying out to the mountains and rocks, "FALL ON US AND HIDE US from the presence of Him who sits on the throne, and from the wrath of the Lamb, for the great DAY OF their WRATH has come, and who is able to stand?" (Rev 6:16–17).

In addition to these rhetorical questions, Nahum added two reminders to stress the might of God's vengeance. First, the prophet exclaimed, **"His wrath is poured out like fire."** God's burning wrath against sin overwhelms the wicked like a volcano eruption that is **poured out** from the heavens (cf. Exod 9:23, 33; 2 Sam 21:10; Ezek 22:21), and it spreads **like fire,** destroying everything it encounters. Second, Nahum declared, **"And the rocks are torn down by Him."** If mountain boulders disintegrate before God's wrathful presence, then certainly no mortal can withstand His indignation. The irresistible force of God's power meant that God's judgment against Nineveh was impossible to resist or prevent. Nineveh, which was once shown mercy, should have never thought that it could escape God's wrath, for God rules heaven and earth with irresistible might.

THE GOD OF IMPECCABLE JUSTICE

ט TETH
Yahweh is good,
A strong defense in the day of distress,

י YODH
And He knows those who take refuge in Him.
But with an overflowing flood

כ KAPH
He will make a complete destruction of its place
And will pursue His enemies into darkness. (1:7–8)

In introducing God's justice, Nahum proclaimed that **Yahweh is good,** doing what is right, kind, and even beneficial to others. The psalmist recounted that God is good and does good in that He forgives sins, heals sickness, redeems life from the pit, and demonstrates patience (Ps 119:68; cf. Ps 103:1–5). Psalm 136 mentions that God's goodness is seen in numerous ways, including His work of creation, His deliverance of Israel from Egypt, His guidance of the people through the wilderness, His giving of the Promised Land to them, and His provision of food to meet their daily needs. God's abundant goodness is seen in both everyday matters and dramatic deliverances. Most of all, it is manifested in the gift of His Son through whom sinners might have eternal salvation.

In highlighting God's goodness, Nahum emphasized that Yahweh is **a strong defense in the day of distress.** The word **strong defense** often refers to a heavily fortified location (cf. Isa 17:9; 23:13–14), one completely secure against enemy assault. God is such a defense for His people. He provides perfect peace and security **in the day of distress,** when His people find themselves in dismay or surrounded by danger. The Lord not only protects His own (cf. Ps 62:1–3) but **knows those who take refuge in Him.** To **know** someone is to enjoy intimate fellowship with that person (cf. Gen 4:1; Exod 2:25), and the Lord knows by name **those who take refuge in Him** (cf. John 10:14; 2 Tim 2:19; Rev 21:27). All those who run to the Lord for safety, placing their full trust in Him (cf. Pss 2:12; 7:1; 16:1; 17:7; 18:3, 30; 25:20; 31:2), will find Him eager to welcome and care for them (cf. John 6:37; Heb 4:14–16).

For those who love the Lord, He will unequivocally stand in their defense as a strong fortress. But such is not God's disposition toward unrepentant sinners. Nahum continued by noting Yahweh's attitude toward wicked Nineveh: **With an overflowing flood, He will make a complete destruction of its place.** The term **flood** metaphorically denotes an unstoppable force that covers everything (Ps 32:6; Prov 27:4), with the word **overflowing** describing the magnitude of this torrent. This was precisely how the Assyrian army moved through Israel as it attacked the nation (cf. Isa 8:6–8), creating a river of destruction. Because Assyria treated Israel this way, Nahum prophesied that God would do the same to the Ninevites, raising up a relentless foe to sweep through their capital city. However, the imagery of the **flood** was not merely a metaphor. The Lord would literally level the city with an actual flood (cf. Nah 2:6). In this way, God **will make a complete destruction of its place,** bringing the city to its end (cf. Jer 30:11).

The Lord would further execute His wrath by pursuing **His enemies into darkness.** In Hebrew, the phrase **His enemies** stands at the beginning of the sentence, accentuating God's total focus on His foes. With such fixation, the Lord would **pursue** and hunt down His adversaries until the enemy was eliminated entirely (cf. Exod 15:9; Lev 26:7–8).) As a result of their destruction, the wicked Ninevites would be plunged into **darkness.** God would send them into divine wrath, a darkness felt (Exod 10:21–23) in eternal judgment (cf. Matt 25:30). Thus, Nahum proclaimed that God would exact justice and achieve vengeance for His people as He propelled His enemies into eternal darkness.

To illustrate the decisive and sudden death of the wicked, the prophet used a vivid poetic construction known as an acrostic, in which each line or stanza of the poem begins with a sequential letter of the Hebrew alphabet in order to advance the message of the author. Though acrostics normally run from the beginning to the end of the alphabet, in this passage, the acrostic is suddenly and unexpectedly cut off at the letter *kaph,* in the middle of the alphabet. In the same way, Nahum illustrated that God would end Nineveh's existence abruptly and completely. One moment the city would exist, and the next, it would be gone. Thus Nahum continued to reinforce the lesson that God is not only supremely good and gracious but also supremely righteous and wrathful. While the Lord had in the past shown mercy to the repentant Ninevites, Nahum declared that He would not do so for this generation of impenitent sinners.

From the ancient Ninevites on to the people in the present day, all humanity has experienced an abundance of God's mercy and patience (2 Pet 3:4–8). However, no one should ever presume upon God's grace or conclude that the Lord's wrath against the unrighteous is avoidable. To those who spurn the thought of divine righteousness and judgment, Nahum's description of God's fearsome power serves as a timely warning. Unless sinners repent, they will perish (Luke 13:3–5; Heb 9:27). As the author of Hebrews rightly observed, "It is a terrifying thing to fall into the hands of the living God" (Heb 10:31). Though the Lord has always demonstrated great patience with sinners, providing them with ample time to repent (2 Pet 3:9), He will one day execute judgment against His enemies, pouring out His wrath suddenly and when they least expect it (cf. Matt 24:36–41; 1 Thess 5:2; 2 Pet 3:10).

Comfort through Judgment

10

NAHUM 1:9–15

Whatever you devise against Yahweh,
He will make a complete destruction of it.
Distress will not rise up twice.

Like tangled thorns,
And like those who are drunken with their drink,
They are consumed
As stubble fully dried up.

From you has gone forth
One who devised evil against Yahweh,
A vile counselor.

Thus says Yahweh,
"Though they are at full *strength* and likewise many,
Even so, they will be cut off and pass away.
Though I have afflicted you,
I will afflict you no longer.

So now, I will break his yoke bar from upon you,
And I will break your bands apart."

And Yahweh has commanded concerning you:
"There will no longer be seed from your name.
From the house of your gods,
I will cut off graven image and molten image.
I will prepare your grave,
For you are contemptible."

Behold, on the mountains the feet of him who proclaims good news,
Who announces peace!
Celebrate your feasts, O Judah;
Pay your vows.
For never again will the vile one pass through you;
He is cut off completely.

The theme of Nahum's prophecy is judgment. Yet, the meaning of his name is "comfort." These details may initially seem incompatible. However, in the book of Nahum, comfort and judgment are not in opposition. Rather, they complement one another in keeping with the prophet's purpose. Nahum sought to comfort God's people after the northern kingdom of Israel had been violently conquered and exiled by the Assyrians. By declaring that the Lord would not allow such brutality to go unpunished (cf. Deut 6:15; 2 Pet 3:7), Nahum's prophecy offered hope to God's people by assuring them that Yahweh would bring the wicked to justice.

That the judgment of God can bring comfort to His people is a theme found throughout Scripture. The saints have often cried out to the Lord asking Him to hold evildoers accountable. David did so, beseeching God to pour out His burning indignation on the enemies of Israel (Ps 69:24). The psalmist called such vindication the salvation of Zion (69:35–36; cf. Pss 5, 6, 11, 12,

35, 37, 40, 52, 54, 56, 57, 58, 59, 79, 83, 94, 137, 139, and 143). Looking to the future, Ezekiel prophesied that God will judge Gog in order to "return the fortunes of Jacob and have compassion on the whole house of Israel" (Ezek 39:25). The Apostle John, seeing a vision of the fall of eschatological Babylon, urged the saints to celebrate, saying, "Rejoice over her, O heaven, and you saints and apostles and prophets, because God has pronounced judgment for you against her" (Rev 18:20; cf. 6:9–10; 19:1–2). As these examples illustrate, the Lord's holy judgment fulfills His promises by avenging His people and righting the wrongs done against them. Divine judgment is therefore a great consolation to the righteous.

Nahum's revelation also provided comfort in another important way. It demonstrated the veracity of divine prophecy because the events it predicted regarding Nineveh came to pass exactly as they were foretold. The precise fulfillment of Nahum's predictions (near prophecies) confirmed that the Lord will keep every promise He has made, including His revelations about the end of the age (distant prophecies). Per Old Testament law, a true prophet was one whose predictions came to pass with perfect accuracy (Deut 18:21–22). Because prophets often made predictions that went beyond their lifetimes, they would also give a more immediate prediction to certify their credibility. For example, in 1 Kings 13:1–5, a man of God prophesied that nearly three centuries later the righteous king Josiah would come to the throne and remove false religion from the land. To verify this distant prophecy, the man of God also declared that the altar before him would split open and ashes would pour out. Because that immediate prediction took place, the people knew that his distant prophecy would also occur.

The promise of the Messiah provides an even greater example of this relationship between near and distant prophecies. The Old Testament reveals that the Messiah will conquer all His enemies and reign on earth during the millennial kingdom (cf. Ps 110:1; Zech 14). But Scripture also predicted that before

Christ's ultimate victory, He would suffer, die, and rise again (cf. Gen 3:15; Ps 16:10; Isa 53; Zech 12:10–13:1). Because the Lord Jesus perfectly fulfilled the prophecies regarding His first coming, He proved the veracity of those prophecies related to His second coming. Believers can therefore rest with certainty in the truthfulness of those promises which are yet to be fulfilled. As the angels declared to the disciples on the Mount of Olives, "Men of Galilee, why do you stand looking toward heaven? This Jesus, who has been taken up from you into heaven, will come in just the same way as you have watched Him go into heaven" (Acts 1:11).

With the language "Behold, on the mountains the feet of him who proclaims good news" (Nah 1:15), Nahum linked his prophecy with the words of Isaiah (cf. Isa 52:7). Nahum's message of Nineveh's fall was the near prophecy that served as a guarantee for the distant prophecies of Isaiah and other prophets concerning the eschatological destruction of Israel's enemies and establishment of Messiah's earthly kingdom. In detailing Nineveh's demise, God confirmed the certainty of His plan (1:9–13), His promises (v. 14), and His prophecies (v. 15). All of this brought comfort to God's people, both in the immediate and for all time.

Judgment Affirms God's Plan

Whatever you devise against Yahweh,
He will make a complete destruction of it.
Distress will not rise up twice.

Like tangled thorns,
And like those who are drunken with their drink,
They are consumed
As stubble fully dried up.

From you has gone forth
One who devised evil against Yahweh,
A vile counselor.

Thus says Yahweh,
"Though they are at full *strength* and likewise many,
Even so, they will be cut off and pass away.
Though I have afflicted you,
I will afflict you no longer.

So now, I will break his yoke bar from upon you,
And I will break your bands apart." (1:9–13)

Nahum began this portion of his prophecy by declaring that God's plan will always stand. What the Lord ordained would certainly take place despite **whatever you,** the wicked Ninevites, might **devise against Yahweh.** The specific form of the word **devise** denotes intensive thinking and the deliberation to strategize (cf. Prov 16:9; 24:8; Hos 7:15). The city of Nineveh concocted various schemes to resist and oppose what the Lord had determined. Like all of God's enemies, they thought they could thwart His plan (cf. Ps 2:1–3). But despite Nineveh's best efforts, Yahweh promised to **make a complete destruction of it** (cf. 1:8). Nothing of the city would be left. In fact, the Lord would destroy the city in a single blow so that **distress** or adversity would **not rise up twice.** They would be utterly defeated and completely silenced the first time.

Though the city appeared to be an impregnable fortress surrounded by water, God declared that Nineveh was **like tangled thorns,** a reference to kindling and ready to ignite in fiery destruction (cf. Isa 9:18). Though Assyria had a cruel and formidable army, the Lord described them **like those who are drunken with their drink,** incapable of defending themselves against His attack. The violence and brutality in which they had imbibed would become the very cup that God would make them drink. In their defeat, they would be **as stubble fully dried up. Stubble,** or any dry straw, is easily ignited, especially when it is **fully dried up.** The God who can mercifully lead sailors to dry land (Jonah 1:13, 16), and who can dry the sea and the rivers

(Nah 1:4), can also make Nineveh like dry straw ready to be incinerated. This description was no hyperbole. Nineveh was destroyed quickly, and the devastation was so extensive that the location remained undiscovered until the nineteenth century. Benjamin of Tudela, a rabbi in the twelfth century, observed that, "Nineveh now lies in utter ruins, but numerous villages and small towns occupy its former space."[1] Despite its military prowess, Nineveh was powerless to stop God's plan from being executed.

Nahum further revealed that the ruler of Nineveh would be overthrown. This prediction was fulfilled in 612 BC, when the king of Nineveh was killed during Nineveh's defeat. The Assyrian ruler was an opponent of God. As Nahum declared of him, **"From you** [Nineveh] **has gone forth one who devised evil against Yahweh, a vile counselor."** The king of Nineveh had **gone forth** from the city as its commander. As the entire city **devised** schemes against the Lord (Nah 1:9), so its king was the chief architect **who devised evil against Yahweh.** Thus, Nahum referred to him as **a vile counselor. Vile** is the Hebrew term *belial,* which not only denotes egregious human wickedness but is also used in Scripture to refer to Satan himself. In 2 Corinthians, the Apostle Paul wrote, "What harmony has Christ with Belial," using Belial there to refer to the devil (2 Cor 6:15). Nahum's description indicated that the king of Nineveh was satanic, leading his people into blasphemous idolatry, violence, and gross iniquity. In calling him a vile **counselor,** the prophet even depicted the ruler as an antichrist, contrasting him with Christ, the Wonderful Counselor (Isa 9:6; cf. 1 John 2:18). Though so depraved and defiant, the king of Nineveh would not escape divine judgment. He would fall and be destroyed with his city (Nah 1:9–10), foreshadowing the destruction of the ultimate Antichrist (cf. Rev 19:20) and demonstrating that God's purpose against evil will not fail.

Nineveh's judgment also confirmed God's purpose to show mercy to His chosen people. The prophet boldly attributed this mercy directly to Yahweh by declaring, **"Thus**

1 See T. Wright, ed., *Early Travels in Palestine* (London: Henry G. Bohn, 1848), 94; and see Fritsch, "Nineveh," 3:540.

says Yahweh." In promising to demonstrate mercy to Israel, God first acknowledged that the Assyrians were **at full strength and likewise many.** From a human perspective, they seemed to be too mighty and too many to be defeated. But, in reality, they were nothing compared to the Lord. Hence, Nahum declared that **even so, they will be cut off and pass away.** The Lord would **cut off** the Assyrian army, mowing them down as if they were the wool of a sheep (Gen 31:19; Deut 15:19) or the hair of a man (Jer 7:29; Mic 1:16; cf. Job 1:20). Under divine judgment, Nineveh's military would **pass away,** an allusion to being washed away in a flood (cf. Nah 1:8). The Assyrian army was but a passing shadow before God (cf. Pss 90:4, 9; 103:15–16; 144:4; Jas 4:14).

Because Nineveh could not survive God's assault, the Lord declared to His people Israel, **"Though I have afflicted you, I will afflict you no longer."** God recounted that in the past He had **afflicted** Israel, using Assyria to discipline His people (Isa 5:13, 24–30; 10:5–6, 12, 15; cf. 2 Kgs 16–17; 2 Chr 32–33; Jer 27:6). Assyria's barbarism against nations, including Israel, was well known as they destroyed cities and enslaved or tortured their captives. But the God who sovereignly used Assyria in His judgment of Israel (***I* have afflicted you**) would also judge Assyria and show compassion to His people (***I* will afflict you no longer**). Thus, the Lord promised to Israel: **"So now, I will break his yoke bar from upon you, and I will break your bands apart."** The **yoke bar** refers to the sturdy frame of a yoke and was often used to describe the unbreakable bond of foreign subjugation (cf. Lev 26:13; Jer 27:2, 6–11; 28:10, 12–13). God's declaration that He **will break** the yoke bar meant that He would destroy Nineveh to deliver His people from Assyrian oppression. The Lord then added, **"I will break your bands apart."** In Psalm 107:14, this same statement described God's deliverance of despairing people, even those in the shadow of death (cf. v. 10). Here in Nahum, this promise to **break your bands apart** indicated that the Lord would remove the heavy shackles of despair that weighed His people down. As the psalmist declared:

When Yahweh returned the captive ones of Zion,
We were like those who dream.
Then our mouth was filled with laughter
And our tongue with shouts of joy;
Then they said among the nations,
"Yahweh has done great things for them."
Yahweh has done great things for us;
We are glad. (Ps 126:1–3)

By declaring His intention to destroy Nineveh, the Lord made it clear that Assyria would afflict Israel **no longer.** The promise foreshadowed Israel's ultimate salvation at the end of the age. When the Lord Jesus returns, God will not **afflict** His people in discipline anymore (Jer 50:29; 51:56; Obad 15) but will rather free Israel permanently from the **yoke** of every enemy (cf. Isa 10:27; Ezek 34:27). In that day, Israel will enjoy only the Lord's blessing. The destruction of Nineveh proved that God will keep His promises to Israel, both to judge Israel's enemies and to preserve His people immediately and ultimately. The Lord will accomplish His plan precisely as He has ordained it.

Judgment Affirms God's Promises

And Yahweh has commanded concerning you:
"There will no longer be seed from your name.
From the house of your gods,
I will cut off graven image and molten image.
I will prepare your grave,
For you are contemptible." (1:14)

Having prophesied Nineveh's demise, Nahum then described specifically the death of its king, saying, **"Yahweh has commanded concerning you."** While the prophet had earlier addressed the city (using a feminine pronoun; cf. v. 11), here he addressed the city's ruler (using a masculine pronoun). The king may have given many commands during his reign, but it was

Yahweh who gave the final **command concerning** the king. As the King of kings and Israel's covenant God, **Yahweh** issued this decree against the king of Nineveh to demonstrate that He would keep His promises to His own.

The Lord condemned the Assyrian king with the judgment that **there will no longer be seed from your name,** indicating that he would not have a descendant to sit on his throne. Destroying the ruler's **seed** and **name** directly contrasted with God's promise to establish Abraham's seed and name (cf. Gen 12:3; 12:7; 22:18) as well as to sustain the messianic Seed of the woman (cf. Gen 3:15; Gal 3:16). By eradicating the king's **seed** and **name,** the Lord demonstrated that the seed of evildoers wwill perish (cf. Isa 14:20; Jer 22:30; 29:32; 49:10), that Israel's seed and name will endure forever (cf. Isa 6:13; 66:22), and that the messianic Seed will triumph (cf. Gen 3:15; Rom 16:20; Rev 12). Though the **seed** and the **name** of Nineveh's king would perish, Israel could rejoice in knowing that God was upholding His promises to His people.

The death of Nineveh's ruler also confirmed God's promise to judge idolatry, for the Lord declared, **"From the house of your gods, I will cut off graven image and molten image."** Just as the lofty reputation of the Ninevites would not continue, neither would their false religion survive. The **house of your gods** refers to the pagan temple, which would have been filled with many images of the deities that the Ninevites worshiped. Ashur was the patron god, and Ishtar, the goddess of love and war, was the patron goddess. Nabu was the god of scribes and writing. Nergal was the god of the underworld. Tiamat was the sea goddess. There were also Marduk, Enlil, Ninlil, Nisroch, and other deities. The king's life revolved around these many pagan deities which he worshiped as his (**your**) gods (cf. 2 Kgs 19:36–37; Isa 37:37–38). But they would all be eliminated, for as the Lord decreed, **"I will cut off graven image and molten image."** A **graven image** referred to an idol carved out of wood or stone (cf. Isa 44:9–10, 15, 17), and a **molten image** described an idol cast in metal (cf. Exod 32:4; 2 Kgs 17:16; Isa 42:17). In His judgment of Nineveh and the king of Nineveh, God would **cut off** and hew to pieces every expression of idolatry in the city (cf. Deut 7:5; 12:3; 27:15). Nineveh's coming destruction was a powerful expression of God's wrath against idolatry.

Moreover, Yahweh's punishment of Nineveh would uphold His promises in the Abrahamic Covenant. As the Lord had declared that He would curse those who oppressed Israel (cf. Gen 12:3), so Yahweh proclaimed to the king of Nineveh, **"I will prepare your grave, for you are contemptible."** Well known for its magnificent palace (cf. Nah 2:6), the royal city magnified the power and splendor of its king. But in His wrath and destruction of Nineveh, God would **prepare** the city to become **your** (the king's) **grave.** The king would be perpetually enshrined in shame. Such desecration would occur because God viewed the king as **contemptible,** which describes an object that is worthless, detestable, and even cursed. The same root appeared in God's promise to Abraham, in which God decreed, "I will bless those who bless you, and the one who curses you [or, treats you as contemptible] I will curse" (Gen 12:3). Since Assyria cursed Israel, treating them as **contemptible,** God declared that He would curse the king with unceasing shame, thereby upholding the Abrahamic covenant. The prophesied death of Assyria's king displayed God's unfailing commitment to the promises He had made to His people.

Judgment Affirms God's Prophecies

Behold, on the mountains the feet of him who proclaims good news,
Who announces peace!
Celebrate your feasts, O Judah;
Pay your vows.
For never again will the vile one pass through you;
He is cut off completely. (1:15)

In addition to prophesying about the judgment against Nineveh and its king, Nahum also foretold the comfort Israel would receive over the news of this judgment. He exclaimed: **"Behold, on the mountains the feet of him who proclaims good news, who announces peace!"** Nahum called all of God's people to turn their focus (**behold**) to **the mountains** that surrounded Jerusalem over which messengers would travel to bring news to the city (cf. Isa 40:9; Judg 9:7). Nahum was urging the people to watch for the first glimpse of these bearers of good news, the appearance of **the feet** of those running to report Nineveh's defeat. While in the past Israel had received bad news on these hills (cf. Judg 9:25, 36; Zech 11:1–3; Rev 16:16), this time the report would be triumphant. Israel would receive the messenger who **proclaims** the **good news** of Assyria's defeat and who **announces peace** because the oppressor was removed.

This prophetic scene was designed to resemble the prophecy announced previously in Isaiah 52:7:

> How lovely on the mountains
> Are the feet of him who proclaims good news,
> Who announces peace
> And proclaims good news of good things,
> Who announces salvation,
> *And* says to Zion, "Your God reigns!"

Isaiah's prophecy was not about the fall of Assyria; it rather foresaw Israel's future victory and restoration after the battle of Armageddon (cf. Rev 19:11–21). Nahum intentionally paralleled Isaiah's prophecy to make a simple point: the comfort Israel would experience over Nineveh's defeat prefigured Israel's ultimate joy in response to Messiah's victory at the end of the age (cf. Ps 110:1; 1 Cor 15:25–26). Even the meaning of Nahum's name ("comfort") contributed to this prophetic message. This very name is the word Isaiah used to introduce his prophecy to encourage Israel, saying, "Comfort, O comfort My people" (Isa 40:1). Nahum, the prophet of comfort, gave the near prophecy that provided assurance that the comfort anticipated in Isaiah's distant prophecy will be realized (cf. 1 Kgs 13:2–3). Such comfort and **good news** are inextricably tied together with the gospel, the greatest message of good news. As Paul declared, "How will they preach unless they are sent? Just as it is written, 'HOW BEAUTIFUL ARE THE FEET OF THOSE WHO PROCLAIM GOOD NEWS OF GOOD THINGS!'" (Rom 10:15; cf. Eph 2:17; 6:15). The prophet Nahum instructed God's people that when they saw Nineveh's demise, they would know that God's promise of good news and final victory was certain.

Because of the assurance of God's plan of redemption, Nahum commanded the Israelites: **"Celebrate your feasts, O Judah."** The mention of the **feasts** is a likely reference to the three yearly celebrations during which Israel would journey to Jerusalem—the Passover (*Pesach*, or the Feast of Unleavened Bread), the Feast of Weeks (*Shavuot*), and the Feast of Booths (*Sukkot*) (Exod 23:14–17; 34:18–23; Deut 16:1–17). As pilgrimage feasts, these three festivals were the major events of Israel's yearly calendar that the people would observe to commemorate God's deliverance. They worshiped the Lord for His past redemption of Israel from Egypt and the wilderness (cf. Exod 12:14; 13:3; Deut 16:1–8; 2 Kgs 23:21–23; 2 Chr 35:1–19; Ezra 6:19–21), His present provision of food (cf. Exod 34:22; Deut 16:9–12), and His future salvation and restoration of the nation (cf. Deut 16:13–15; Zech 14:16–19). In celebrating the salvation of the Lord, the Israelites arranged their entire lives around their worship of God, recognizing their dependence on His grace. Nahum exhorted Israel to commit themselves to this way of living because God's salvation was so sure.

The nation was called to devote not only their lives but also their resources to commemorate God's deliverance. Nahum urged Israel, **"Pay your vows."** A **vow** was an offering made in recognition of God's saving intervention in one's life. The sailors in Jonah's day offered vows to Yahweh in response to His willingness to deliver them (Jonah 1:16). Jonah himself paid vows because

God rescued him from the sea and the fish (2:9). Nahum similarly called Israel to pay their vows and give praise to God specifically for His judgment on Nineveh. While in Jonah the vows were paid for God's mercy to sinners, in Nahum they would be paid for God's judgment of sinners. Though opposite circumstances, the only proper response was to worship God. When Israel would hear of the wicked city's destruction, they were to offer exuberant and continual worship to the Lord for their deliverance.

In urging Israel to pay their vows, Nahum elaborated on the lasting effects of God's deliverance, explaining, **"For never again will the vile one pass through you; he is cut off completely."** The **vile one** (*belial*) referred to the king of Nineveh in all his depravity, and placed him in the ranks of an antichrist-type figure who opposes God and His people (cf. 2 Cor 6:15; 1 John 2:18). The Lord promised that upon the Assyrian capital's destruction, this wicked ruler would **never again pass through** Israel. God's people would find satisfaction in God's justice, as this evil king would be **cut off completely. Cut** in this case is different than the term used earlier (Nah 1:12), emphasizing here not only physical destruction but also divine fury and judgment (Lev 17:4, 9; 22:3; cf. Exod 12:15; 31:14; Num 15:31; 19:20). Such definitive condemnation of this **vile one,** a strategic tool of Satan (see discussion on Nah 1:11), was a sign of what God would do against the ultimate vile one, Satan himself (cf. 2 Cor 6:15). Just as Israel's liberation from Nineveh prefigured their ultimate rescue (see discussion on Nah 1:15), so the defeat of Nineveh's king prefigured the defeat of Israel's ultimate enemy, Satan. The Lord will prevail over all His enemies, just as He prevailed over the wicked ruler of Nineveh and the violent Assyrian army.

Given the close connection between comfort and judgment in this passage, commentators designate this portion of Nahum's prophecy, and particularly Nahum 1:15, as the key to the entire book.[2] Though the book describes Nineveh's catastrophic judgment, it does so to demonstrate that God's plan is certain,

2 Barker, *Micah, Nahum, Habakkuk, Zephaniah*, 190.

His promises true, and His prophecies sure. By predicting the spectacular destruction of Nineveh that would soon come to pass, Nahum provided irrefutable evidence of God's sovereignty over the nations and the events of world history. The Lord demonstrated that He would complete His good purposes for His people. In this way, the book of Nahum embodies the meaning of its author's name: comfort.

A Prophetic Judgment

11

NAHUM 2:1–7

The one who scatters has come up against you.
Guard the fortification, watch the road;
Strengthen your loins, instill *your* power with exceeding courage.

For Yahweh will restore the majesty of Jacob
Like the majesty of Israel,
Even though those who empty *them* have emptied them to destruction
And ruined their vine branches.

The shields of his mighty men are *colored* red,
The valiant men are dressed in scarlet,
The chariots are *enveloped* in flashing steel
When he is set up *to march*,
And the cypress *spears* are brandished.

The chariots race madly in the streets;
They rush wildly in the squares;
Their appearance is like torches;
They dash to and fro like lightning flashes.

He remembers his mighty ones;
They stumble in their march;
They hurry to her wall,
And the mantelet is set up.

The gates of the rivers are opened,
And the palace is melted away.

So it stands fixed:
She is exiled, she is carried away,
And her maidservants are moaning like the sound of doves,
Beating on their hearts.

The Word of God is more certain than any human experience. As the Apostle Peter declared, "We have as more sure the prophetic word, to which you do well to pay attention as to a lamp shining in a dark place" (2 Pet 1:19a; cf. Ps 119:105). Peter emphasized this truth about Scripture after recounting his experience at the Transfiguration (cf. Matt 17:1–8; Mark 9:2–13; Luke 9:28–36). Though Peter vividly recalled that unforgettable event, he understood that God's Word is more sure than even the most sublime experience.

The Lord Jesus also affirmed the absolute reliability of Scripture, reminding the religious leaders that "Scripture cannot be broken" (John 10:35; cf. 17:17). In the Sermon on the Mount, He explained that "until heaven and earth pass away, not the smallest letter or stroke shall pass from the Law until all is accomplished" (Matt 5:18). Christ's point was that Scripture cannot fail, not even at the level of the smallest letter, a *yodh* in Hebrew, or a "stroke," a small mark to distinguish one Hebrew letter from another. Every detail of God's Word will be fulfilled perfectly and precisely. After His resurrection, Jesus reiterated that "all things which are written about Me in the Law of Moses and the Prophets and the Psalms must be fulfilled" (Luke 24:44). Because Scripture is God-breathed, it is inspired, authoritative, inerrant, infallible, and all-sufficient (2 Tim 3:16). Given the certainty of divine revelation, believers are called to "remember the words spoken beforehand by the holy prophets and the commandment of the Lord and Savior *spoken* by [the] apostles" (2 Pet 3:2).

Scripture is absolutely certain because its Author is God, the One who knows all things (1 John 3:20) and declares the end from the beginning (Isa 46:9–10). Accordingly, the Word of God not only records the past but also reveals the future (cf. 2 Pet 1:19). Nahum's predictions about Nineveh demonstrate this truth, foretelling details of God's judgment on the city before its destruction took place. The prophet recounted the purpose of this judgment (Nah 2:1–2), the people subjected to it (2:3–5), the place it would first fall on the city (2:6), and the plight of the Ninevites as a result (2:7). The prophecy of Nahum was accurate down to the specific details. While an enemy would typically besiege a city to starve its inhabitants, invading only after the people became weak, Nahum indicated that Nineveh's defenses would instead be wrecked by a flood of water (2:6). Only God could have foreknown that Assyria's capital city would be destroyed in that way. Thus, Nahum's prophecy provides an astounding testimony to the divine inspiration and veracity of Scripture.

The Purpose of Judgment

The one who scatters has come up against you.
Guard the fortification, watch the road;
Strengthen your loins, instill *your* power with exceeding courage.

For Yahweh will restore the majesty of Jacob
Like the majesty of Israel,
Even though those who empty *them* have emptied them to destruction
And ruined their vine branches. (2:1–2)

Nahum introduced God's prophetic description of Nineveh's destruction by putting the city on notice. He warned the Ninevites that **the one who scatters has come up against you. The one who scatters** referred to the Babylonian army, which implemented a strategy of attacking and decimating enemy nations by sending their inhabitants into exile (cf. Gen 11:4; Deut 4:27; cf. 2 Kgs 25:1–21). Approximately forty years before Babylon destroyed Assyria in 612 BC, the prophet Nahum announced that the Babylonians would **come up against** Nineveh to destroy the city and scatter its residents.

In predicting Assyria's coming demise, Nahum rhetorically challenged the Ninevites to prepare their defenses. First, they were to **guard the fortification.** Since the Hebrew words for **guard** (*natzor*) and **fortification** (*matzor*) sound similar, Nahum used these two terms to emphasize his call to the Ninevites to attempt to reinforce their defenses. Second, the people were to **watch the road.** With their city secured, they were to be on constant alert for the approaching enemy, to avoid a surprise attack (cf. 1 Sam 4:13; Jer 48:19).

Third, Nahum rhetorically urged the people to **strengthen** their **loins.** In keeping with the typical military imperative to "gird up the loins" (cf. 1 Kgs 18:46; 2 Kgs 4:29; 9:1; 1 Pet 1:13), Nahum's admonition to the Ninevite warriors was for them to summon their mental fortitude and physical strength for battle (cf. 2 Kgs 9:1; Isa 45:1). Fourth, the citizens of Nineveh were to **instill** their **power with exceeding courage,** infusing their fighting ability (**power**) with the utmost boldness (**courage**). The Ninevites were not merely to be bold but to possess **exceeding courage,** having the greatest degree of ferocity a fighter could muster. By linking the terms **strong** and **courageous,** Nahum referenced a theme commonly found in Scripture regarding warfare (cf. Deut 31:6, 7; Josh 1:6, 7, 9; Ps 31:24). With this familiar refrain, Nahum urged the Assyrians to try to defend their capital.

The prophet's call to Nineveh to prepare for battle (presented as a charge to guard, watch, strengthen, and instill) made a powerful rhetorical point. No matter how well-prepared the Ninevites might be, they could not overcome or resist the judgment of God against them (cf. Joel 3:9–17). The Lord's decree was to destroy Assyria and avenge Israel. Thus, Nahum exclaimed, **"For Yahweh will restore the majesty of Jacob, like the majesty of Israel."** Nineveh's destruction served as a guarantee that God would preserve His people, and one day exalt Israel to a position of **majesty** and lofty dignity (cf. Job 38:11). At the end of the age, the Lord will elevate Israel above all the nations so that they will be the pride and joy of the world (cf. Isa 24:14; 60:15; Mic 5:4). God's chosen nation will then become distinguished like the patriarch **Jacob** and live up to the God-given name **Israel.** The man **Jacob** prevailed in his trouble-filled life (cf. Gen 47:9), so God gave him the name **Israel,** meaning "he who strives with God" or "God strives." That name served as a constant reminder to Jacob that the only reason he prevailed was because the Lord fought on his behalf (Gen 32:26–28; 35:10; Hos 12:5; cf. Gen 31:7; Exod 14:14, 25). Through Nahum, the Lord similarly promised to cause His people to prevail, so that one day Israel also will be exalted among the nations (cf. Isa 2:3; Zech 8:23; 14:16–19) just as Jacob formerly was (Gen 47:10).

Nahum proclaimed that God's plan for Israel will be fulfilled **even though those who empty *them* have emptied them to destruction.** Assyria's violence against God's people, which **emptied** the northern kingdom of Israel to the point of **destruction** and desolation, did not thwart God's purpose for His own. Yahweh's promises for Israel would not fail even though Nineveh had **ruined** Israel's **vine branches** by destroying its vineyards. While Israel was often depicted as a vine (cf. Ps 80:8; Isa 5:1–7; Jer 2:21), this term for **vine branches** describes literal vineyards and, specifically, the luscious and fruitful boughs of a mature grapevine. In the book of Numbers, when the twelve spies surveyed the Promised Land, they cut down one of these **vine branches** to show the Israelites the bounty of the land that God promised them (Num 13:23). Israel's land was famous for its abundant agriculture, but Assyria **ruined** and destroyed the countryside. Despite this, Yahweh promised to restore the majesty of Jacob. As Amos described, one future day Israel "will also plant vineyards and drink their wine and make gardens and eat their fruit" (Amos 9:14). The Lord assured His people that neither the Assyrians' conquest of Israel nor their efforts to defend their capital city could thwart the sovereign purposes of God. In the end, Nineveh would be destroyed, and Israel will be exalted and blessed during the millennial kingdom.

It is noteworthy that Nahum repeated the word "empty" to describe the destruction the Assyrians carried out against Israel. In Hebrew, the word "empty" is *baqaq*, which is the sound of water emptying from a bottle or jug. This was particularly appropriate given that Nineveh would be destroyed by water flooding the city (cf. Nah 2:6). Just as God promised to curse those who curse Israel (cf. Gen 12:1–3; see discussion on Nah 1:14), so He would empty those who had emptied Israel. Nahum impressed upon his readers that as they saw this prophecy fulfilled, they ought to recognize Yahweh as the one true God, who alone declares the end from the beginning (Isa 46:10).

THE PEOPLE UNDER JUDGMENT

The shields of his mighty men are *colored* red,
The valiant men are dressed in scarlet,
The chariots are *enveloped* in flashing steel
When he is set up *to march,*
And the cypress *spears* are brandished.

The chariots race madly in the streets;
They rush wildly in the squares;
Their appearance is like torches;
They dash to and fro like lightning flashes.

He remembers his mighty ones;
They stumble in their march;
They hurry to her wall,
And the mantelet is set up. (2:3–5)

In exacting detail, Nahum described the battle scene that would unfold between the Babylonians and the Assyrians. Portraying the Ninevite military brigade, Nahum indicated that **the shields of his mighty men are *colored* red** as the Ninevites exuded their strength against the coming foe. Assyria's **mighty men,** the elite soldiers of the Ninevite king himself (cf. 2 Sam 23:8), took up **shields** that were **red,** overlaid either with copper to reflect sunlight and terrify the enemy, or with red leather designed to extinguish fiery arrows. Likewise, **the valiant men are dressed in scarlet,** adorned for battle and ready to intimidate the approaching enemy. The term **valiant men** referred to the most competent and courageous troops, the leaders of the elite units (cf. Exod 18:21; Judg 20:44; 2 Sam 11:16; 2 Kgs 24:16). As these **dressed in scarlet,** or crimson, these troops would have been immediately recognizable as exceptional warriors. In detailing this formidable scene, Nahum conveyed Nineveh's confidence as its military prepared to wage war against Babylon.

Nineveh would also ready its war machines. As Nahum predicted, **the chariots are *enveloped* in flashing steel** in preparation for battle. **Chariots** were powerful instruments of war on the ancient battlefield. They were swift and capable of overrunning infantry. Being ***enveloped* in flashing steel** indicated that the chariots and their horses were heavily armored with steel fittings. Thus, both man and machine were strategically arranged along with the king who was **set up *to march*** with his troops against the oncoming foe.

Nahum further described the Assyrian weapons by observing that **the cypress *spears* are brandished.** Cypress, a type of fir tree that produced a hearty wood for various construction projects, was even used by Solomon to build the temple (cf. 1 Kgs 5:8; 6:15, 34). **Brandished** conveys a quivering motion like that of an arrow that reverberates after striking its target. These sturdy spears were primed to thwart the charge of enemy forces, or to hurl at opposing soldiers as they advanced on the city.

Describing the fervency of the battle, Nahum noted that **the chariots** of the Ninevites would **race madly in the streets.** Though the previous verse depicted Nineveh's chariots assembled in military formation, they would **race madly** once the fighting began. Nineveh's chariots would **rush wildly in the squares,** a reference to the city center where business and civic activity normally took place (cf. Gen 19:2; Deut 13:16; 2 Sam 21:12). With the streets filled with chariots, **their appearance** glistened **like torches** as their shiny steel coverings reflected the sun. As they drove through the city, they would **dash to and fro like lightning flashes,** displaying force and projecting confidence that Nineveh's military could repel the imminent threat.

The king of Nineveh committed all his resources to defend the city. Nahum remarked that **he** [the king] **remembers his mighty ones.** The "mighty men" mentioned earlier were Nineveh's veteran warriors (Nah 2:3), but the **mighty ones** in this context referred to the city's distinguished nobles. The king assigned these illustrious heroes to lead the counteroffensive, which they would do with such fervency and haste that some would even **stumble in their march** as **the** rushed to **hurry to** Nineveh's **wall.** Without hesitation, they inspired their troops to defend the most vulnerable areas of the city and even reinforce the perimeter, so that **the mantelet** was **set up.** The mantelet likely referred to the defensive towers of Nineveh, which, according to the Greek historian Diodorus Siculus, were 1,500 in number and up to 200 feet tall.[1] Nahum portrayed the entire city rallying behind its leaders to resist the enemy invasion.

1 Diodorus Siculus, "Diodori Bibliotheca Historica," *Bibliotheca Historica* (Medford, MA: Teubneri, 1888–1890), 1:173; see G. Booth, trans. *The Historical Library of Diodorus the Sicilian: In Fifteen Books* (London: Edward Jones, 1700), 55; and Smith, *Micah–Malachi*, 83.

Thus, the city's troops were prepared, the chariots readied, the leaders resolved, and the defenses strengthened for the approaching adversary. With perfect accuracy, Nahum foretold the opening moments of the Battle of Nineveh in 612 BC. From a human perspective, Assyria's capital appeared unassailable, but just as God raised up Pharaoh to crush him for His glory (cf. Exod 9:16; Rom 9:17), so the Lord elevated Nineveh so that His majesty would be displayed in its downfall.

The Place of Judgment

The gates of the rivers are opened,
And the palace is melted away. (2:6)

Though Nineveh felt secure in its defenses, the Lord would intervene and **the gates of the rivers** would be **opened.** The city of Nineveh was located at the convergence of three rivers. The Tigris flowed outside the city, while the Khosr and Tebiltu ran through it. All three waterways were sources of Nineveh's pride.[2] These rivers provided life for Nineveh and beautified the city, as Sennacherib utilized them to irrigate magnificent gardens. The rivers also formed a natural defense against foreign invaders. However, as **the gates of the rivers** were **opened,** God used the very strength and security of the city—its rivers—as the primary means of its destruction. Nahum foresaw that the dams, which regulated the flow of water in and out of the capital, would break, and a catastrophic flood would destroy the city's defenses.[3]

As Nahum described the devastation, he added that even **the palace** would be **melted away.** The **palace** of Nineveh was spectacular, named by Sennacherib as "the palace without rival."[4] It contained approximately seventy rooms, with a footprint of

2 Carl E. Armerding, "Nahum," in *The Expositor's Bible Commentary: Daniel–Malachi,* revised edition (Grand Rapids: Zondervan, 2008), 584–85; Timmer, *Nahum,* 130.

3 Robertson, *The Books of Nahum, Habakkuk and Zephaniah,* 90.

4 Grayson, "Nineveh," 4:1118–19; Anna Sieges, "Nineveh," *Lexham Bible Dictionary* (Bellingham, WA: Lexham, 2016).

1,650 by 794 feet.[5] The palace was filled with artwork and reliefs depicting Assyrian warriors hunting lions, seizing spoil, and savagely conquering other peoples.[6] This imposing structure was not merely destroyed; it **melted away** as the water eroded its foundation and the invading army burned it to the ground (cf. Nah 3:13).[7] The principal center and preeminent symbol of the strength of Nineveh and Assyria would crumble, signifying the collapse of its imperial power. Though Nineveh was fully braced for an intense conflict, it was to no avail. God would use the irresistible power of flood waters to accomplish His sovereign purposes.

Though false prophets of ancient times oftentimes uttered oracles that would prove untrue (cf. 1 Kgs 13:18; 22:13–28; Jer 28:10–17), Nahum declared a prophecy that was historically fulfilled. Ancient records report that Nineveh's demise came to pass just as the prophet foretold:

> The Assyrian and Babylonian records are silent with regard to the fall of the city, but Alexander Polyhistor, Abydenus and Syncellus all speak of it. The best account, however, is that of Diodorus Siculus, who refers to a legend that the city could not be taken until the river became its enemy. Arbaces, the Scythian, besieged it, but could not make any impression on it for 2 years. In the 3rd year, however, the river (according to Commander Jones, not the Tigris, but the Khosr), being swollen by rains, and very rapid in its current, carried away a portion of the wall, and by this opening the besiegers gained an entrance.[8]

The fulfillment of Nahum's prophecy, delivered about forty years before it occurred, is compelling evidence that God's Word is infallible and inerrant. Because God sovereignly predetermines the future, He predicts it with flawless precision. His Word is always true and His promises certain. Nahum's prophecy of

5 Ibid.

6 Ibid.

7 Timmer, *Nahum*, 130; Renz, *The Books of Nahum, Habakkuk, and Zephaniah*, 128.

8 T. G. Pinches, "Nineveh," *International Standard Bible Encyclopedia* (Chicago: Howard-Severance, 1915), 4:2151.

Nineveh's demise intended to encourage the ancient Israelites (Nah 1:15; 2:1–2), especially those who saw his predictions come to pass four decades after they were issued. For believers in any age, these fulfilled prophecies serve as evidence that God is always faithful to keep His promises to His people (see discussion on 1:15).

The Plight of Those under Judgment

So it stands fixed:
She is exiled, she is carried away,
And her maidservants are moaning like the sound of doves,
Beating on their hearts. (2:7)

Having detailed Nineveh's fall, Nahum proceeded to describe the plight of the Assyrian people as a result of this judgment. Reiterating the certainty of his prophecy, Nahum declared, **"So it stands fixed."** The verb for **stands fixed** describes an object that is firmly positioned and remains immovable (cf. Gen 28:12). This decree, like everything revealed in God's Word, was absolutely fixed and definite (cf. Num 23:19; Eccl 7:13; Isa 14:24–27; 46:9–11).

Nahum made three pronouncements about Nineveh and its residents. First, he declared that **she is exiled** in disgrace. The pronoun **she** refers not only to the city but also to its false goddess Ishtar (see discussion on Nah 1:14; cf. Judg 6:25–32; 1 Sam 4:1–11; 5:1–7).[9] Nineveh's destruction would be fulfilled precisely as Nahum had prophesied: its survivors carried away from their land as captives, and their gods shown to be impotent. **Exiled** connotes the idea of exposing or laying something bare or naked (Nah 3:5; cf. Isa 47:2–3; Ezek 16:37). It was used as a technical term for exile because captivity exposed a nation in its shame (cf. 2 Kgs 17:6, 11, 23; 18:11). The proud city of Nineveh and its gods would be humiliated, which would be God's retribution

9 Timmer, *Nahum*, 133–34.

against Assyria's exile of the northern kingdom of Israel (cf. 2 Kgs 17; 18:11; Isa 10:5–12). The Lord promised through Nahum that He would seek vengeance for His people.

Second, in addition to experiencing shame, Nineveh would also be made desolate, as **she is carried away,** meaning that both the city's population and its possessions were taken into captivity. **Carried away** means to "go up," and can refer to going up to a city and even to being offered up as a sacrifice (Judg 6:28; cf. Gen 8:20; 22:2, 13; Exod 24:5). Those who had "gone up" to take Israel into exile (cf. 2 Kgs 17:3, 5) and to besiege Jerusalem (cf. 18:13) would themselves experience the same. As the smoke of Nineveh's ruins rose into the sky and her citizens were deported, Nahum called Israel to recognize that Nineveh was like a sacrifice to satisfy God's wrath (cf. Zeph 1:7–13). The Ninevites would be **carried away** never to return again, while their former home became a place of permanent desolation (cf. 2:13).

Third, in describing the Ninevites' captivity, Nahum explained that **her maidservants** would be **moaning like the sound of doves, beating on their hearts.** A **maidservant** identified any female servant or slave. At the time of Nineveh's defeat, all the military warriors and common men would be either killed or deported as slaves, and all the nobility would also be carried away (cf. 2 Kgs 24:14). So, any remaining individuals in the city would include the **maidservants,** who, in the face of such distress, would be overcome by **moaning** and weeping. Shocked by the devastations of war, these women would respond with a shuddering wail, one **like the sound of doves.** They would not only shed tears, but also beat **on their hearts.** This term **beating** is used one other time in the Old Testament, but in reference to beating on tambourines with joy (Ps 68:25). The opposite emotions conveyed by the term **beating** in these two instances is insightful. While the beating of tambourines signified heartfelt celebration, the **beating on their hearts** reflected heartbroken agony. In the days of Jonah, the city heard a message of destruction but was spared (Jonah 3:4–10). But in Nahum's prophecy, divine wrath was unleashed on Nineveh, resulting in a city reduced to the wailing of weeping women. Unlike in Jonah's time, the Lord would not relent from His judgment.

Given Nahum's deliberate parallels with Jonah, that this passage concludes with women moaning like **doves** is fitting, since the Hebrew word for **dove** is the very name of the prophet Jonah. The city that experienced mercy at the preaching of the prophet Jonah would experience a different *jonah* as the maidservants mourned like doves (*jonah*) in response to divine judgment. While God sent Jonah to Nineveh to give them comfort (*nahum*, Jonah 3:10), He later sent Nahum to condemn the city and cause them to mourn like doves (*jonah*, Nah 2:7). The symmetry presents two vastly different outcomes. Either the sinner repents in light of God's warning and receives His grace, or the sinner ignores God's warning and receives His wrath (cf. Rom 2:3–6). While God may extend mercy after mercy for a period, He will ultimately execute judgment against the unrepentant. Because of such sure judgment, sinners must never presume on God's grace (cf. 2 Pet 2:3–4). Conversely, God calls His people to wait on Him patiently, knowing He will avenge them in due time (cf. Jas 5:7–9; 2 Pet 3:9).

A Definitive Judgment

12

NAHUM 2:8–13

Though Nineveh *was* like a pool of water throughout her days,
Now they are fleeing;
"Stand! Stand!"
But no one turns back.

Plunder the silver!
Plunder the gold!
And there is no limit to the treasure—
Wealth from every kind of desirable object.

She is emptied! Yes, she is emptied out and eviscerated!
Hearts are melting and knees knocking!
Also anguish is in all *their* loins,
And all their faces turn pale!

Where is the den of the lions
And the feeding place of the young lions,
Where the lion, lioness, and lion's cub prowled,
With nothing to make *them* tremble?

The lion tore enough for its cubs
And strangled *enough* for its lionesses
And filled its lairs with torn up prey
And its dens with torn up flesh.

"Behold, I am against you," declares Yahweh of hosts. "And I will burn up her chariots in smoke, and a sword will devour your young lions; and I will cut off your prey from the land, and no longer will the voice of your messengers be heard."

The enemies of God may presume they can oppose Him, but the Lord promises to obliterate them. Psalm 2 captures the arrogance of the wicked with these words: "The kings of the earth take their stand and the rulers take counsel together against Yahweh and against His Anointed" (Ps 2:2). In response, God declares their destruction, saying to the Messiah: "You shall break them with a rod of iron, You shall shatter them like a potter's vessel" (v. 9).

Throughout human history, wicked rulers have challenged the supremacy of God, only to be crushed by Him. When Moses announced to Pharaoh that Yahweh commanded the Israelites to leave Egypt, Pharaoh responded, "Who is Yahweh that I should listen to His voice to let Israel go?" (Exod 5:2). The Lord answered Pharaoh's question by decimating Egypt with severe plagues and drowning the Egyptian army in the sea. When Goliath came against the Israelites and "reproached" the God of Israel, the Lord sent David to kill him (cf. 1 Sam 17:25–26, 36, 45). The king of Tyre said of himself, "I will make myself like the Most High" (Isa 14:14), and even declared, "I am a god" (Ezek 28:2). But Yahweh replied, "You are a man and not God.... You will die the death of the uncircumcised.... And you will cease to be forever" (28:2, 10, 19). God's chief enemy Satan will rise up against God in the final battle of Gog and Magog, but God will cast the devil into the lake of fire and brimstone (Rev 20:7–10). Yahweh's victory over His enemies will be so definitive that He will destroy even death itself. As Paul explained, "The last enemy to be abolished is death" (1 Cor 15:26; cf. Heb 2:14–15; Rev 20:14). Any adversary who dares to oppose God will be irrevocably vanquished by Him.

Nahum proclaimed that God would judge Nineveh with that kind of power. As the greatest military power of the ancient Near East, Assyria assumed itself to be invincible even from the wrath of Yahweh. When the Assyrian commander Rabshakeh came against Jerusalem in the time of Hezekiah, he defied God and claimed the Lord was powerless to defend Jerusalem. Rabshakeh's message was:

> Do not let your God in whom you trust deceive you, saying, "Jerusalem will not be given into the hand of the king of Assyria." Behold, you have heard what the kings of Assyria have done to all the lands, devoting them to destruction. So will you be delivered? Did the gods of those nations which my fathers brought to ruin deliver them, *even* Gozan and Haran and Rezeph and the sons of Eden who *were* in Telassar? Where is the king of Hamath, the king of Arpad, the king of the city of Sepharvaim, and *of* Hena and Ivvah? (2 Kgs 19:10–13; cf. 18:32–35)

The Assyrians not only declared their king superior to Yahweh, but they also mocked God and likened Him to false and impotent idols. While this taunt was meant to intimidate God's people (18:26, 37; cf. 19:1–3), the Lord encouraged them with the simple words, "Do not be afraid" (19:6). To show that the Assyrians could not oppose Him and that He would defend Jerusalem, God sent the Angel of Yahweh to single-handedly put to death 185,000 Assyrian soldiers in one night (19:35). Because Nineveh set itself against the Lord, He set Himself against Nineveh and declared to them through Nahum: "Whatever you devise against Yahweh, He will make a complete destruction of it" (Nah 1:9; cf. 1:10–13).

Through Nahum, God prophesied that He would destroy Nineveh's pride (2:8), prosperity (2:9), power (2:10), and preeminence (2:11–12), which were all decreed by His divine prosecution of the city (2:13). The Lord's comprehensive judgment would devastate the city and the surrounding empire, so that Assyria would never again wreak havoc against Israel. By destroying the mightiest nation in the ancient Near East, God demonstrated His power to judge His enemies, protect His own, and keep every promise He made to His people.

Destruction of Pride

Though Nineveh *was* like a pool of water throughout her days,
Now they are fleeing;
"Stand! Stand!"
But no one turns back. (2:8)

Before describing Nineveh's downfall, Nahum recognized the city's pride of place in the ancient world. Nineveh was one of the largest and most magnificent cities in the ancient Near East. It enjoyed thriving trade and abundant agriculture. A literal oasis in the desert, **Nineveh *was* like a pool of water throughout her days.** The prophet depicted Nineveh as **a pool of water,** like a reservoir or lake created by a spring (cf. 2 Sam 2:13; 4:12; 1 Kgs 22:38; 2 Kgs 18:17; Isa 22:11). For a city to survive and prosper, it needed water nearby. Nineveh not only enjoyed such a benefit, being located near various rivers (Tigris, Khosr, and Tebiltu; see discussion on Nah 2:6), but it was even considered self-sustaining because it was so well supplied with water. Nineveh was known for its riches and abundant natural resources **throughout her days,** starting from the dawn of civilization (cf. Gen 10:11). Because of its prime location, the Assyrians made the city their capital (cf. 2 Kgs 19:36; Isa 37:37) and established it as a center for culture (with the libraries of Ashurbanipal), agriculture, and trade (see "Historical Setting" in the Introduction). That **Nineveh *was* like a pool of water** explained its prosperity and self-sufficiency.

But God would turn Nineveh's strength into weakness—the water that sustained its life would become the force of its destruction, as floodwaters collapsed the city's defenses. Depicting the response of the people, Nahum stated, **"Now they are fleeing."** Though people had flocked to Nineveh to escape the desert, at Nineveh's fall, they would flee from the city to escape destruction. As prophesied in Nahum 2:6, "the gates of the rivers" would open and a torrent of water would flood the city, destroying key defenses and allowing the enemy to pour in. While the people would flee, shouts would be heard, **"Stand! Stand!"** as military leaders barked out orders for their soldiers to hold their positions (cf. 2 Kgs 3:21; Neh 13:19; Hab 2:1). But such a summons to bravery would have no effect. Despite the calls to stop running, **no one turns back.** In a full retreat, both the common people and the military forces would seek a way of escape. Nineveh's pride would be brought low. As the Lord illustrated in Assyria's destruction, pride comes before a fall (Prov 16:18; 29:23).

Destruction of Prosperity

Plunder the silver!
Plunder the gold!
And there is no limit to the treasure—
Wealth from every kind of desirable object. (2:9)

While the Ninevites fled the flood and the foe, the Babylonians invaded the city, celebrating with shouts, **"Plunder the silver! Plunder the gold!" Silver** and **gold,** when used in parallel, represent the sum total of one's precious possessions. Having won the battle, Babylon would **plunder** and loot the city, not resting until every treasure was taken. As Assyria's adversaries gleefully stripped Nineveh of its wealth, the Ninevites experienced what they had done for 200 years to other nations, including Israel (cf. Amos 3:11). Nahum's prophecy assured God's people that He had not forgotten their affliction but that He would soon require an eye for an eye and a tooth for a tooth from Nineveh (cf. Exod 21:24; Lev 24:20).

As Babylonian forces ransacked the city, they cheerfully exclaimed, **"And there is no limit to the treasure."** Because Assyria was a superpower in the ancient world, Nineveh amassed a vast treasure as the Assyrian army overcame city after city. Their riches increased further as conquered nations paid tribute to Assyria. As a result, **there** was **no limit** to Nineveh's wealth, since **treasure** from various lands filled its storehouses to the brim. But when the city fell, the invaders collected all this wealth for themselves.

Assyria's enemies observed that the Ninevites obtained **wealth from every kind of desirable object. Wealth** is the same Hebrew word for "glory" or "honor," conveying the idea of weightiness. The items Assyria possessed and Babylon plundered were genuine riches of magnificent quality, and Assyria had accumulated valuable treasures of all types, representing **every kind of desirable object.** Reveling in their success, Assyria kept a record of its treasures, including chariots, precious metals, copper, iron, brightly colored fabrics, exotic animals, finely crafted furniture, and jewels.[1] This list contained essentially any object that was **desirable,** a word sometimes translated as "covet" (cf. Gen 3:6; Deut 5:21). The treasures people longed for Assyria possessed in abundance. Yet under devastating divine judgment, Nineveh lost all it had acquired. The richest city in the world was reduced to poverty.

The Lord's judgment against Nineveh would prove thorough, and archaeology attests to the accuracy of this prophecy. After its destruction, the city has remained a desolate ruin for centuries, serving as a testimony to the truthfulness of God's Word and the exhaustive nature of His judgment power.[2] The ancient ruins of Nineveh are located by the Tigris River near

1 Robertson, *The Books of Nahum, Habakkuk and Zephaniah*, 93.

2 Grayson, "Nineveh," 4:1118.

Mosul in northern Iraq. Nineveh's destruction has stood as a witness to the fulfillment of God's promise to avenge His people.

Nineveh's economic destruction also assured God's people of His promises to Israel. While Assyria would lose all its **gold** and **silver,** God declared that Israel would gain this treasure. In Isaiah 60:9, the Lord proclaimed: "Surely the coastlands will hope in Me; and the ships of Tarshish *will come* first, to bring your sons from afar, their silver and their gold with them, for the name of Yahweh your God, and for the Holy One of Israel because He has adorned you with beautiful glory." Likewise, though Nineveh would lose **every kind of desirable object,** Haggai later predicted that in the Millennium, "the desirable things of all nations" will flow into Jerusalem, where the Messiah will reign supreme (Hag 2:7–8). Nahum's prophecy demonstrated that all silver and gold belong to Yahweh (cf. 2:8). He can remove them from the wicked whenever He wishes, and He will ultimately give them to His people.

Destruction of Power

She is emptied! Yes, she is emptied out and eviscerated!
Hearts are melting and knees knocking!
Also anguish is in all *their* loins,
And all their faces turn pale! (2:10)

Having foreseen Nineveh's defeat and plundering, Nahum concluded that **she** [Nineveh] **is emptied! Yes, she is emptied out and eviscerated!** In describing the utter devastation of the city, the Hebrew alliterates the words **emptied** (*buqah*), **emptied out** (*mebuqah*), and **eviscerated** (*mebulaqah*). The thrice-repeated sound in these words marks the threefold destruction of the city. First, Nineveh would be **emptied** as the population was exiled. Second, the city would be **emptied out** as the Babylonians carried off its riches, leaving nothing behind. Third, as a result, the city would be **eviscerated,** being completely destroyed and left in ruin. Earlier in the chapter, the word "emptied" described how Assyria had emptied the northern kingdom of Israel of its people and wealth (cf. Nah 2:2). Here, the prophet declared that those who had emptied Israel would themselves be emptied. With this reversal, God's justice would be served.

As they watched their city collapse, the Ninevites would be paralyzed by fear. Just as the palace had "melted" away (Nah 2:6; cf. Exod 15:15; 16:21; Josh 2:9, 11), so would the **hearts** of the people—**melting** with dread while their **knees** began **knocking** together. As they trembled in terror, losing all their resolve, **anguish** swelled within **all *their* loins. Anguish** is associated with the word for childbirth and thus conveys the agony of labor pains (cf. Isa 21:3). Though Nineveh's army was supposed to have had strength in their loins to wield their weapons in battle (cf. Nah 2:1), they would be debilitated from the distress of their defeat.

Nahum further described that **all their faces** would **turn pale,** evidencing no hope of survival. **Pale** conveys the idea of glowing, indicating that their faces would radiate dismay and despair. Though Nineveh boasted in its military power and might, its soldiers would be reduced to dread as a result of God's judgment. The same depiction of pale-faced fear appears elsewhere only in Joel 2:6, in response to divine judgment in the Day of the Lord. In Nineveh's destruction, Israel saw a foreshadowing of what will take place at the end of the age when Yahweh destroys all His enemies. Nahum's prophecy assured God's people of the future judgment of the wicked and served as a warning that sinners must repent or likewise perish (cf. Luke 13:3).

With language similar to Nahum, Isaiah declared: "Behold, Yahweh empties the earth to destruction [and] eviscerates it" (Isa 24:1). While Nahum's prophecy pertained to a specific time and nation in history, Isaiah's prophecy pointed to God's final judgment of the world. Because all creation is filled with idolatry (cf. 2:7–8), the Lord will empty the world of all vestiges of wickedness so that His glory will fill the earth (cf. 6:3). As God's people beheld the emptying of Nineveh, they saw a glimpse of what God would one day do on a global scale.

Destruction of Preeminence

Where is the den of the lions
And the feeding place of the young lions,
Where the lion, lioness, and lion's cub prowled,
With nothing to make *them* tremble?

The lion tore enough for its cubs
And strangled *enough* for its lionesses
And filled its lairs with torn up prey
And its dens with torn up flesh. (2:11–12)

Nahum emphasized Assyria's fall from preeminence by posing a rhetorical question to Nineveh's leadership: **"Where is the den of the lions?"** In ancient times, the **lion,** representing the top of the food chain, signified nobility, supremacy, and military might (cf. Num 23:24; 24:9; Judg 14:18). The lion was a fitting symbol both for warriors (cf. 2 Sam 1:23) and for rulers (cf. Ezek 19:2, 6). Nahum's use of this metaphor to depict Assyria's royalty was particularly appropriate. Assyrian kings hunted lions (as ancient carvings depict), portrayed themselves as lions, and even imagined the Assyrian empire as a lion on account of its ferocity and cruelty.[3] Nahum's rhetorical question drove home the reality of the Ninevites' defeat. Thus, he asked **where** their **den** or home had gone. Those who once boasted in their supremacy and strength had become lowly and weak. Those who formerly lived in palaces were either killed or homeless captives.

Nahum continued by inquiring whether **the feeding place of the young lions** still existed. The prophet's point was that, in addition to forfeiting their home, the Ninevites would

3 A. Kirk Grayson, "Mesopotamia," *The Anchor Yale Bible Dictionary* (New York: Doubleday, 1992), 4:748–49; Elnathan Weissert, "Royal Hunt and Royal Triumph in a Prism Fragment of Ashurbanipal (82-5-22,2)," in *Assyria 1995: Proceedings of the 10th Anniversary Symposium of the Neo-Assyrian Text Corpus Project* (Helsinki: The Neo-Assyrian Text Corpus Project, 1997), 339–58.

also lose their future leaders. **Young lions** are older cubs or subadult lions learning to hunt their prey. A young lion would be particularly aggressive (cf. Judg 14:5; Jer 25:38), loud (cf. Isa 5:29; 31:4), and hungry (cf. Ezek 19:3; Hos 5:14). In like manner, the royal youths of Assyria were bloodthirsty warriors-in-training, eager to conquer nations and amass riches. To continue Assyria's tradition of conquest, these young men were raised in Nineveh as their **feeding place,** the location where they learned the skill of warfare. With the destruction of the capital, Assyria would no longer be able to raise up future generations of violent warriors.

Nahum further described Nineveh as a place **where the lion, lioness, and lion's cub prowled.** This phrase portrayed an entire family of lions, from the father **lion,** to the mother **lioness** (cf. Gen 49:9), to the **lion's cub.** In Nineveh, the royal families **prowled** and walked about freely. They did so without fear and **with nothing to make *them* tremble** or feel dread (cf. 27:33). Prior to Nineveh's destruction, the rulers moved freely and confidently throughout the city. But when Nineveh fell, those leaders became powerless and were subjected to the conquering enemy.

Nineveh's humiliation would be particularly shameful for the king of Assyria. Formerly, the king could have boasted, **"The lion tore enough for its cubs and strangled *enough* for its lionesses and filled its lairs with torn up prey and its dens with torn up flesh."** Appearing three times in this verse, **tore** or **torn up** emphasizes Assyria's brutality against other nations to enrich itself. Prior to Nineveh's destruction, the king was able to provide for his **cubs**—the royal princes and young nobles of Assyria. He was able to please the **lionesses**—the queen and other noble women—with **strangled** prey, that is, the spoils and treasures of conquests.

The king of Assyria had also **filled its lairs with torn up prey and its dens with torn up flesh,** as the city of Nineveh prospered from conquering and subjugating other nations. In other Old Testament passages, the term **lairs** is used not only of an animal's dwelling but also in reference to a chest or hole where treasure was stored (cf. 2 Kgs 12:10; Ezek 8:7). The king had **filled** his storehouses with loot captured from those whom he had **torn up** as **prey.** The Ninevites celebrated such barbary as they filled their **dens with torn up flesh. Torn up flesh** is the third time the root "torn up" appears in this verse. This reference is the most graphic use of the verb, describing an animal being eviscerated by predators and scavengers (cf. Lev 7:24; 17:15; 22:8; Ezek 4:14). Assyria delighted in brutal violence, filling their **dens,** or palaces and homes, with artwork that commemorated their barbarism. But Nahum prophesied that the king who used such violence to provide for his young, to please his women, and to prosper his city, would himself become the object of such brutality and humiliation. Just as the Assyrians tore up their enemies, so their enemies would tear them to pieces as God would judge the lion of Assyria for his savagery.

The dominant imagery of the lion throughout these verses establishes Nahum's words as a near prophecy that guarantees the fulfillment of more-distant biblical prophecies. Similar lion imagery is used by other prophets to demonstrate that the strength of God's enemies will fail while the Lord claims all authority (cf. Jer 50:7; Ezek 32:2). Nahum's announcement of Nineveh's destruction affirmed that every nation which resists God will ultimately be destroyed. While these powers imagined as lions will perish, the Messiah will one day reign as the ultimate Lion (cf. Num 24:9; Ezek 19:1–6; Hos 11:10). Only one Lion will stand in the end, the "Lion that is from the tribe of Judah, the Root of David" (Rev 5:5; cf. Mic 5:8). Nineveh's demise illustrates that God will ultimately destroy all human competitors who present themselves as lions, so that the Messiah, the Lion of Judah, will triumph in glory and power.

Divine Prosecution

"Behold, I am against you," declares Yahweh of hosts. "And I will burn up her chariots in smoke, and a sword will devour your young lions; and I will cut off your prey from the land, and no longer will the voice of your messengers be heard." (2:13)

Though the destruction of Nineveh might be attributed to Assyria's foes, the Lord stated that it was ultimately His doing. **"Behold, I am against you," declares Yahweh of hosts.** Nineveh fell because of God's sovereign intervention. On account of Assyria's atrocities against His people, the Lord declared Nineveh to be His enemy. As Israel's covenant God and the Captain of heaven's armies, **Yahweh of hosts** announced His zeal to avenge His people.

The Lord proclaimed that He would ensure every aspect of Nineveh's downfall. First, He would destroy their military: **"I will burn up her chariots in smoke."** The **chariots,** which once symbolized Nineveh's invincibility (Nah 2:3) and swiftness (2:4), would become an ash heap, signaling not only the army's defeat but its annihilation (cf. Josh 8:21; Judg 20:38).

Second, Yahweh would bring down the next generation of Nineveh's nobility, exclaiming that **"a sword will devour your young lions."** Nahum had earlier prophesied that Nineveh's young lions, the princes and noble youths (cf. Nah 2:11), would become homeless and destitute. Here, the Lord reiterated that promise. Though these young men thrived on devouring others, God would cause the **sword** of Babylon's military to **devour** them.

Third, God announced He would end Nineveh's prosperity, saying, **"I will cut off your prey from the land."** Nahum recounted that Nineveh had grown wealthy by preying on other nations, subjugating their people and pillaging their goods (cf. 2:12). But God decreed that He would **cut off** such **prey from the land,** abolishing Assyria's ability to conquer and oppress others. Just as a lion without its prey starves, so

Nineveh would collapse and come to nothing. The Lord would use the Babylonians as His instrument of judgment against Assyria. Nonetheless, He would be the One behind each part of Nineveh's colossal fall. Vengeance belongs to the Lord and He is the One who repays (cf. Deut 32:35; Rom 12:19; Heb 10:30).

Nahum issued a fourth act of divine judgment with these words: **"No longer will the voice of your messengers be heard."** Assyria had often sent its **messengers** to other lands on diplomatic and military ventures. Judah experienced this when Assyria sent messengers to intimidate them and insult Yahweh (cf. 2 Kgs 19:9, 14, 23). In response to that particular provocation, God sent His own "messenger," the Angel of Yahweh, to put to death 185,000 Assyrian soldiers in one night (19:35). As part of its military strategy, Assyria used its messengers to herald its supremacy throughout the ancient Near East. But after the destruction of Nineveh, those messengers disappeared. Their deafening silence was a resounding testimony to Assyria's total dissolution.

While He destroyed the Assyrian messengers who promoted their own glory, God would one day send His own messenger as a forerunner to the Messiah. Recording God's announcement concerning this, Mark wrote, "Behold, I send My messenger ahead of You, who will prepare Your way; the voice of one crying in the wilderness, 'Make ready the way of the Lord, make His paths straight'" (Mark 1:2–3; cf. Isa 40:3; Mal 3:1; 4:5, 6). God sent John the Baptist to be that messenger before Christ's first coming (Luke 3:4–6). In the future, He will again send a messenger before Christ returns to establish His kingdom.

God designed Nineveh's destruction to prefigure the culmination of His plan for redemptive history. When the Lord Jesus Christ returns, the desirable treasures of the nations will be given to Israel (Nah 2:9; cf. Hag 2:8), the world will be emptied so that God's glory will fill it (Nah 2:10; cf. Isa 6:3), the lions of the nations will be put down and the Lion of Judah will be exalted (Nah 2:11–12; Rev 5:5), and the messengers of this world will be silenced so that the only message proclaimed will be the good news of Jesus Christ. While Nineveh's desolation was grave, it previewed for Israel the Lord's ultimate victory over all His enemies, providing comfort that God can and will fulfill all His promises.

An Avenging Judgment

13

NAHUM 3:1–7

Woe to the city of bloodshed, completely full of deception *and* pillage;
***Her* prey never departs.**

The sound of the whip,
And the sound of the rumbling of the wheel,
Galloping horses,
And bounding chariots!

Horsemen charging,
And swords flaming, and spears flashing,
Many slain, a mass of corpses,
And there is no end to dead bodies—
They stumble over the dead bodies!

***All* because of the many harlotries of the harlot,**
The charming one, the mistress of sorceries,
Who sells nations by her harlotries
And families by her sorceries.

"Behold, I am against you," declares Yahweh of hosts;
"And I will uncover your skirts over your face
And show to the nations your nakedness
And to the kingdoms your disgrace.

I will throw detestable *filth* on you
And display you as a wicked fool
And set you up as a spectacle.

And it will be that all who see you
Will flee from you and say,
'Nineveh is devastated!
Who will console her?'
Where will I seek comforters for you?"

The righteousness of God demands perfect justice. For divine justice to be satisfied, all God's enemies must be punished. Those who love the Lord, celebrate His righteousness, and desire that He be glorified—they will rejoice when evil is judged and His impenitent enemies are justly punished. As the psalmist exclaimed:

> Let God arise, let His enemies be scattered, and let those who hate Him flee before Him. As smoke is driven away, *so* drive *them* away; as wax melts before the fire, *so* let the wicked perish before God. But let the righteous be glad; let them exult before God; and let them rejoice with gladness. (Ps 68:1–3)

The psalmist called on the Lord to take action because He alone executes true justice (cf. 10:12). He causes the wicked to perish and the righteous to rejoice. This is not an indifferent attitude toward those who perish; it is the joy of the souls that love God and seek His glory. When God is dishonored, those who love Him feel the pain, as the psalmist said: "For zeal for Your house has consumed me, and the reproaches of those who reproach You have fallen on me" (69:9). The Apostle Paul applied this attitude to the Son of God, saying, "For even Christ did not please Himself; but as it is written, 'THE REPROACHES OF THOSE WHO REPROACHED YOU FELL ON ME'" (Rom 15:3). Paul then conveyed the truth of God's righteous judgment in 2 Thessalonians 1:5–7, when he wrote:

> *This is* a plain indication of God's righteous judgment so that you will be considered worthy of the kingdom of God, for which indeed you are suffering. Since it is right for God to repay with affliction those who afflict you, and *to give* rest to you who are afflicted and to us as well at the revelation of the Lord Jesus from heaven with His mighty angels in flaming fire.

The apostle assured the Thessalonians that the Lord Jesus will return to judge the wicked, and to establish His righteous kingdom. During His millennial reign, He will enact His rule with perfect justice over the whole earth (cf. Isa 9:7).

But Scripture is also clear that until His earthly kingdom is established, justice is perverted. David expressed that reality when he cried out, "How long, O Yahweh? Will You forget me forever? How long will You hide Your face from me? How long shall I take counsel in my soul, *having* sorrow in my heart all the day? How long will my enemy be exalted over me?" (Pss 13:1–2; 10:1; Jer 12:1). When justice is delayed, distress abounds in the hearts of the righteous (cf. Prov 28:12). Job expressed a similar concern, observing that the wicked are not always punished in this life. He lamented: "How often is the lamp of the wicked put out, or does their disaster fall on them?" (Job 21:17; cf. 20:28–29; 21:1–16). In Revelation, when the martyred saints in heaven observe the injustice against the righteous on earth, they cry out to God, "How long, O Master, holy and true? Will You not judge and avenge our blood on those who dwell on the earth?" (Rev 6:10). In response to this plea, "it was told to them that they should rest for a little while longer, until *the number of* their fellow slaves and their brothers who were to be killed even as they had been, would be completed also" (6:11). While justice in the hands of sinners is not guaranteed in this life, God has promised to render righteous and impartial judgment to every person in the life to come (cf. Heb 9:27).

Though the wicked seem to prosper for a little while, the Lord will not let their injustice go unpunished (cf. Exod 34:7). The book of Nahum serves as a vivid illustration of that reality. Nahum's prophecy concerned a nation that had long prospered while exacting violence, immorality, and idolatry. But at the appointed time, according to God's sovereign plan, the Lord would unleash His wrath on Assyria for its gross unrighteousness. In describing the coming fall of Nineveh, Nahum explained that this vile city and the empire it represented would be punished in proportion to its wickedness. But as discussed previously, Nahum delivered a near prophecy that, being perfectly fulfilled, proved the reliability of every divine promise, including those regarding the end of the age. By judging Nineveh, God gave His people a glimpse of what He will one day do to all who oppose Him.

In this passage (Nah 3:1–7), Nahum declared that God would bring Nineveh to justice on account of the city's savage brutality (vv. 1–3) and spiritual harlotry (vv. 4–7). Nineveh would be an object lesson for every other nation throughout subsequent history. While justice may seem to be delayed from a human standpoint, God has not forgotten. In His perfect time, He will ensure that pure justice is meted out, resulting in the condemnation of the wicked and the comfort of the righteous.

Vengeance for Savage Brutality

Woe to the city of bloodshed, completely full of deception *and* pillage;
***Her* prey never departs.**

The sound of the whip,
And the sound of the rumbling of the wheel,
Galloping horses,
And bounding chariots!

Horsemen charging,
And swords flaming, and spears flashing,
Many slain, a mass of corpses,
And there is no end to dead bodies—
They stumble over the dead bodies! (3:1–3)

With a cry of lament, **"Woe,"** Nahum signals God's vengeance upon Nineveh. The term expresses the emotion of intense disapproval and condemnation. Nineveh, as a **city of bloodshed,** had become an object of the wrath of God. The Hebrew word for **bloodshed,** occurring first in the context of Abel's murder (cf. Gen 4:10), was a euphemism for vicious murder and violent death. Nineveh was characterized by savage brutality, as illustrated by the words of one of its kings, Shalmaneser III:

> I slew their warriors with the sword, descending upon them like Adad when he makes a rainstorm pour down. In the moat (of the town) I piled them up, I covered the wide plain with the corpses of their fighting men, I dyed the mountains with their blood like red wool. I took away from him many chariots (and) horses broken to the yoke. I erected pillars of skulls in front of his town, destroyed his (other) towns, tore down (their walls) and burnt (them) down.[1]

Nahum continued by noting that Nineveh was **completely full of deception and pillage. Deception** fundamentally means "empty" (cf. Job 16:8), describing Nineveh's political trickery as they made deceitful promises to achieve political objectives (cf. 2 Kgs 18:31–32). After deceiving other nations through treachery, the Ninevites would **pillage** their lands, stripping

1 Pritchard, ed., *The Ancient Near Eastern Texts Relating to the Old Testament*, 277; Barker, *Micah, Nahum, Habakkuk, Zephaniah*, 220.

away property and resources by violence. When Nineveh conquered other nations, they looted homes, storehouses, treasuries, palaces, and every kind of depository, plundering everything of value.

Every level of Ninevite society celebrated its culture of cruelty and covetousness, so that the city was **completely full** of such depravity. Because Assyria captured city after city, the supply of riches and resources was seemingly endless. Thus, Nahum observed of Nineveh that **her prey never departs.** With the word **prey,** used earlier to describe Assyria's enemies (cf. Nah 2:12), Nahum once again employed animal imagery to convey the relentless brutality of Assyria's military tactics (cf. Num 23:24; Isa 5:29). For Nineveh, violence and indulgence were a way of life.

But God would hold the city accountable for its sins. Nineveh would be overcome with **the sound of the whip, and the sound of the rumbling of the wheel, galloping horses, and bounding chariots!** The city that once cruelly whipped and enslaved its captives would itself be filled with **the sound of the whip** as Assyrian riders would drive their horses to meet the enemy. The city whose chariots once intimidated other nations would now reverberate with **the sound of the rumbling of the wheel** as its chariots desperately raced into the battle (cf. Nah 2:4). The city whose cavalry had previously overrun opposing armies would hear the clamor of **galloping horses** and **bounding chariots** frantically rushing through the streets. The **sound** that once struck fear in the hearts of Nineveh's foes would become the **sound** of Nineveh's own destruction. With such resounding reversals, God would inflict judgment on Assyria for its atrocities.

Nahum moved from describing the vivid sounds of the battle to depicting the violent scene. The epic conflict would include **horsemen charging, and swords flaming, and spears flashing.** As the future battle is described, the **horsemen** and charioteers of Assyria's cavalry would begin **charging** the enemy, in an effort to defend the city. Their unsheathed **swords** would be **flaming** in the sun and their **spears flashing** like bolts of lightning as they would thunder to meet their attackers. The imagery was fearsome yet familiar to Nahum's audience, since Assyria had engaged in many such military operations. But this time would be different. The Assyrians would no longer be on the offensive. They would find themselves in a desperate struggle to defend their capital city and the heart of their empire.

Nineveh would suffer an outcome that, for them, was both unfamiliar and unthinkable—catastrophic defeat. The prophecy given to Nahum painted a shocking scene of **many slain, a mass of corpses, and there is no end to dead bodies—they stumble over the dead bodies!** The Assyrians would be severely defeated, resulting in **many** of their soldiers being **slain.** Just as Nineveh had often stacked the lifeless bodies of their defeated foes, so **a mass of** their own **corpses** would fill the city (cf. Gen 15:11; Num 14:32–33). **There** would seemingly be **no end to** the **dead bodies** strewn as far as the eye could see. The carnage would be so extensive that those who survive and seek to flee would **stumble over the dead bodies.** Nahum's repetition of **dead bodies** served to amplify the gruesome image of layered corpses. While Nineveh's military at first "stumbled" in their eager rush to defend the city (cf. Nah 2:5), in the end, they would **stumble** in their efforts to flee from it. At that time, the Ninevites would become like the nations they previously conquered and terrorized. Through this dramatic reversal, the Lord would avenge His people for the violence Assyria had committed against them.

Vengeance for Spiritual Harlotry

***All* because of the many harlotries of the harlot,**
The charming one, the mistress of sorceries,
Who sells nations by her harlotries
And families by her sorceries.

"Behold, I am against you," declares Yahweh of hosts;
"And I will uncover your skirts over your face
And show to the nations your nakedness
And to the kingdoms your disgrace.

I will throw detestable *filth* on you
And display you as a wicked fool
And set you up as a spectacle.

And it will be that all who see you
Will flee from you and say,
'Nineveh is devastated!
Who will console her?'
Where will I seek comforters for you?" (3:4–7)

Of the many atrocities Nineveh committed, Nahum identified the particular evil that primarily incited God's wrath: **"*All* because of the many harlotries of the harlot."** While harlotry can refer to sexual immorality, it was often used in the Old Testament as a metaphor for the spiritual adultery of false religion and idol worship (cf. Hos 1–3; Ezek 16; 23). In this context, spiritual harlotry is in view since the remainder of the verse parallels **harlotries** with **sorceries,** indicating that the focus of this condemnation relates to idolatry and pagan worship. In 2 Kings 9, a similar parallel between "harlotries" and "sorceries" appears in reference to Jezebel, the wicked queen who seduced Israel to follow Baal (2 Kgs 9:22). In a similar way, Assyria seduced many nations to embrace their false gods and to engage in despicable acts of pagan worship. Even the southern kingdom of Judah fell prey to this spiritual harlotry, as King Ahaz gave up the treasures of the temple of Yahweh in Jerusalem to the king of Assyria. Ahaz then installed a replica of the Assyrian altar in the temple court and led the people of Judah into false religion (2 Kgs 16:7–18; cf. Isa 7–8). As the example of Ahaz illustrates, Assyria used its influence to promote spiritual apostasy and pagan worship (cf. 2 Kgs 21). That God singled out spiritual harlotry as Assyria's most grave offense against Him accentuates His hatred for all idolatry (cf. Exod 20:2–5; Jer 16:18).

Nahum then described Nineveh as **the charming one,** a reference to Assyria's refined craft of spiritual seduction by which the empire lured its subjects and vassal states into false religion. In doing this, Assyria became guilty of the weightiest crime against God (cf. Deut 13:1–3; Matt 18:6; Mark 9:42; 1 Cor 8:9). Nahum further depicted Nineveh as **the mistress of sorceries.** The term **sorceries,** though not frequent in Hebrew, has the idea of practicing magic. Its Greek translation in the Septuagint is the term *pharmakos,* from which the English word "pharmacy" is derived. The Assyrian use of magic likely involved hallucinogenic compounds and intoxicating drugs designed to facilitate ecstatic and grotesque expressions of idolatrous worship. By designating Nineveh as a **mistress,** Nahum portrayed the city as both a seducer and a subjugator, using her wiles to entice and enslave her victims to the Assyrian religion.[2]

The results of such spiritual harlotry were abominable. As Nahum declared, Nineveh **"sells nations by her harlotries and families by her sorceries."** The prophet likened the city to a **harlot** marketing her services for financial gain. In this case, however, Assyria seduced other **nations** into spiritual bondage so that she might reap the economic and political benefits. Enslaving cities and nations by **her sorceries,** Assyria conquered these lands and destroyed **families,** selling men, women, and children into slavery. The Ninevites also used their captives to build structures dedicated to Assyria's gods.[3] This program of exile and enslavement not only coerced many to worship the pagan deities of Assyria but also contributed to the wealth and prosperity of the Assyrian empire (cf. Isa 49:25; Nah 3:10). As noted above, when Ahaz turned to Assyria for political support, he demonstrated his loyalty by installing an Assyrian altar in

2 Timmer, *Nahum*, 154.

3 Renz, *The Books of Nahum, Habakkuk, and Zephaniah*, 160.

the temple court (2 Kgs 16; cf. Isa 7–8). When Rabshakeh later came with the Assyrian army to capture Jerusalem, he attempted to lure the Judeans away from trusting Yahweh and instead to follow the king of Nineveh (2 Kgs 18:22–25, 30–35; 19:4–6, 10–13, 36–37; Isa 36:7–8, 14–21). As a harlot entices a man and leads him off like an ox to the slaughter (cf. Prov 7:21–22), so the Assyrians brought nations to destruction through their campaign of exile, enslavement, and idolatry (cf. 2 Chr 32:9–19).

In response to Assyria's iniquity, Nahum pronounced God's words: **"Behold, I am against you," declares Yahweh of hosts.** The Lord declared those same harrowing words earlier in Nahum 2:13, claiming divine responsibility for Nineveh's destruction. In this instance, God emphasized that He would judge the Ninevites particularly for their vile spiritual abominations. The Lord expressed His personal opposition to Nineveh (**Behold, I am against you**), His fixed decree (**declares**), and His power to execute judgment (**Yahweh of hosts**). This divine declaration against Nineveh displayed the Lord's fervent disdain for idolatry and His fixed determination to punish those who engaged in it.

God promised to judge Nineveh in three ways. First, He would humiliate the pride of Assyria. Yahweh declared, **"I will uncover your skirts over your face and show to the nations your nakedness and to the kingdoms your disgrace."** Such a graphic act of shameful degradation and public humiliation illustrated the way God would expose Nineveh as a whore before the watching world. The Lord's judgment would **uncover** the city's corruption and weakness, thereby showing **to the nations your nakedness** and bringing perpetual shame on it (cf. Gen 3:7–10, 21; 9:20–25). With dead bodies (cf. Nah 3:3) and burning chariots (cf. 2:13) strewn about, the formerly formidable capital, and the empire it represented, would be seen as pitiful and pathetic. As God would bring Nineveh low, He would display **to the kingdoms your disgrace.** The root of the word **disgrace** literally means to be made small and often refers to being cursed and reviled (cf. Deut 21:22–23; Hos 4:7; Hab 2:16). The surrounding **kingdoms** would be shocked and revolted to see Nineveh's shame. With comprehensive divine judgment, the city that had been great in Jonah's day (cf. Jonah 1:2; 3:2) would become greatly disgraced.

Second, Nineveh would serve as an object lesson on the futility of idolatry. God declared to the nation, **"I will throw detestable *filth* on you."** While **detestable *filth*** certainly relates to the physical ruin of the defeated city, the word primarily conveys the despicable nature of idolatry (Deut 29:17; 1 Kgs 11:5, 7; 2 Kgs 23:13, 24; Isa 66:3; Jer 4:1). In using this particular expression, God indicated He was condemning the spiritual filth of the city's false religion. Formerly, the nations may have found Nineveh's gods, pagan rituals, and religious alliances to be alluring and desirable. But the city's ruin and squalor would demonstrate that its deities were impotent and its idolatry as repugnant as excrement (cf. Phil 3:8). Nineveh's demise would punctuate the point that destruction, not delight, is the true end of false religion (cf. Prov 16:25; Ezek 32:16–32; Rom 6:23; Rev 18:1–24).

The Lord would use Nineveh to demonstrate that idolatry is not only filthy (cf. Ezek 16:16–34; Hos 8–9) but also foolish, as He declared He would **"display you** [Nineveh] **as a wicked fool."** In Scripture, the **wicked fool** is the worst of all fools, the apostate who rejects God and makes reprehensible and destructive choices in accordance with his wicked character (cf. Ps 14:1; 53:1). Nabal, whose name means **wicked fool,** was the embodiment of such irrationality, dying of shock upon being informed of the recklessness of his actions (cf. 1 Sam 25:10–38). Nineveh acted in folly as it placed its hope in idolatrous worship (cf. 2 Kgs 19:37), military might (cf. 2 Kgs 18:28–35; 19:11–13; 2 Chr 32:13–19), and national prosperity (cf. 2 Kgs 18:31–32; Nah 2:8). God exposed this folly, desecrating Nineveh's idolatrous worship (Nah 1:14; 3:6), devastating its military force (1:12–13; 2:13), and deploying its rivers to decimate its defenses (cf. 1:8; 2:6). Idolatry may promise insight and sophistication but in reality leaves one completely unfit (cf. Isa 44:9–20; Rom 1:28). God would **set** Nineveh **up as a spectacle** of devastation and disgrace, literally in Hebrew as "something to see," so that the city would become a permanent reminder of the catastrophic consequences of rejecting the true God for false deities.

Third, the city would serve as an historic object lesson of the vengeance of the Almighty. Describing the outcome of His judgment, the Lord proclaimed, **"And it will be that all who see you will flee from you." Flee** conveys the act of frantically trying to escape from danger (cf. Gen 31:40; Esth 6:1). Though Nineveh was once an oasis in the desert to which travelers came (see discussion on Nah 2:8), it would become a place that people purposely avoided, being horrified by the aftermath of God's judgment. Those who bypassed the city would **say** in astonishment, **"Nineveh is devastated!"** recognizing its irrevocable ruin (cf. Isa 23:14). Reflecting on the severity of God's judgment, the onlookers would ask, **"Who will console her?" Console** carries the idea of shaking one's head out of sympathy or empathy. The question being asked is rhetorical. No one would come alongside Nineveh to soothe its anguish for fear that divine judgment would fall on them also. Emphasizing the city's devastation, the Lord Himself added: **"Where will I seek comforters for you?"** Nineveh's abandonment would be so comprehensive that not even God would seek a comforter for the ruined city. **Comforters** in Hebrew comes from *naham,* the same root of the prophet's name *Nahum*. If the only comforter God could send to Nineveh was the prophet Nahum, the one who delivered this message of Nineveh's devastation, then any hope of comfort for the city was certainly lost. No one would comfort the doomed city after God's judgment fell.

On the other hand, *naham* also appears in Isaiah 40:1, in which God said concerning Israel, "Comfort, O comfort My people." In keeping with other portions of Nahum's prophecy, this near prophecy about the destruction of Nineveh guarantees that the more distant prophecies will also be fulfilled with equal precision (see discussion on Nah 1:14–15; cf. Isa 52:7). The Lord demonstrated through Nineveh that while the wicked will ultimately have no comfort, He will provide comfort for His people. Moreover, while the destruction of Nineveh would bring temporary comfort to Israel, Isaiah prophesied of the everlasting comfort that includes the forgiveness of sins and restoration of all things in Christ (Isa 40–53). As the Israelites would behold the fulfillment of Nahum's prophecy, they would know that God is faithful both to avenge and to comfort His people.

A Certain Judgment

14

NAHUM 3:8–19

Are you better than No-amon,
Which sits along the waters of the Nile,
With water surrounding her,
Whose rampart *was* the sea,
Whose wall *consisted* of the sea?

Ethiopia was *her* might,
And Egypt too, without end.
Put and Lubim were among her helpers.

Yet she became an exile;
She went into captivity;
Also her infants were dashed to pieces
At the head of every street;
They cast lots for her honorable men,
And all her great men were bound with fetters.

You too will become drunk;
You will be hidden.
You too will search for a strong defense from the enemy.

All your fortifications are fig trees with ripe fruit—
When shaken, they fall into the eater's mouth.

Behold, your people are women in your midst!
The gates of your land are opened wide to your enemies;
Fire consumes your gate bars.

Draw for yourself water for the siege!
Strengthen your fortifications!
Go into the clay and tread the mortar!
Take hold of the brick mold!

There, fire will consume you;
The sword will cut you down;
It will consume you as the locust *does*.
Multiply yourself like the creeping locust,
Multiply yourself like the swarming locust.

You have increased your traders more than the stars of heaven—
The creeping locust strips and flies away.

Your guardsmen are like the swarming locust.
Your marshals are like a locust-swarm
Encamping in the stone walls on a cold day.
The sun rises, and they flee,
And the place where they are is not known.

Your shepherds are sleeping, O king of Assyria;
Your mighty ones are lying down.
Your people are scattered on the mountains,
And there is no one to regather *them*.

There is no relief for your breakdown,
Your wound is incurable.
All who hear the report about you

Will clap *their* hands over you,
For on whom has not your evil passed continually?

The wicked assume they will never face God's judgment. Describing the mindset of such a person, the psalmist wrote, "He says in his heart, 'God has forgotten; He has hidden His face; He will never see it'" (Ps 10:11). The unbelieving fool thinks he can avoid divine accountability, saying to God, "You will not require *it*" (10:13). Those who practice evil also insist that the Lord will never return to this world in judgment, stating, "Where is the promise of His coming? For since the fathers fell asleep, all continues just as it was from the beginning of creation" (2 Pet 3:4; cf. Isa 5:19). But as Peter explained, while God may delay His wrath in keeping with His patience, the full fury of His judgment will certainly come. When it does, the result will be the "destruction of ungodly men" (2 Pet 3:7). Though the wicked mock the Lord in their unbelief, they will ultimately be put to everlasting shame (cf. Ps 2:4).

In pronouncing the prophecy of Nineveh's destruction, Nahum confronted the arrogant presumption of an empire that denied the reality of divine judgment. The Assyrians believed they were immune to the wrath of God. But Nahum declared that their judgment was inevitable (Nah 3:8–13), inescapable (3:14–17), and irreversible (3:18–19). To prove this point, the prophet pointed to the then recent destruction of Thebes, a city much like Nineveh. If God could destroy Thebes, He could also destroy the capital of Assyria. Though Nahum's prophecy against Nineveh was fulfilled many centuries ago, it serves as a timeless reminder that no unrepentant sinner is exempt from the holy judgment of God.

Inevitable Judgment

Are you better than No-amon,
Which sits along the waters of the Nile,
With water surrounding her,
Whose rampart *was* the sea,
Whose wall *consisted* of the sea?

Ethiopia was *her* might,
And Egypt too, without end.
Put and Lubim were among her helpers.

Yet she became an exile;
She went into captivity;
Also her infants were dashed to pieces
At the head of every street;
They cast lots for her honorable men,
And all her great men were bound with fetters.

You too will become drunk;
You will be hidden.
You too will search for a strong defense from the enemy.

All your fortifications are fig trees with ripe fruit—
When shaken, they fall into the eater's mouth.

Behold, your people are women in your midst!
The gates of your land are opened wide to your enemies;
Fire consumes your gate bars. (3:8–13)

The opening words **"Are you better than"** set the tone for God's rebuke of Nineveh in this final section of Nahum's prophecy. The question emphasized that despite Assyria's arrogance, its capital city would not escape God's judgment. In its pride, Assyria even considered itself to be like God. As Zephaniah declared: "This is the exultant city which inhabits securely, who says in her heart, 'I am, and there is no one besides me'" (Zeph 2:15; cf. Isa 14:13–14; 45:5–6; Ezek 28:2, 6). The Ninevites never imagined that they would be the objects of God's wrath. They saw themselves as supreme and invincible. But they were profoundly mistaken.

To expose the folly of their overconfidence, Nahum referred to the city of **No-amon,** which translated means "the city of Amon" (the chief god of Egypt).[1] This town, which is modern-day Thebes, was destroyed by the Assyrians in 663 BC (see "Date" in the Introduction). Describing his victory over Thebes, the Assyrian king Ashurbanipal wrote:

> Upon a trust (-inspiring) oracle of Ashur and Ishtar, I, myself, conquered this town completely. From Thebes [I] carried away booty, heavy and beyond counting: silver, gold, precious stones, his entire personal possessions, linen garments with multicolored trimmings, fine horses, (certain) inhabitants, male and female. I pulled two high obelisks, cast of shining *zaḫalû*-bronze, the weight of which was 2,500 talents, standing at the door of the temple, out of their bases and took (them) to Assyria. (Thus) I carried off from Thebes heavy booty, beyond counting. I made Egypt (*Muṣur*) and Nubia feel my weapons bitterly and celebrated my triumph. With full hands and safely, I returned to Nineveh, the city (where I exercise) my rule.[2]

Since this conquest had been recent to Nahum's generation, the Ninevites would have readily remembered the destruction of No-amon, especially because the parallels between No-amon and Nineveh were striking. The two cities were both situated near rivers. No-amon sat **along the waters of the Nile,** just like Nineveh was surrounded by three rivers (the Tigris, Khosr, and Tebiltu). As Nineveh's rivers brought the city prosperity, so the **waters of the Nile,** including the network of waterways that

1 Theodore J. Lewis, "Amon (Deity)," *The Anchor Yale Bible Dictionary* (New York: Doubleday, 1992), 1:197.

2 Pritchard, ed., *The Ancient Near Eastern Texts Relating to the Old Testament*, 295.

branched out from the Nile, brought wealth to Thebes. Being in a prime location, Thebes, like Nineveh, was its nation's capital, containing key monuments of Egypt's grandeur and housing the royal family.[3] The city had numerous temples, streets lined with sphinxes, and even one hundred gates.[4] The military successes of their armies gave both Nineveh and Thebes great renown.

Thebes also boasted of the protection provided by the **water surrounding her.** Like Nineveh, the waters around No-amon acted as a natural moat, keeping potential enemies at a distance. Thebes also had a **rampart** which ***was* the sea** itself. The **rampart** is the most outward fortification or defensive structure of a city. For Thebes, the **sea** provided a formidable buttress, since the Mediterranean and the Nile delta formed a natural obstacle against foreign invaders. These bodies of water, which were north of Thebes, were such an effective protection that Nahum declared that No-amon's **wall *consisted* of the sea.** To bring troops, war machines, and weapons against Thebes through such waters presented an immense challenge for any invading force.

Thebes also had additional protection through political alliances, in that **Ethiopia was *her* might.** Around the time of Nahum, **Ethiopia,** a Cushite dynasty, was the dominant power in the region, ruling even over Egypt. Ethiopia's strength provided security for Thebes on its southern and southeastern sides.[5] On the northern flank of No-amon, **Egypt** was their defense **without end.** Though Egypt was not as strong at that time as it had been in prior generations, it was still a constant thorn in Assyria's side, putting up resistance seemingly **without end** (cf. 2 Kgs 18:21, 24). Rounding out No-amon's protection to the west and southwest, **Put and Lubim were among her helpers. Put** referred to the country of Libya which is west and southwest of Egypt (cf. Jer 46:9; Ezek 30:5). The term **Lubim,** infrequent in the

3 See Donald B. Redford, "Thebes (Place)," *The Anchor Yale Bible Dictionary* (New York: Doubleday, 1992), 6:443; Lewis, "Amon (Deity)," 1:197–98.

4 Robertson, *The Books of Nahum, Habakkuk and Zephaniah*, 113; Redford, "Thebes," 6:443.

5 Renz, *The Books of Nahum, Habakkuk, and Zephaniah*, 170.

Old Testament, described the Lybians of North Africa including the military forces of Put (cf. 2 Chr 12:3; 16:8). Like Nineveh, No-amon enjoyed economic prominence, physical protection, and political support.

Though Thebes had these formidable advantages, **yet she became an exile** and **went into captivity** as her citizens were defeated and became prisoners of war (cf. Exod 12:29; Num 31:26; Isa 20:4). If the Ninevites thought their city was indestructible (cf. Nah 2:7, 11; 3:5), they would have done well to remember what happened to No-amon, a city much like their own.

Nahum then recounted the details of Thebes' destruction, beginning with the Assyrian attack on the most vulnerable. The prophet explained that **her infants were dashed to pieces at the head of every street.** This brutal act of violence against **infants** was a horrifying form of cruelty. That such atrocities occurred **at the head of every street,** the main public junctures of the city, reveals the savage extent of Assyria's war crimes. Nahum continued by describing the cruelty against the most honorable. The Assyrians **cast lots** for the **honorable men and** all the **great men were bound with fetters.** The most respected and **honorable men** of the city were shamefully mistreated as the Assyrians **cast lots** for them, treating them like property or cattle. The **great men,** or members of the ruling class, also **were bound with fetters** to be led away as prisoners of war and slaves.

With the words **you too,** Nahum moved from discussing Thebes to confronting Nineveh directly. Just as No-amon was toppled, God promised that Nineveh **too will become drunk** and incapacitated, unable to defend itself from its assailants (cf. Isa 29:9; Zech 12:2). Though the Ninevites thought they could avoid God's wrath, having previously experienced His mercy (cf. Jonah 3:9–10), the Lord assured them they would become like Thebes. Nineveh would **be hidden** as divine wrath would obliterate the city, causing the people to **search for a strong defense** as they would flee **from the enemy.** If the Ninevites thought such judgment impossible, Yahweh assured them that what He did to

Thebes, He would do to them **too**. Indeed, the massacre that took place at Thebes in 663 BC paralleled the slaughter that occurred at Nineveh in 612 BC. These ancient cities both serve as memorials to the certainty and severity of God's judgment on the wicked.

From God's perspective, Nineveh's defenses were feeble and useless. The Lord declared, **"All your fortifications are fig trees with ripe fruit."** God compared Nineveh's outer wall and perimeter defenses to a grove of **trees** full of delectable fruit (cf. Isa 28:4; Mic 7:1). Instead of repelling the enemy, God ordained that Nineveh—like a fruit tree—would entice enemies to desire the city as a prize worth taking. Moreover, Nineveh's foes would conquer it with ease, like gathering figs from a tree that **when shaken, they fall into the eater's mouth.** The Babylonians would only have to give the city a little shake, as small as nodding the head (cf. 2 Kgs 19:21; Ps 22:7), and Assyria's capital would collapse.

Describing the helpless state of Nineveh's citizens, God declared, **"Behold, your people are women in your midst!"** Nineveh considered itself to be valiant (Nah 2:3), mighty (2:5), and even like a lion (2:11). But the Lord assessed the Ninevite people as being like **women.** In ancient Near Eastern culture, women generally lacked fighting ability (cf. Jer 50:37; 51:30), dominant physical strength (cf. Isa 19:16), and leadership training (cf. Isa 3:12). The weak and cowardly citizens of Nineveh would succumb fully to their enemies when **"the gates of your land are opened wide to your enemies."** Not only would the gates be **opened** but they would be **opened wide,** giving Nineveh's **enemies** full access to the city. Having entered with force, the Babylonians would set fire to the city so that the **fire consumes your gate bars,** destroying the beams used to seal and secure the gates (cf. 2 Chr 14:7; Neh 3:14, 15). Once the gates were destroyed, stopping the invasion was no longer possible.

The reference to Thebes set a historical precedent for God's judgment of Nineveh. Because it was fresh on his mind, Nahum likely proclaimed his prophecy shortly after Thebes fell (see "Date" in the Introduction).[6] Thebes was conquered around 663 BC, but partially rebuilt around 654 BC. It is likely that Nahum prophesied between those two dates, since the image he painted of Thebes was that of a city still in ruins.[7] At this time, approximately forty years prior to the destruction of Nineveh (in 612 BC), Assyria was still a prominent power.[8] By predicting Nineveh's fall decades before it took place, Nahum's prophecy testifies both to God's perfect knowledge of the future and His inexorable judgment on the wicked.

Inescapable Judgment

Draw for yourself water for the siege!
Strengthen your fortifications!
Go into the clay and tread the mortar!
Take hold of the brick mold!

There, fire will consume you;
The sword will cut you down;
It will consume you as the locust *does.*
Multiply yourself like the creeping locust,
Multiply yourself like the swarming locust.

You have increased your traders more than the stars of heaven—
The creeping locust strips and flies away.

Your guardsmen are like the swarming locust.
Your marshals are like a locust-swarm
Encamping in the stone walls on a cold day.
The sun rises, and they flee,
And the place where they are is not known. (3:14–17)

6 See Timmer, *Nahum*, 33; Barker, *Micah, Nahum, Habakkuk, Zephaniah*, 137–38; Robertson, *The Books of Nahum, Habakkuk and Zephaniah*, 31.

7 See Timmer, *Nahum*, 34, n. 2; Spronk, *Nahum*, 13; Smith, *Micah–Malachi*, 66.

8 Barker, *Micah, Nahum, Habakkuk, Zephaniah*, 137–38.

Nahum's prophecy then emphasized that no amount of preparation would spare the city from God's judgment. While the Ninevites would make every effort to prepare for battle, they would be destroyed. Conveying this rhetorically, Nahum taunted the people to **draw for** themselves **water for the siege,** storing up a supply in case their access to water was cut off by the enemy (cf. 2 Kgs 20:20; 2 Chr 32:30). They were also to **strengthen** their **fortifications** by reinforcing the outermost walls. To do this, the prophet directed them to **go into the clay,** or the clay pits, to acquire the materials to make bricks. They were then to **tread the mortar** to create grout for binding bricks together. Nahum also told them to **take hold of the brick mold** to shape the bricks into the proper size. With clay bricks and mortar, they could build fortifications and reinforce their armaments. The Hebrew word for **take hold** shares the same root with **strengthen,** reinforcing Nahum's taunting call to the Ninevites to do all they can to defend themselves. But the prophet's message was clear: no matter how masterfully they buttressed their defenses, defeat was inescapable. Their efforts would fail, as any attempt to resist the decree of God fails (Nah 1:9, 14–15; 2:6–7; 3:15; cf. Isa 47:12–15).

Nahum proceeded to declare that the very places where Nineveh reinforced their fortifications, prepared their defenses, and drew water, **there, fire will consume you. There,** the prophet declared, as if emphatically pointing to the places Nineveh thought would protect them; **there** would be the very places where the city's defenses would collapse. Nahum predicted that **fire will consume you** as flames engulfed the gates and outer walls while spreading to the inner city. Though Nahum had previously predicted that the city would be flooded by water (cf. Nah 2:6), here he also announced that it would be burned by fire.[9] Could both be true? Historical accounts record that the palaces of the city, including the palace of Sennacherib, were

9 Robertson, *The Books of Nahum, Habakkuk and Zephaniah*, 90, 124.

burned to the ground.[10] Historical accounts also indicate that Nineveh was flooded, and that "the king, recognizing in this the fulfilment of the oracle, gathered together his concubines and eunuchs, and, mounting a funeral pyre which he had caused to be constructed, perished in the flames."[11] Despite the incompatibility of fire and water, God's Word was fulfilled and His prophecy confirmed as Nineveh fell both by flood and by flame.

With their defenses destroyed, the Ninevites would be slaughtered as **the sword will cut you down. Cut down** referred not simply to being killed but to being slaughtered in a shameful execution (Lev 17:10; 26:22; Deut 12:29; Josh 7:9; Jer 44:7). The devastation would be so comprehensive that Nahum compared it to a locust plague. He exclaimed that the fire and the sword **will consume you as the locust *does*.** Locust plagues were common in ancient times and devoured all vegetation, leaving the land utterly barren (cf. Joel 1:4; 2:25; Amos 4:9; 7:1). Even to this day, world governments spend massive sums per year to combat locust infestations, which can decimate food supplies in places like Africa, Arabia, and India. Nahum's prediction was that after flood, fire, and foe ravaged Nineveh, the city would be left as a desolate wasteland.

Having compared their enemies to locusts, Nahum then applied that analogy to the Ninevites. He sarcastically urged Nineveh to **multiply yourself like the creeping locust** and **multiply yourself like the swarming locust.** While the **creeping locust** referred to the locust at its infant stage, the **swarming locust** marked the fully grown insect when it swarms together. The prophet again made it clear that no matter how much Nineveh multiplied its population or military forces, it would be no match for the enemy horde that was coming. Locust plagues can produce so many locusts that they obscure the sky when they swarm. If the Ninevites thought they were invincible because of the size of their city and its army, they had severely miscalculated.

10 Armerding, "Nahum," 599.

11 Pinches, "Nineveh," 4:2151.

The prophet acknowledged that Assyria had indeed amassed immense power throughout its history, observing that **you have increased your traders more than the stars of heaven.** One way Nineveh multiplied its might was by increasing its economic resources. Traders engaged in international commerce, bringing back wares from across the known world (cf. 1 Kgs 10:15; Ezek 17:4; 27:3). Such business allowed Nineveh to acquire the best military hardware, operate as the global center of finance, and become seemingly too mighty to fail. Being more numerous than **the stars of heaven,** an obvious hyperbole to emphasize the size of the Assyrian economy, Nineveh's traders acquired countless riches. They carried out their business, Nahum noted, as **the creeping locust** that **strips and flies away.** The word **strips** can denote ripping a tunic off of a person (cf. Gen 37:23), skinning an animal (cf. Lev 1:6), or removing all the valuables from those slain in battle (cf. 1 Sam 31:8–9). Like a locust devouring every grain of vegetation from the land, so these traders appropriated every treasure from the peoples and places conquered by Assyria.

Moving from economic prosperity to military power, Nahum observed that **your** [Nineveh's] **guardsmen are like the swarming locust. Guardsmen** likely refers to the royal bodyguard **swarming** around the king and other noblemen like the **locust** to shield them from assault. In addition to Nineveh's guardsmen, Nahum also addressed **your marshals** who **are like a locust swarm. Marshals** were field commanders (cf. Jer 51:27) who, like a **locust-swarm,** led their troops forward into battle to overwhelm the enemy (cf. Amos 7:1). Whether on defense or offense, Nineveh's military forces were as dense and devastating as hordes of locusts.

Nonetheless, Assyria's economic and military might would be useless in protecting its empire from God's judgment. Nahum described that initially Nineveh's forces would seem ready for battle like the locust **encamping in the stone walls on a cold day.** Like those destructive insects, dormant and assembled in dense masses, the Assyrian soldiers would camp inside the city's fortifications ready for battle (Nah 2:3–5). But once **the sun rises,** the locusts **flee;** so also, at the dawn of the battle, Ninevite readiness would dissipate. As the locusts feel the heat of the sun and fly far away so that **the place where they are is not known,** so Nineveh's soldiers would scatter and flee. Despite Assyria's economic and military dominance in prior centuries, its attempts to resist the judgment of God would be ineffective (cf. Job 18:5–10; 20:24; Isa 24:17–18; Jer 15:2–3; Amos 5:18–20).

In employing locusts to illustrate the devastation of war, Nahum alluded to the prophet Joel who vividly depicted a locust invasion (Joel 1) to describe God's eschatological judgment on Israel (Joel 2). However, Joel also prophesied that God will reverse that judgment so that those who afflict Israel will be afflicted in the same way (Joel 2:25; 3:1–21). By using such parallel imagery, Nahum indicated that his prediction concerning Nineveh was the near prophecy that guaranteed the fulfillment of Joel's end-time prophecy. The image of Nineveh being consumed by a locust-like army foreshadowed the comprehensive defeat of Israel's enemies at the end of the age (Nah 3:15). In this way, Nahum, a prophet of comfort, used the fall of Nineveh to comfort God's people.

Irreversible Judgment

Your shepherds are sleeping, O king of Assyria;
Your mighty ones are lying down.
Your people are scattered on the mountains,
And there is no one to regather *them.*

There is no relief for your breakdown,
Your wound is incurable.
All who hear the report about you
Will clap *their* hands over you,
For on whom has not your evil passed continually? (3:18–19)

As God concluded Nahum's prophecy, He directed his words to the **king of Assyria.** An earlier king of Assyria had been confronted by the prophet Jonah (cf. Jonah 3:6). But the message of Nahum was different than that of Jonah. While Jonah gave a warning of judgment, Nahum gave the verdict of judgment. God commissioned Nahum to declare that while He gives grace to the humble, He executes definitive judgment on the unrepentant (cf. Exod 34:7; Jas 4:6; 1 Pet 5:5). Because of Nineveh's refusal to turn from sin, the Lord determined to pour out His wrath on the city. Divine judgment could neither be halted nor avoided.

Having demonstrated that the city's defenses (Nah 3:8–14), economic resources (3:16), and military forces (3:17) could not withstand the enemy assault, Nahum declared Nineveh's leadership to be incapable of victory. Nahum proclaimed to the king that **your shepherds are sleeping. Shepherds** commonly refers to those who rule (cf. Num 27:17; 2 Sam 5:2; 7:7; 1 Kgs 22:17; Ezek 34:1–24; 37:24), since leaders must exercise constant vigilance in protecting and providing for their people, as a shepherd does for his flock (cf. Luke 2:8). But the **shepherds** of Nineveh had neglected these responsibilities. Instead of watching, they were **sleeping,** a euphemism for inactivity and a lack of alertness (cf. Isa 56:10). In their pride, Nineveh's leaders became complacent. Their lack of vigilance made them vulnerable. To make matters worse, the king's **mighty ones are lying down,** operating as if they were secure and without any need to be vigilant (cf. Deut 33:12, 28; Prov 1:33; Jer 23:6). In their overconfidence, these leaders were lethargic and apathetic. Such overconfidence would contribute to their downfall.

Due to this failure in leadership, Nineveh would fall and the people would flee. Nahum announced to the king that **your people** would be **scattered on the mountains** as they fled from the city (cf. Jer 50:11; Hab 1:8). They would be like sheep without a shepherd (cf. 1 Kgs 22:17). Nineveh's leadership failure would be total and irreparable as **there** would be **no one to regather *them*.** The foolish shepherds of Nineveh who would be sleeping would be killed and unable to gather their people again (cf. Isa 13:14; Ezek 34:5; Zech 10:2; Matt 9:36; Mark 6:34). Nahum's description of Nineveh's end, with its people in complete disarray, contrasts starkly with how history will end for Israel. Though God will scatter the enemies of His people (cf. Isa 13:14), He will regather Israel (Isa 56:8; Ezek 37:24; Mic 2:12; 4:6) and restore them under the care of the Good Shepherd, the Messiah (cf. Ps 23:1; Ezek 34:10–24; Rev 7:17).

After discussing Nineveh's shepherds, mighty ones, and lost sheep, Nahum proceeded to focus on the king himself. Depicting the king's death, the prophet wrote that **there is no relief for your breakdown. Breakdown** refers to broken bones (cf. Lev 21:19; 24:20) or, figuratively, to the collapse of an entire structure or system (cf. Isa 1:28; 60:19). The Assyrian king would suffer a torturous death when his capital city fell, with his bones crushed and **no relief** for his pain. Nahum further stated of the king that **your wound is incurable,** indicating that the king would incur a fatal injury (cf. 1 Kgs 22:34–35; Jer 10:19). This language not only predicted the ruler's agonizing demise but also underscored that he would suffer the way Israel had suffered under Assyria (cf. Jer 30:12, 15; Mic 1:9). The Lord would avenge His people, in that what the king did to Israel would be done to him.

With the death of the Assyrian king would come the death of the Assyrian empire. The surrounding nations, seeing Assyria fall, would rejoice: **"All who hear the report about you will clap *their* hands over you."** Instead of being mourned, the king of Nineveh would have no honor in his death. Those who hear of his demise would respond not in grief but with joy and celebration. This moment would be the culmination of Nineveh's destruction and shame. But it would also mark the turning of sorrow into joy for those who suffered under Assyrian oppression.

Nahum, whose name means comfort, demonstrated that God would bring His people consolation by judging Nineveh. Nahum's prophecy came to pass when the city fell in 612 BC. Just as the fulfillment of Nahum's prophecy demonstrated the trustworthiness of the more distant biblical prophecies (Nah 1:15; 2:9, 10; 3:17; cf. Isa 52:7; Joel 2:1–32; Hag 2:7–8), so also the joy depicted by Nahum prefigured the future celebration of Christ's victory over all His enemies (cf. Ps 110:1; Rom 16:20; 1 Cor 15:25–26). The only other passage that describes the clapping of hands using the same language as Nahum is Psalm 47, which declares that the world will clap its hands when Yahweh returns and subdues His adversaries (Ps 47:1–4). Thus, Nahum's prophecy not only pointed to comfort in the immediate term but also assured God's people of the ultimate comfort they will experience in the future.

Revealing the reason for the celebration over the death of Nineveh's king and Assyria's fall, the prophet concluded his book with a rhetorical question: **"For on whom has not your evil passed continually?"** People would rejoice at Nineveh's fall because it marked the end of an empire known for its flagrant wickedness. Assyria's atrocities were pure **evil** and they **passed through** the surrounding nations **continually** with violent destruction (cf. 2 Kgs 15:29; 17–19; 2 Chr 32; 33:11; Isa 10:5–14; 14:24–27). The victims of Assyria's brutality would respond to Nineveh's demise with exuberant joy.

This rhetorical question at the end of Nahum corresponds to the rhetorical question at the end of Jonah, the only other biblical book that ends with a question. In Jonah, God asked if He should not have pity upon Nineveh (Jonah 4:11). In Nahum, God asked if people should not rejoice over the destruction of Nineveh. Such a stark contrast illustrates the point that sinners must not presume upon God's grace. While the Lord was ready to show mercy to a people who repented, He was equally ready to render judgment against those who remained impenitent in their sin. As Nineveh was flooded and burned, its people exiled and its king humiliated, the message of Nahum reminded his readers to remember both God's grace and His justice. In Jonah's generation, the Ninevites turned to the Lord and received His kindness and mercy. But in Nahum's generation, they reveled in their sin, refused to repent, and received His wrath. As the author of Hebrews warned, "See to it that you do not refuse Him who is speaking. For if those did not escape when they refused him who warned *them* on earth, much less *will* we *escape* who turn away from Him who *warns* from heaven" (Heb 12:25). Only those who turn away from sin and turn to the Lord in faith will escape His eternal wrath (Rom 10:9–13). Only then will they have true comfort, both in this life and the life to come.

Bibliography

Alexander, T. Desmond. "Jonah: An Introduction and Commentary." In *Obadiah, Jonah, Micah.* Edited by D. J. Wiseman. Tyndale Old Testament Commentaries. Downers Grove, IL: InterVarsity, 1988.

Allen, Leslie C. *The Books of Joel, Obadiah, Jonah and Micah.* New International Commentary on the Old Testament. Grand Rapids: Eerdmans, 1976.

Armerding, Carl E. "Nahum." In *The Expositor's Bible Commentary: Daniel–Malachi.* Revised edition. Volume 8. Edited by Tremper Longman III and David E. Garland. Grand Rapids: Zondervan, 2008.

Barker, Kenneth and Waylon Bailey. *Micah, Nahum, Habakkuk, Zephaniah.* New American Commentary. Nashville: Broadman & Holman, 1998.

Baker, David W. *Nahum, Habakkuk, and Zephaniah: An Introduction and Commentary*. Tyndale Old Testament Commentaries. Downers Grove, IL: InterVarsity, 1988.

Boda, Mark J. and J. Gordon McConville. *Dictionary of the Old Testament: Prophet*s. Downers Grove, IL: InterVarsity, 2012.

Booth, G., trans. *The Historical Library of Diodorus the Sicilian: In Fifteen Books.* London: Edward Jones, 1700.

Bruckner, James. *Jonah, Nahum, Habakkuk, Zephaniah.* The NIV Application Commentary. Grand Rapids: Zondervan, 2004.

Dempster, Stephen G. *Dominion and Dynasty: A Theology of the Hebrew Bible.* New Studies in Biblical Theology. Edited by D. A. Carson. Downers Grove, IL: InterVarsity, 2003.

Feinberg, Charles L. *The Minor Prophets*. Chicago: Moody, 1976.

Fritsch, C. T. "Nineveh." In *The International Standard Bible Encyclopedia*. Revised edition. Edited by Geoffrey W. Bromiley, 3:538–41. Grand Rapids: Eerdmans, 1986.

Grayson, A. Kirk. "Nineveh." In *The Anchor Yale Bible Dictionary*. Edited by David Noel Freedman, 4:1118–19. New York: Doubleday, 1992.

House, Paul R. *Old Testament Theology*. Downers Grove, IL: InterVarsity, 1998.

Hoyt, JoAnna M. *Amos, Jonah, & Micah*. Edited by H. Wayne House and William D. Barrick. Evangelical Exegetical Commentary. Bellingham, WA: Lexham, 2018.

Johnston, Gordon H. "Nahum's Rhetorical Allusions to the Neo-Assyrian Lion Motif." *Bibliotheca Sacra* 158 (July–September 2001): 287–307.

Kaiser Jr., Walter C. and Paul D. Wegner. *A History of Israel: From the Bronze Age through the Jewish Wars*. Revised edition. Nashville: Broadman & Holman Academic, 2016.

Keil, C. F. and F. Delitzsch. *Commentary on the Old Testament*. Peabody, MA: Hendrickson, 1996.

Kobayashi, Yoshitaka. "Elkosh." In *The Anchor Yale Bible Dictionary*. Edited by David Noel Freedman, 2:476. New York: Doubleday, 1992.

Lewis, Theodore J. "Amon (Deity)." In *The Anchor Yale Bible Dictionary*. Edited by David Noel Freedman, 1:197–98. New York: Doubleday, 1992.

Lowery, Daniel DeWitt. "Assyria." In *The Lexham Bible Dictionary*. Edited by John D. Barry et al. Bellingham, WA: Lexham, 2016.

McComiskey, Thomas Edward, ed. *The Minor Prophets: An Exegetical and Expository Commentary*. Vol. 2. Grand Rapids: Baker, 1993.

Merrill, Eugene H. *Kingdom of Priests: A History of Old Testament Israel*. 2nd edition. Grand Rapids: Baker Academic, 2008.

Merrill, Eugene H. *A Commentary on 1 & 2 Chronicles*. Kregel Exegetical Library. Grand Rapids: Kregel, 2015.

Merrill, Eugene H., Mark Rooker, and Michael A. Grisanti. *The World and the Word: An Introduction to the Old Testament.* Nashville: Broadman & Holman Academic, 2011.

Pinches, T. G. "Nineveh." In *The International Standard Bible Encyclopedia.* Chicago: Howard-Severance, 1915.

Peterson, Brian Neil. "Urartu." In *The Lexham Bible Dictionary.* Edited by John D. Barry et al. Bellingham, WA: Lexham, 2016.

Pritchard, James Bennett, ed. *The Ancient Near Eastern Texts Relating to the Old Testament.* 3rd edition, with supplement. Princeton: Princeton University Press, 1969.

Redford, Donald B. "Thebes." In *The Anchor Yale Bible Dictionary.* Edited by David Noel Freedman, 6:442–43. New York: Doubleday, 1992.

Renz, Thomas. *The Books of Nahum, Habakkuk, and Zephaniah.* New International Commentary on the Old Testament. Grand Rapids: Eerdmans, 2021.

Robertson, O. Palmer. *The Books of Nahum, Habakkuk, and Zephaniah.* New International Commentary on the Old Testament. Grand Rapids: Eerdmans, 1990.

Siculus, Diodorus. "Diodori Bibliotheca Historica." In *Bibliotheca Histórica.* Edited by Immanuel Bekker. Medford, MA: Teubneri, 1888–1890.

Sieges, Anna. "Nineveh." In *The Lexham Bible Dictionary.* Edited by John D. Barry. Bellingham, WA: Lexham, 2016.

Simon, Uriel. *Jonah.* JPS Bible Commentary. Philadelphia: Jewish Publication Society, 1999.

Smith, Billy K. and Frank S. Page. *Amos, Obadiah, Jonah.* New American Commentary. Nashville: Broadman & Holman, 1995.

Smith, Ralph L. *Micah–Malachi.* Word Biblical Commentary. Waco, TX: Word, 1984.

Spronk, Klaas. *Nahum.* Historical Commentary on the Old Testament. Kampen: Kok Pharos, 1997.

Stuart, Douglas. *Hosea–Jonah.* Word Biblical Commentary. Dallas: Word, 1987.

Sweeney, Marvin A. *The Twelve Prophets: Hosea, Joel, Amos, Obadiah, Jonah*. Berit Olam. Collegeville, MN: Liturgical, 2000.

Thompson, J. A. *1, 2 Chronicles*. New American Commentary. Nashville: Broadman & Holman, 1994.

Timmer, Daniel C. *Nahum*. Zondervan Exegetical Commentary on the Old Testament. Grand Rapids: Zondervan Academic, 2020.

Timmer, Daniel C. *A Gracious and Compassionate God: Mission, Salvation, and Spirituality in the Book of Jonah*. New Studies in Biblical Theology. Downers Grove, IL: InterVarsity, 2011.

Tozer, A. W. *The Knowledge of the Holy*. San Francisco: HarperCollins, 1961.

Vaillancourt, Ian J. "The Pious Prayer of an Imperfect Prophet: The Psalm of Jonah in Its Narrative Context." *Journal for the Evangelical Study of the Old Testament* 4, no. 2 (2015): 171–89.

Waltke, Bruce K., and Charles Yu. *An Old Testament Theology: An Exegetical, Canonical, and Thematic Approach*. Grand Rapids: Zondervan, 2007.

Walton, John H. "Jonah." In *The Expositor's Bible Commentary: Daniel–Malachi*. Revised edition. Volume 8. Edited by Tremper Longman III and David E. Garland. Grand Rapids: Zondervan, 2008.

Walton, John H. "The Object Lesson of Jonah 4:5–7 and the Purpose of the Book of Jonah." *Bulletin for Biblical Research* 2 (1992): 47–57.

Weissert, Elnathan. "Royal Hunt and Royal Triumph in a Prism Fragment of Ashurbanipal (85-5-22,2)." In *Assyria 1995: Proceedings of the 10th Anniversary Symposium of the Neo-Assyrian Text Corpus Project*. Edited by Simo Parpola and R. M. Whiting. Helsinki: The Neo-Assyrian Text Corpus Project, 1997.

Wright, T., ed. *Early Travels in Palestine*. London: Henry G. Bohn, 1848.

Youngblood, Kevin J. *Jonah*. 2nd edition. Zondervan Exegetical Commentary on the Old Testament. Grand Rapids: Zondervan Academic, 2019.

Index of Scripture

Index of Subjects

Index of Subjects